HOWL'S MOVING CASTLE

FROM THE NOVEL BY DIANA WYNNE JONES
SCREENPLAY WRITTEN AND DIRECTED BY
HAYAO MIYAZAKI

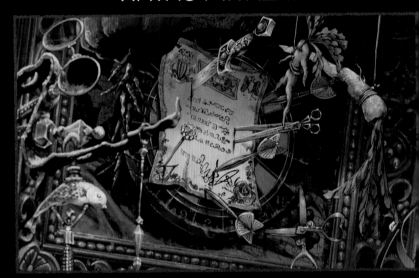

STUDIO
GHIBLI
LIBRARY

Howl's Moving Castle
The Story So Far

In a faraway country in another time, war has started to ravage the city where Sophie manages the hat shop she inherited from her father. One day she encounters a beautiful young man in an alley. Sophie is drawn to this man, even though everyone fears that he eats young women's hearts. He is the wizard Howl. That same evening, the Witch of the Waste shows up at Sophie's hat shop and turns her into a 90-year-old woman. With nowhere else to turn, Sophie embarks alone on a journey and stumbles into Howl's moving castle. She decides she will work there as the cleaning lady, but then...

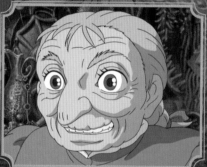

Sophie

As the oldest daughter she looks after her parents' hat shop. The Witch of the Waste turns her into an old lady. Sophie stumbles into Howl's moving castle and stays there as the cleaning lady.

Howl

The lord of the moving castle. He is a very powerful wizard, but he can be overly sensitive, particularly when it comes to his looks. The Witch of the Waste is after him.

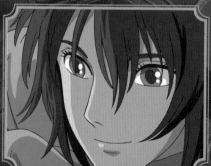

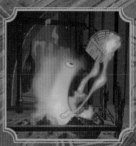

Calcifer

A fire demon. He lives in the fireplace of Howl's castle and powers the castle. He seems bound to Howl by a magical contract.

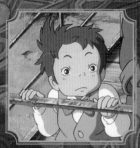

Markl

Howl's apprentice. He studies magic while running errands. He poses as an old man when dealing with clients.

The Witch of the Waste

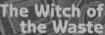

The sorceress who turned Sophie into an old lady. She doggedly sends her magical creations, the spooky blob men, after Howl.

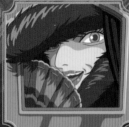

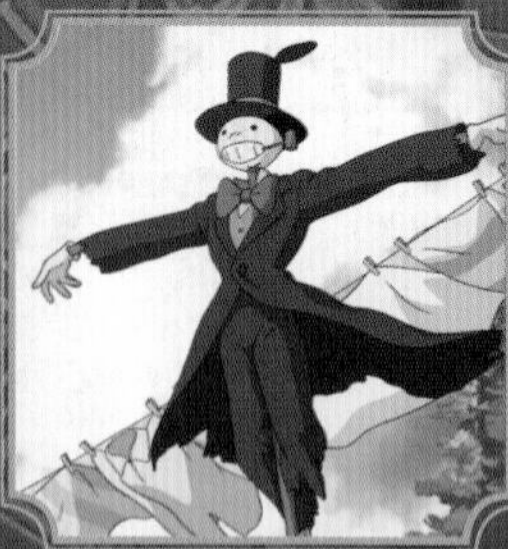

Turnip-head

A scarecrow. He is rescued by Sophie in the wasteland. Sophie came up with this nickname because his head resembles a turnip.

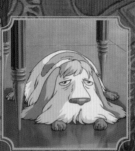

Heen

Suliman's mysterious dog. He guides Sophie to Suliman at the royal palace.

Suliman

The Kingsbury court-appointed wizard. As Howl's former master, she seeks Howl's help in the war.

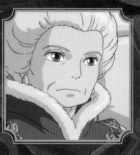

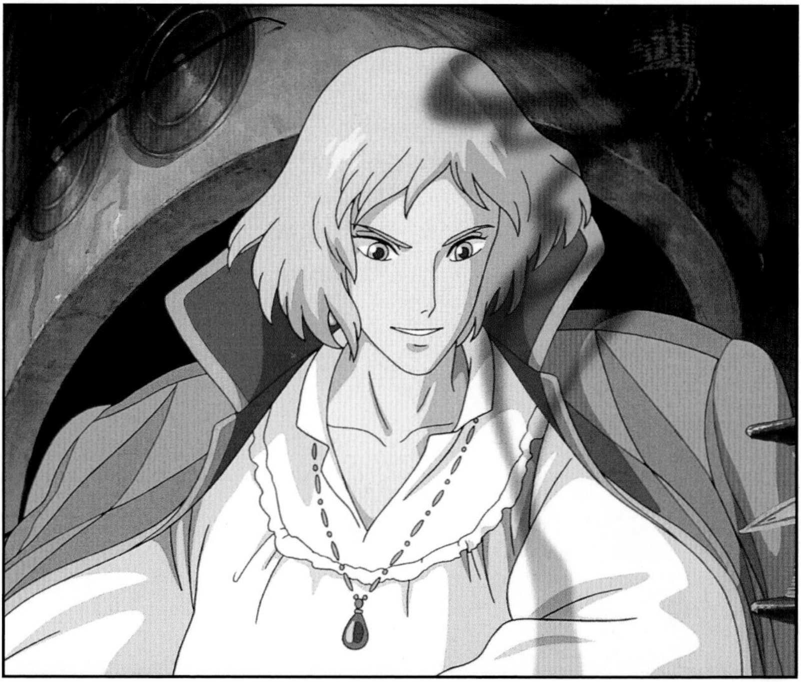

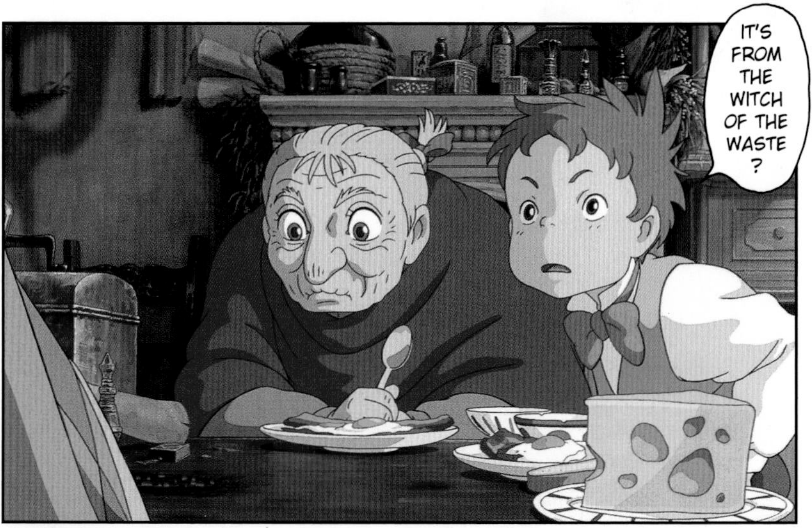
IT'S FROM THE WITCH OF THE WASTE ?

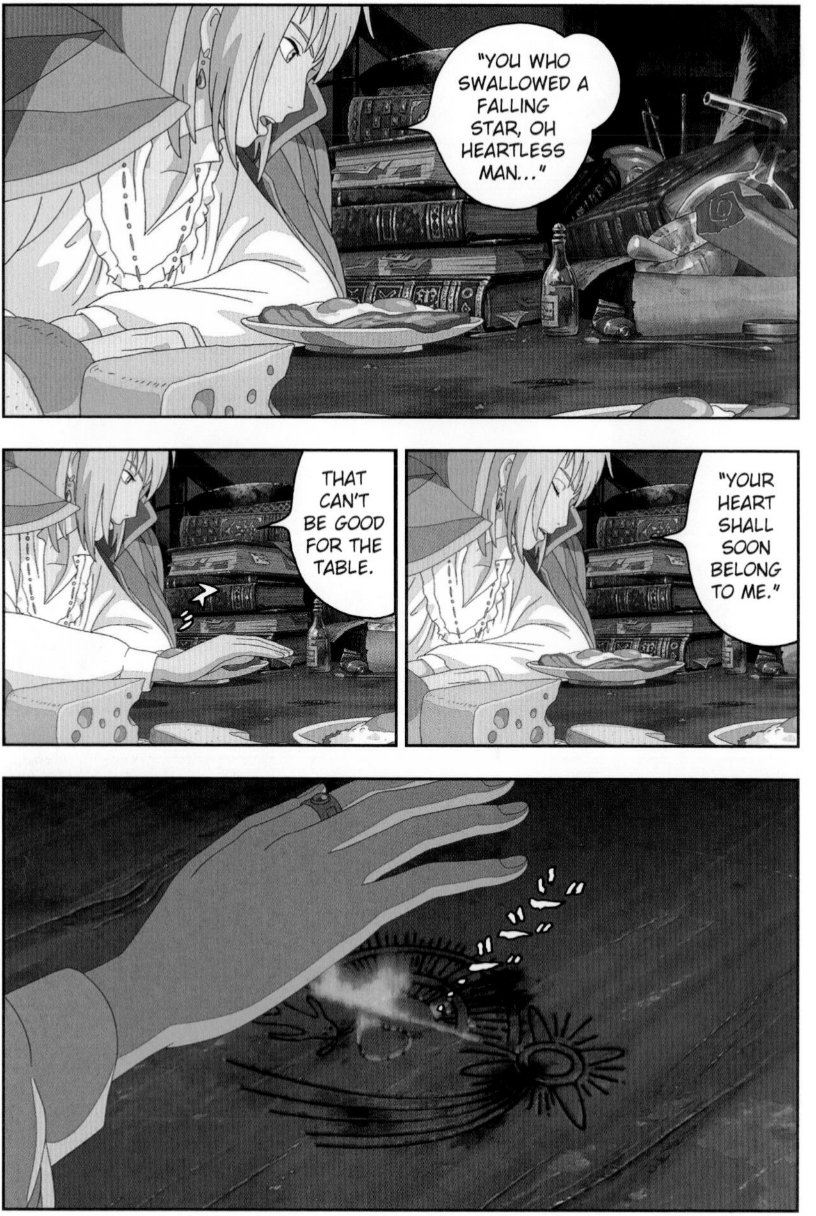
"YOU WHO SWALLOWED A FALLING STAR, OH HEARTLESS MAN..."
"YOUR HEART SHALL SOON BELONG TO ME."
THAT CAN'T BE GOOD FOR THE TABLE.

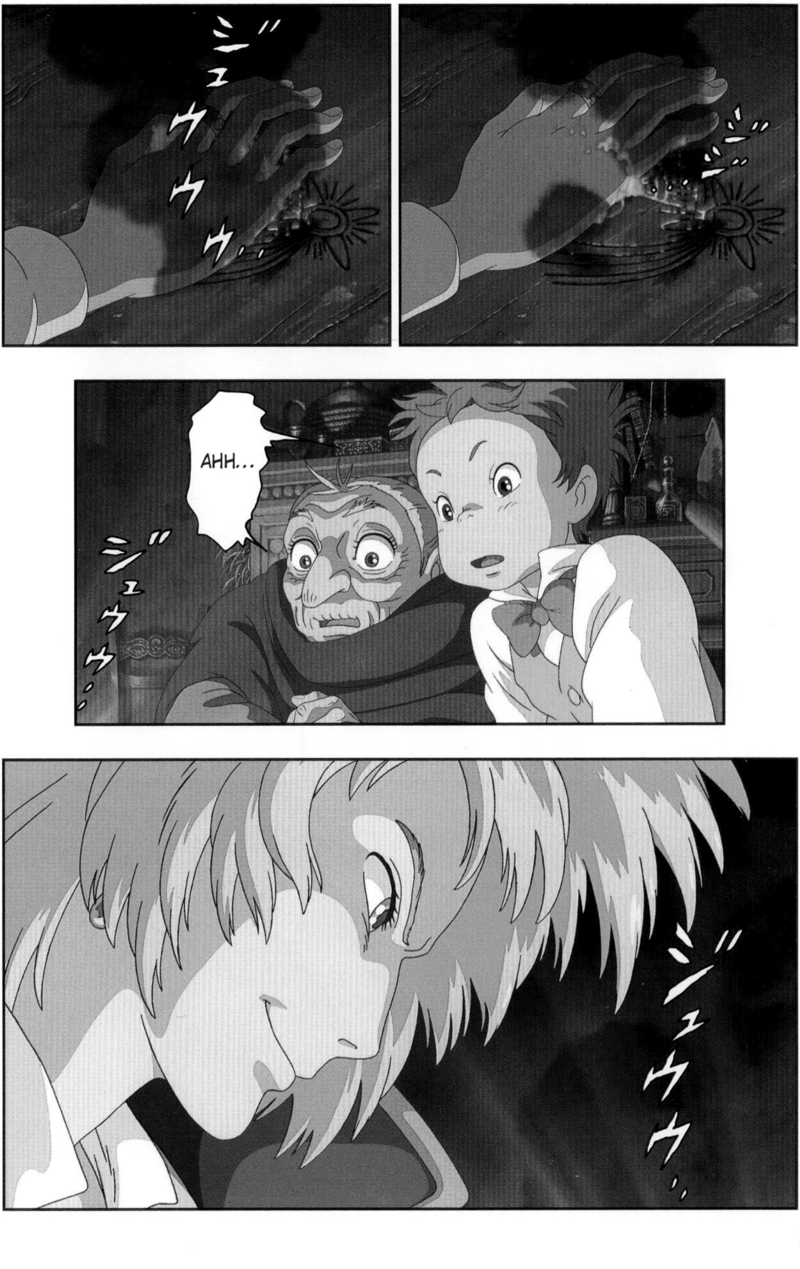

ジュウウウ‥
AHH...
ジュウウ‥
ジュウウ‥

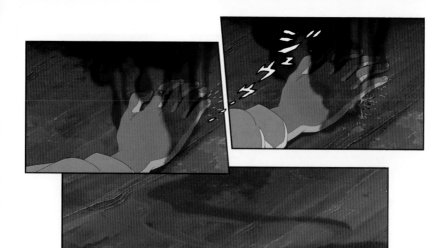

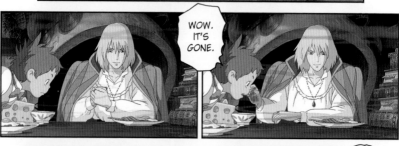

WOW. IT'S GONE.

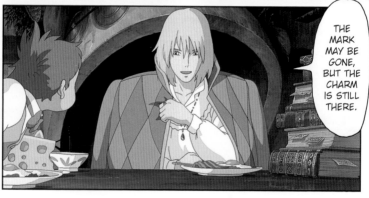

THE MARK MAY BE GONE, BUT THE CHARM IS STILL THERE.

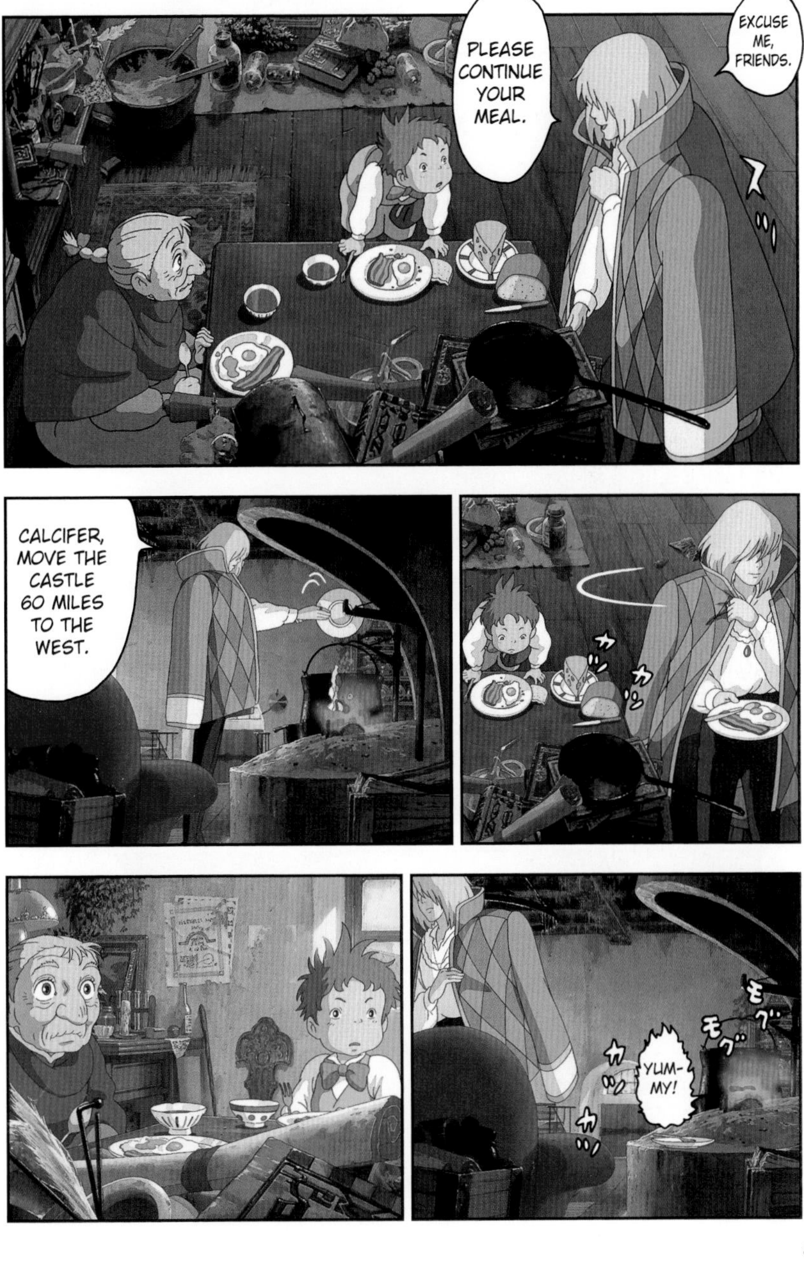
EXCUSE ME, FRIENDS.
PLEASE CONTINUE YOUR MEAL.
CALCIFER, MOVE THE CASTLE 60 MILES TO THE WEST.
モグ
モグ
YUM-MY!

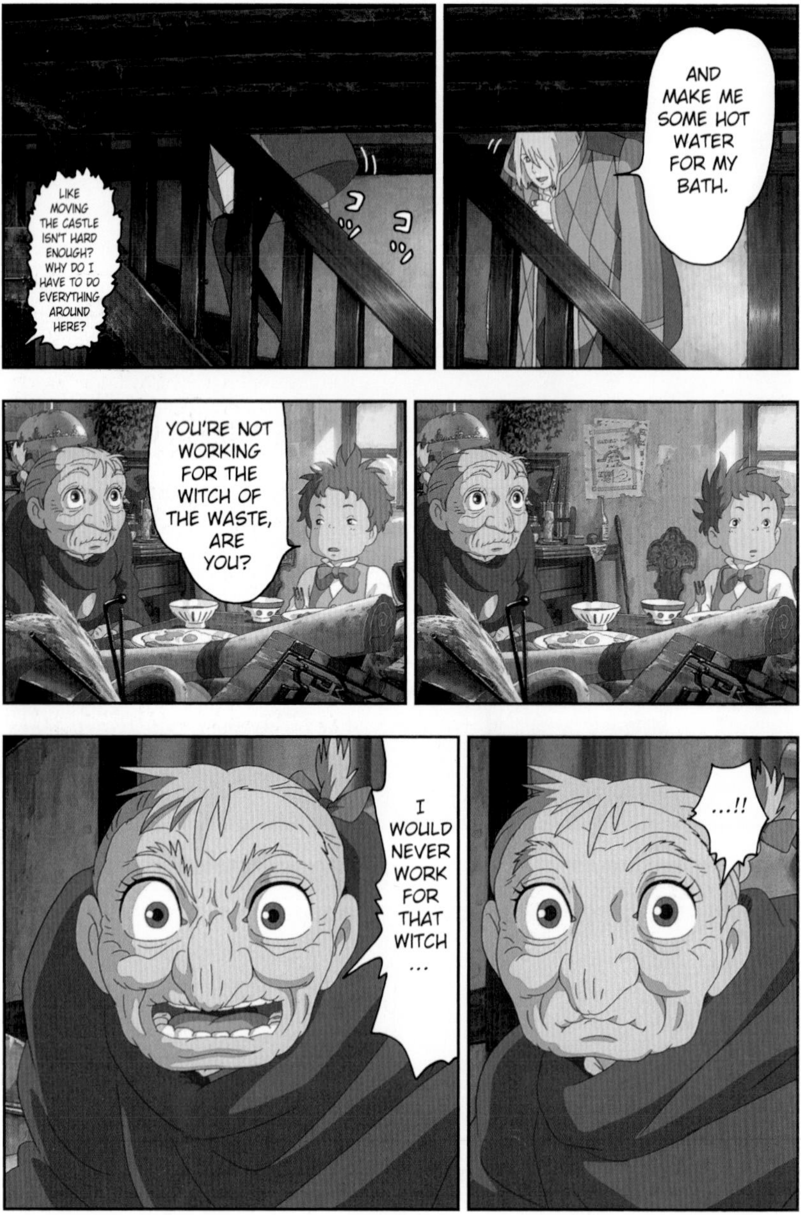
AND MAKE ME SOME HOT WATER FOR MY BATH.
LIKE MOVING THE CASTLE ISN'T HARD ENOUGH? WHY DO I HAVE TO DO EVERYTHING AROUND HERE?
YOU'RE NOT WORKING FOR THE WITCH OF THE WASTE, ARE YOU?
...!!
I WOULD NEVER WORK FOR THAT WITCH ...

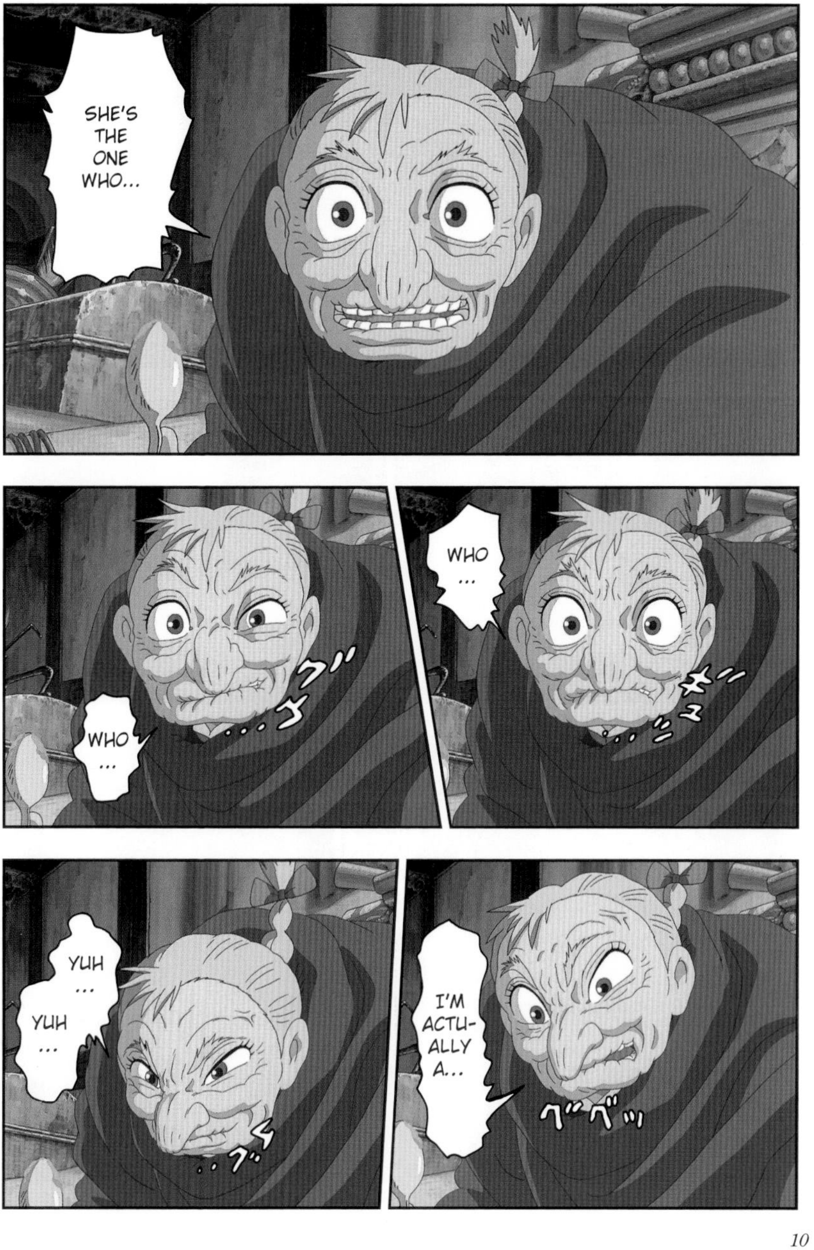
SHE'S THE ONE WHO...
WHO ...
WHO ...
I'M ACTU-ALLY A...
YUH ... YUH ...

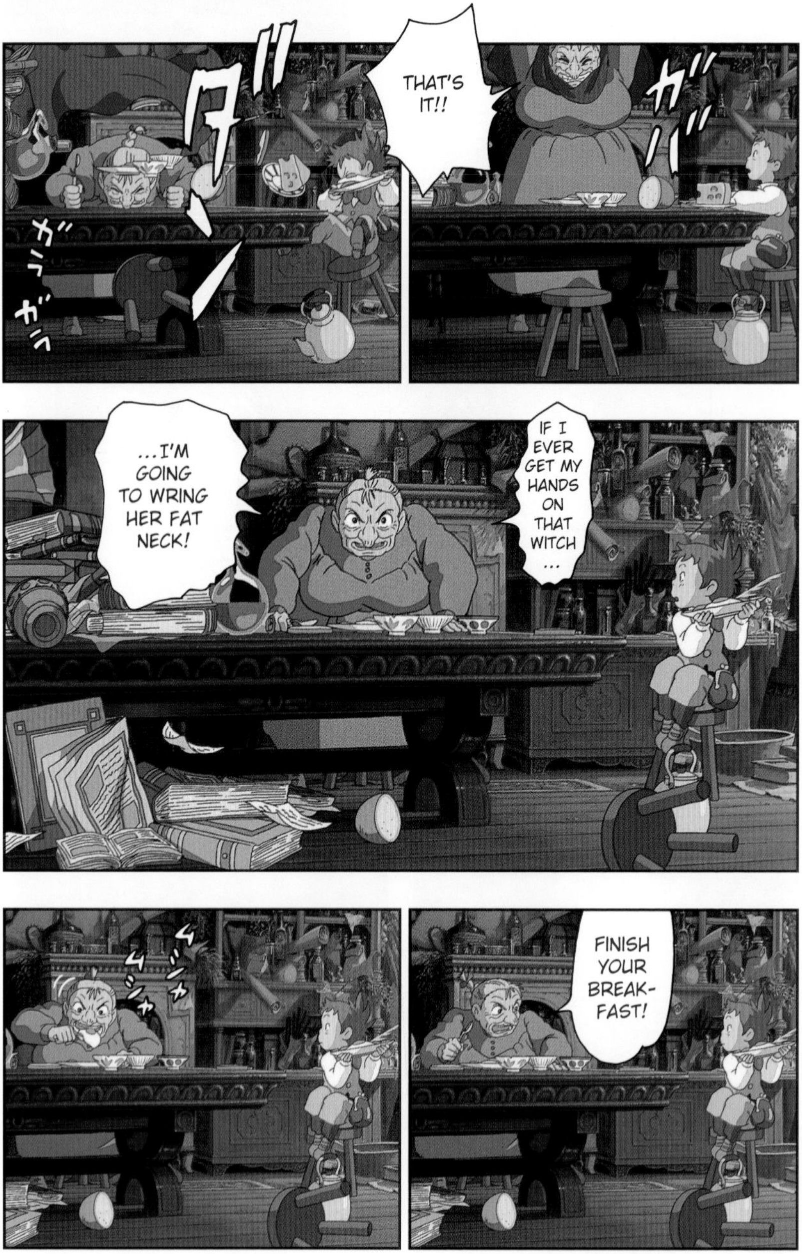
THAT'S IT!!
IF I EVER GET MY HANDS ON THAT WITCH...
...I'M GOING TO WRING HER FAT NECK!
FINISH YOUR BREAK-FAST!

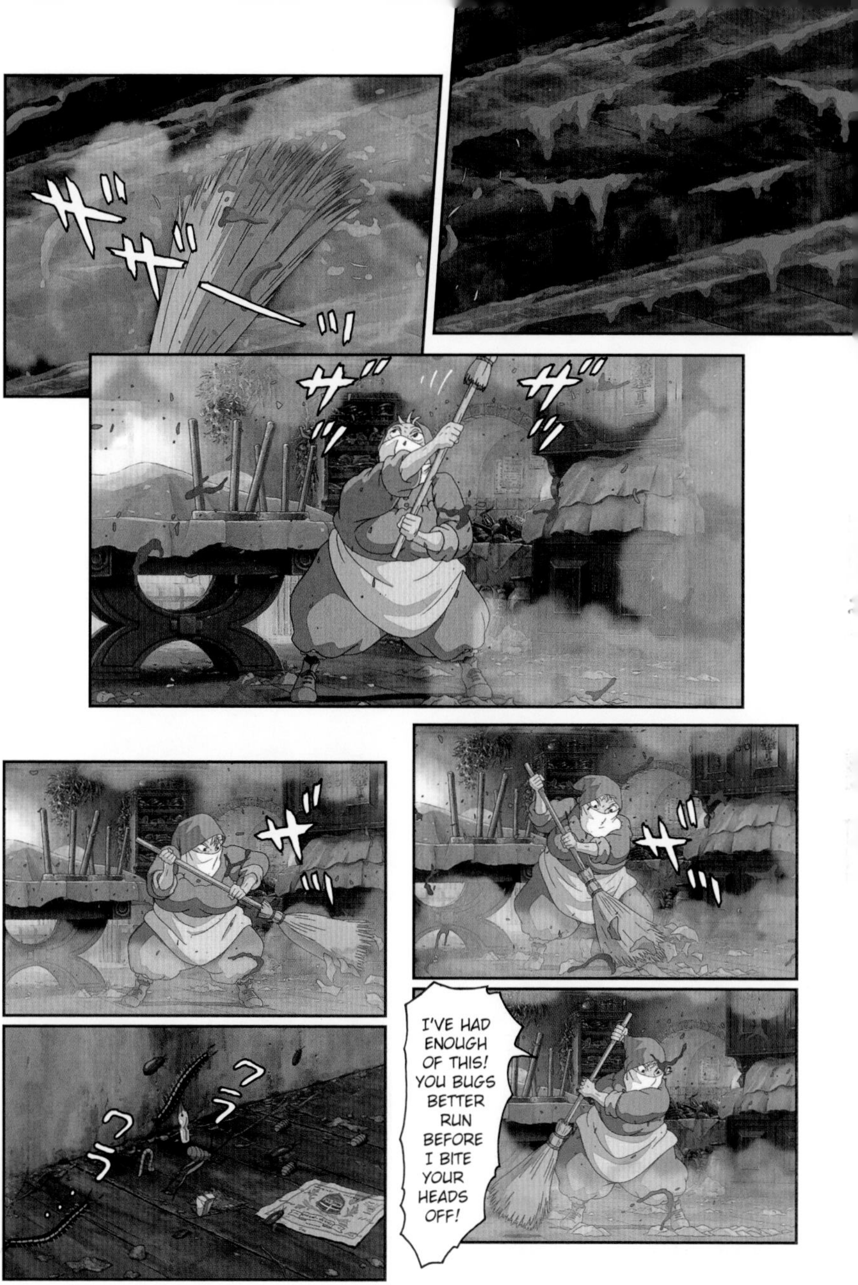
ザザーッ
ザッ
ザッ
ザッ
ザッ
I'VE HAD ENOUGH OF THIS! YOU BUGS BETTER RUN BEFORE I BITE YOUR HEADS OFF!
ワラ
ワラ

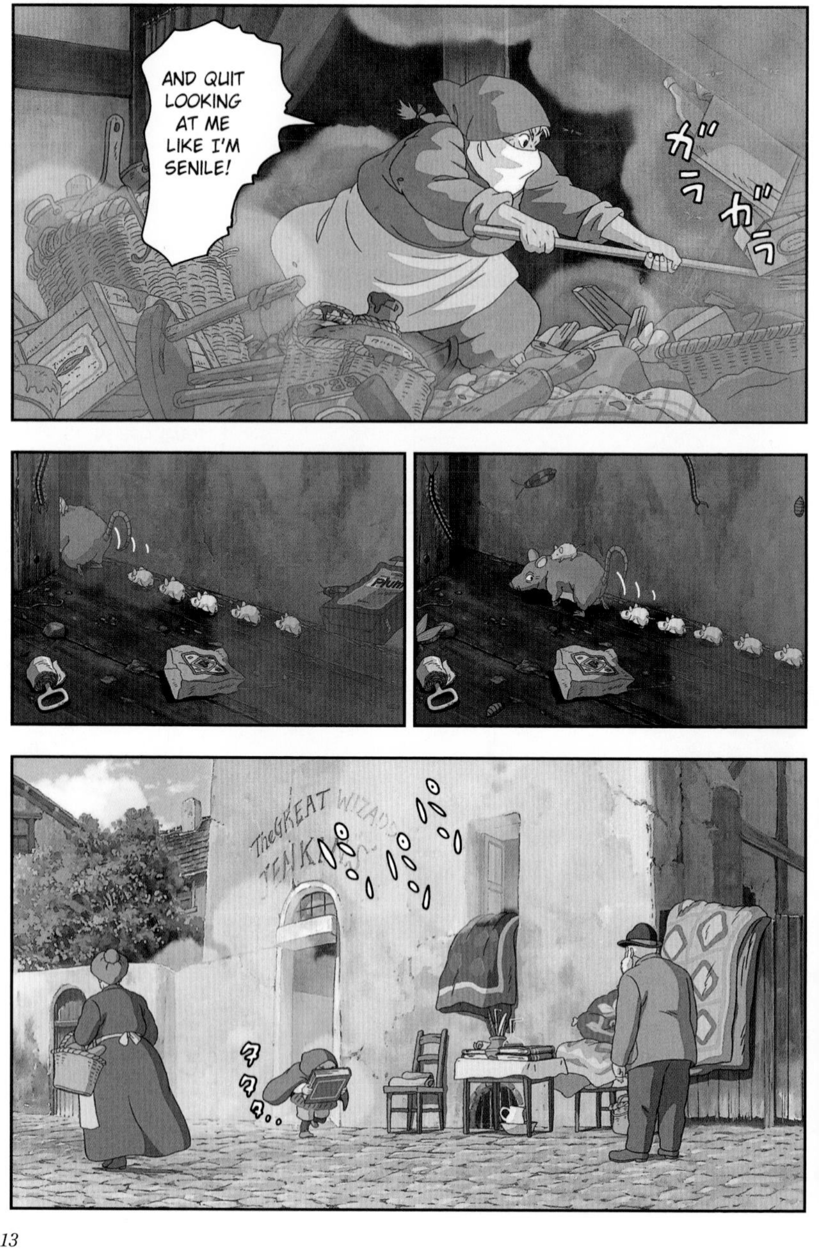

AND QUIT LOOKING AT ME LIKE I'M SENILE!
ガラ ガラ
タタタ

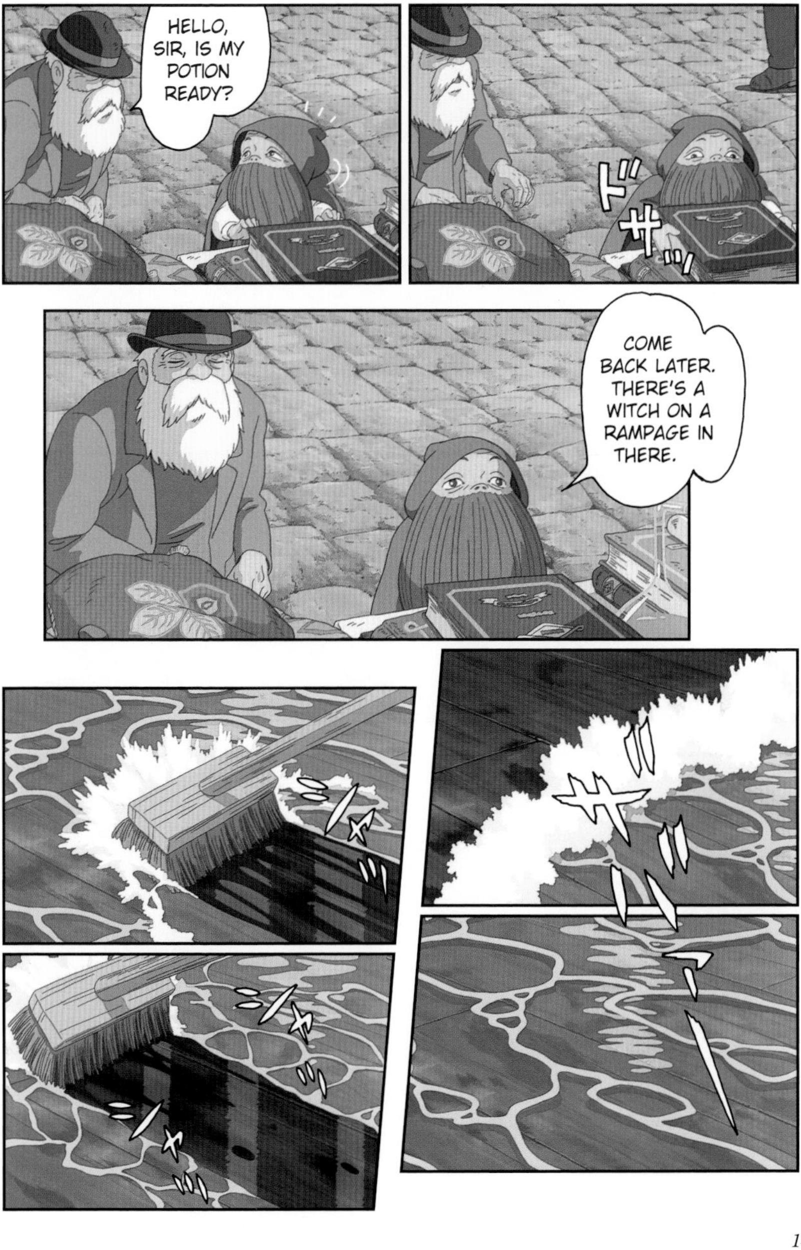
ドサッ
HELLO, SIR, IS MY POTION READY?
COME BACK LATER. THERE'S A WITCH ON A RAMPAGE IN THERE.

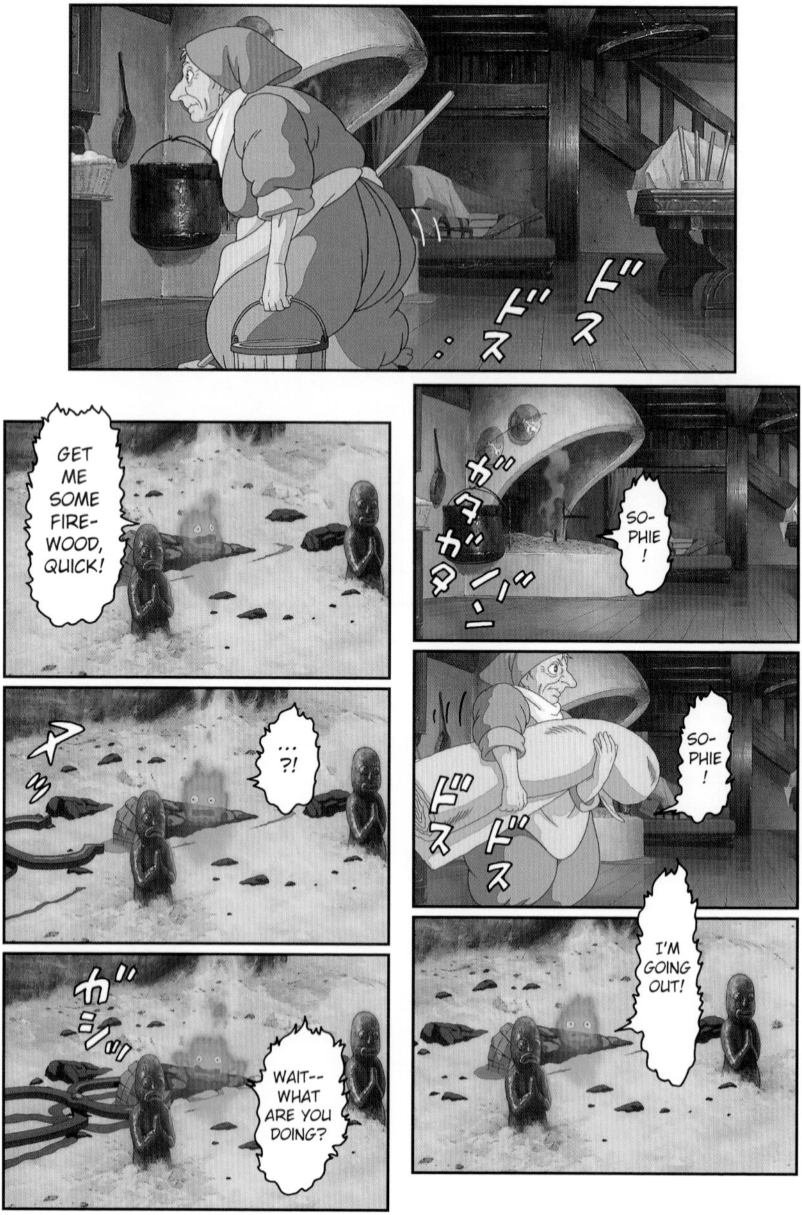
ドス
ドス
SO-PHIE!
SO-PHIE!
ドス
ドス
I'M GOING OUT!
GET ME SOME FIRE-WOOD, QUICK!
...?!
WAIT-- WHAT ARE YOU DOING?

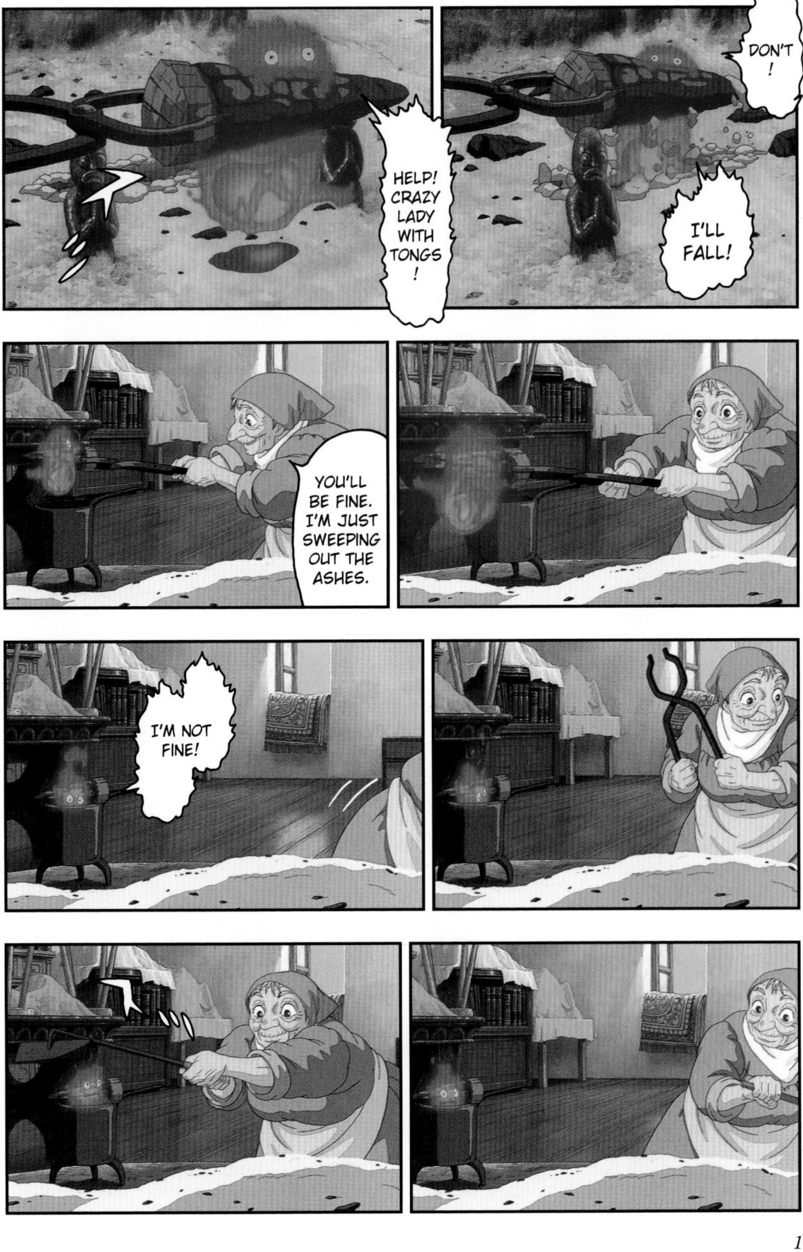
DON'T !
I'LL FALL!
HELP! CRAZY LADY WITH TONGS !
YOU'LL BE FINE. I'M JUST SWEEPING OUT THE ASHES.
I'M NOT FINE!

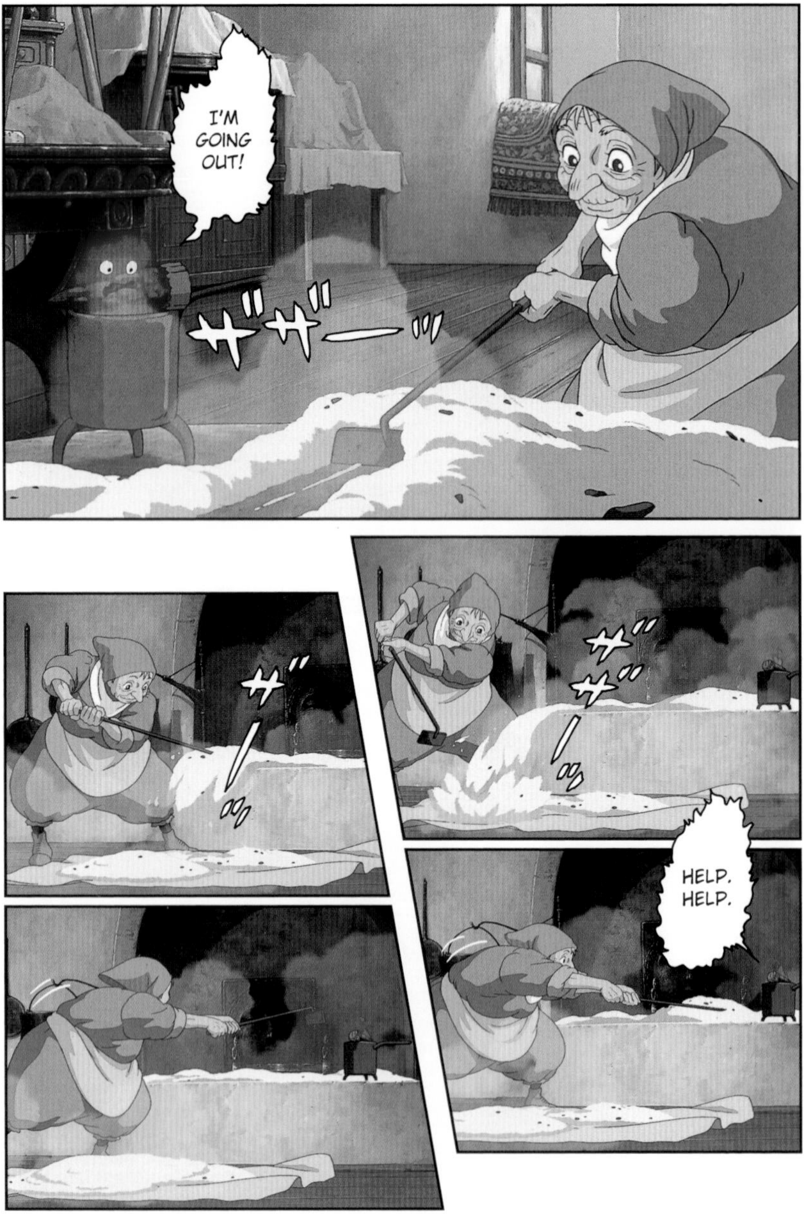

I'M GOING OUT!
ザザーッ
ザザッ
ザッ
HELP, HELP.

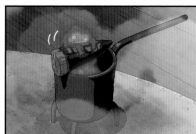

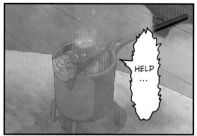

HELP
...

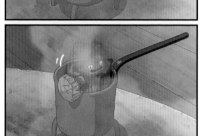

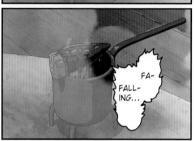

FA-
FALL-
ING...

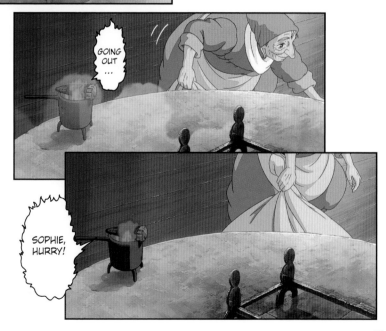

GOING
OUT
...

SOPHIE,
HURRY!

AIEE!
AIEE!
AIEEEEE!
ポワーン
スッ
ゴトン
ゴトン

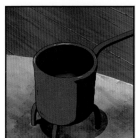

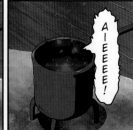

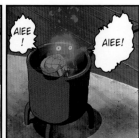

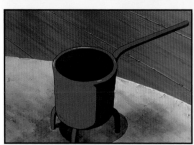

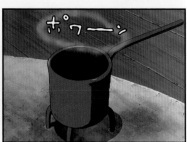

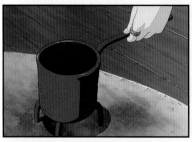

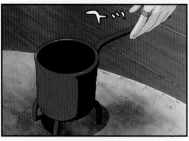

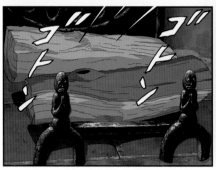

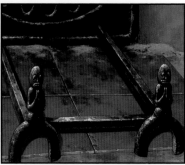

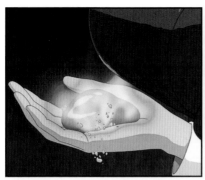
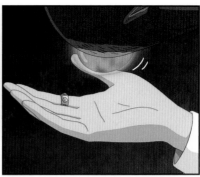
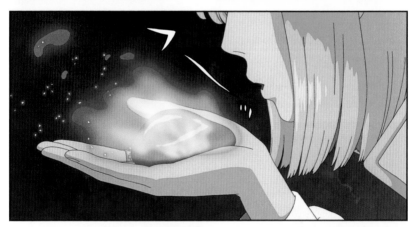
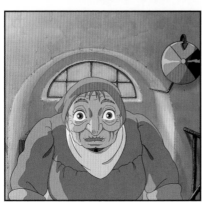
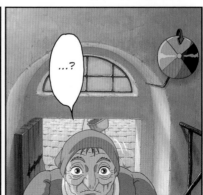

...?

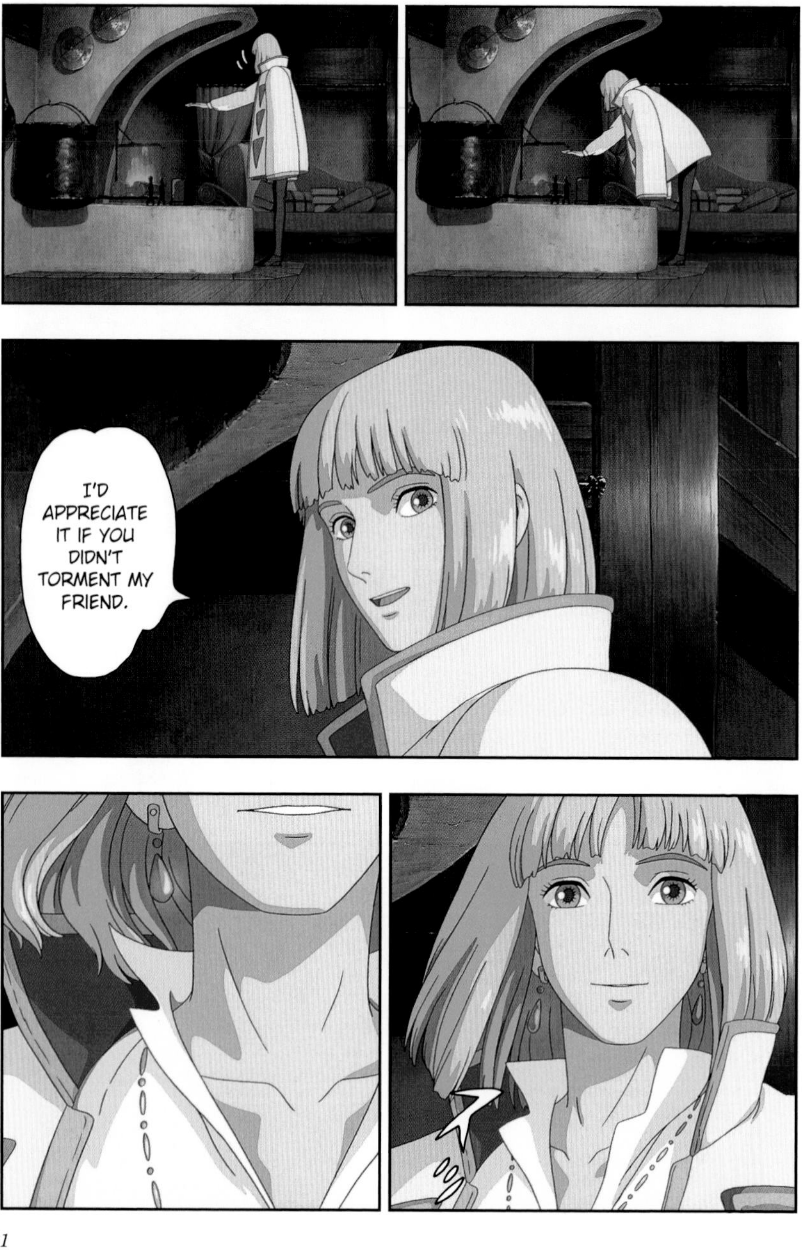
I'D APPRECIATE IT IF YOU DIDN'T TORMENT MY FRIEND.

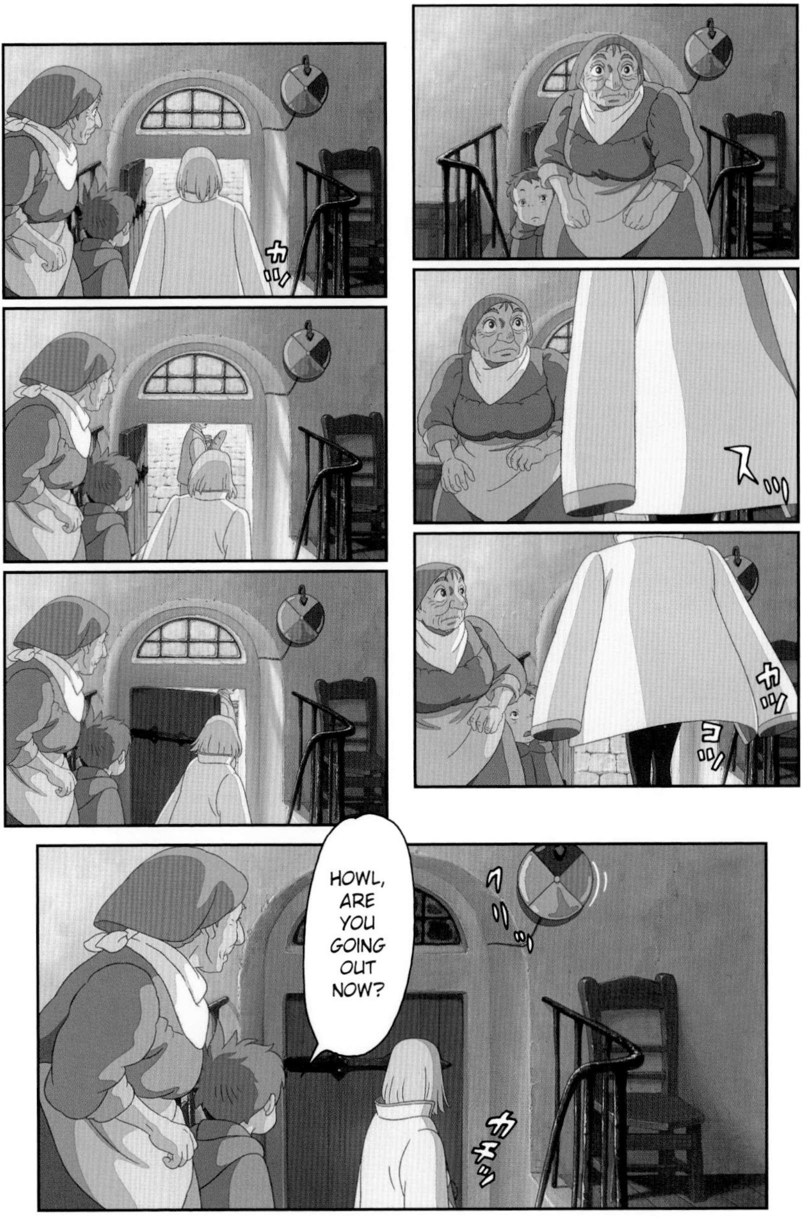
HOWL, ARE YOU GOING OUT NOW?

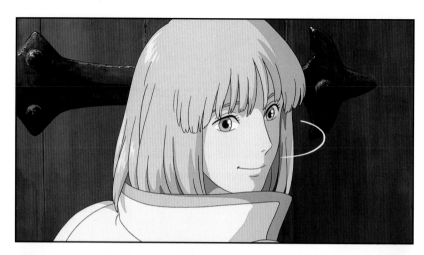

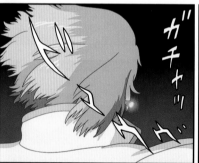

MAKE SURE THE CLEANING LADY DOESN'T GET CARRIED AWAY WHILE I'M GONE.

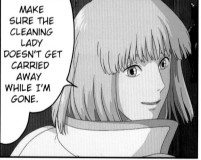

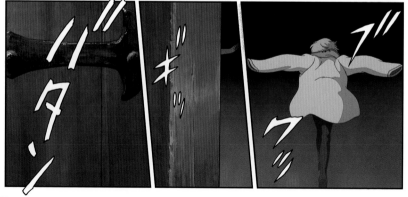

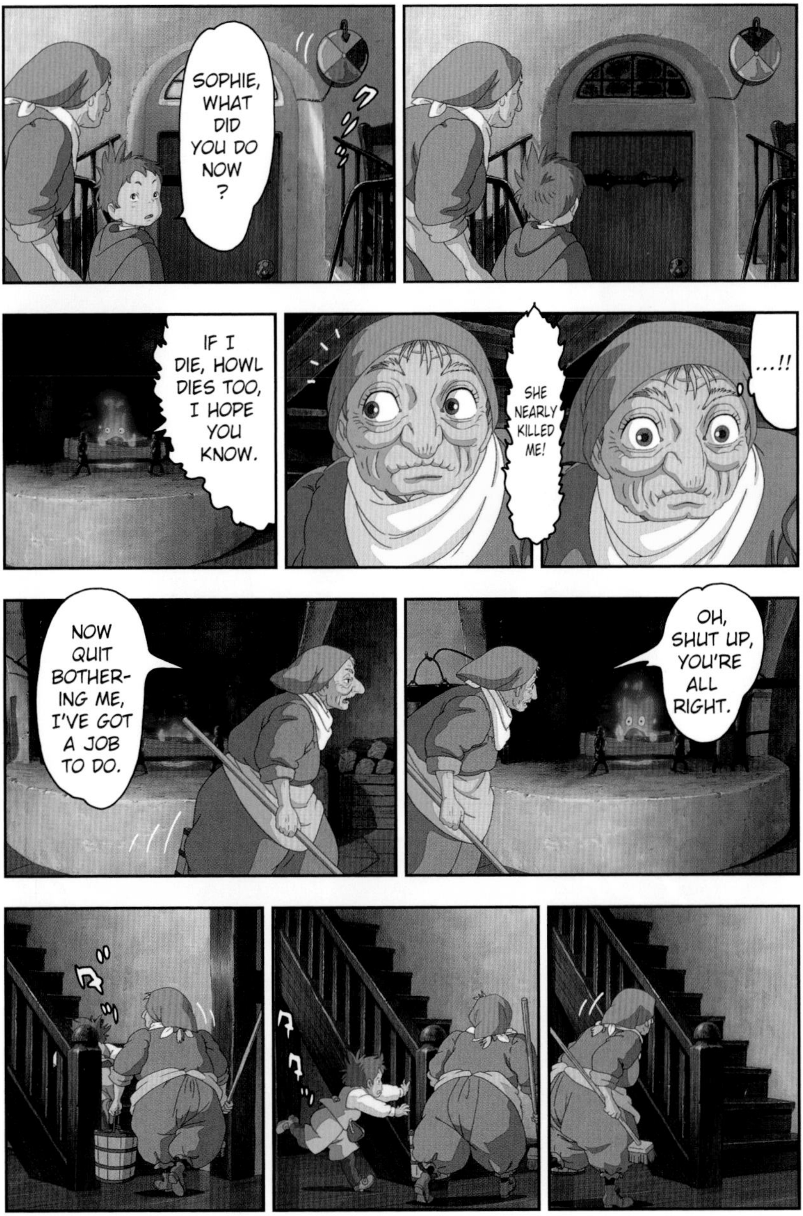
SOPHIE, WHAT DID YOU DO NOW?
...!!
SHE NEARLY KILLED ME!
IF I DIE, HOWL DIES TOO, I HOPE YOU KNOW.
OH, SHUT UP, YOU'RE ALL RIGHT.
NOW QUIT BOTHERING ME, I'VE GOT A JOB TO DO.

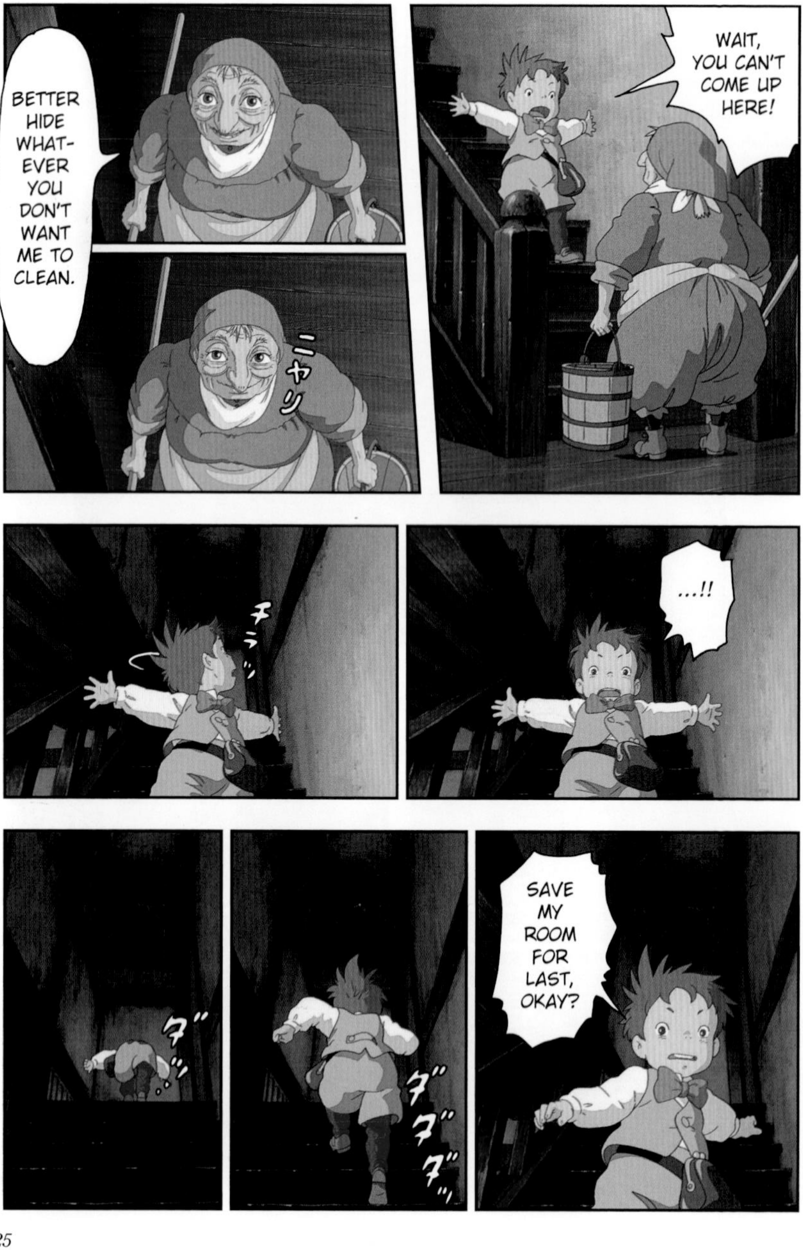
WAIT, YOU CAN'T COME UP HERE!
BETTER HIDE WHATEVER YOU DON'T WANT ME TO CLEAN.
ニヤリ
...!!
チラッ
SAVE MY ROOM FOR LAST, OKAY?
ダダダッ
ダッ

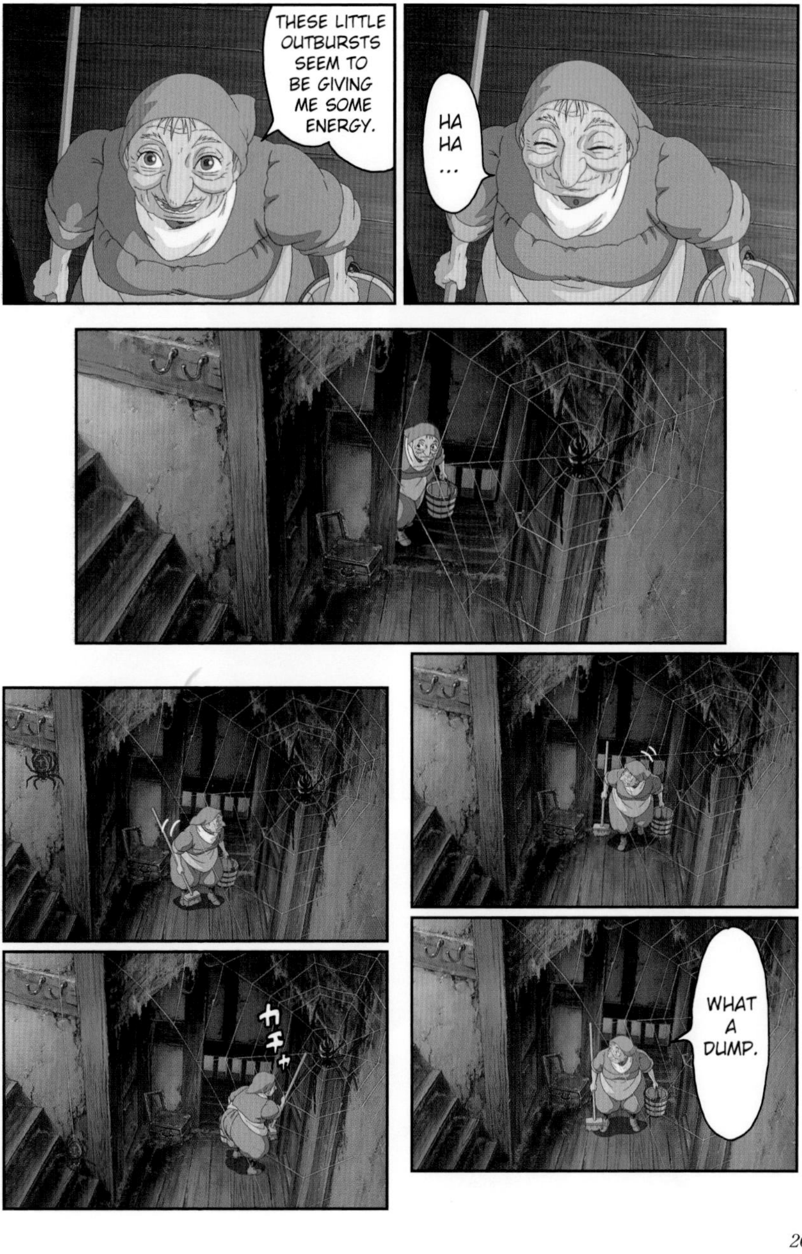
HA HA ...
THESE LITTLE OUTBURSTS SEEM TO BE GIVING ME SOME ENERGY.
WHAT A DUMP.
カチャ

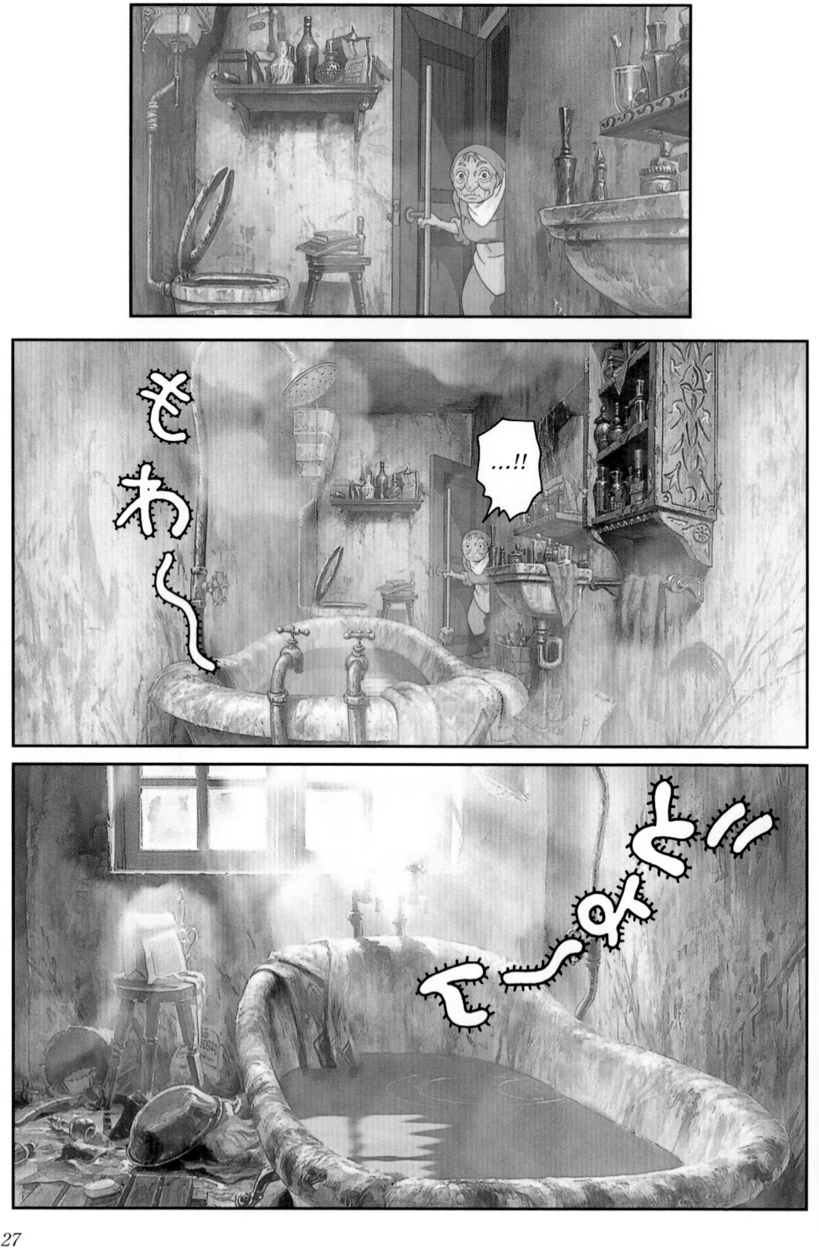
...!!
もわ〜

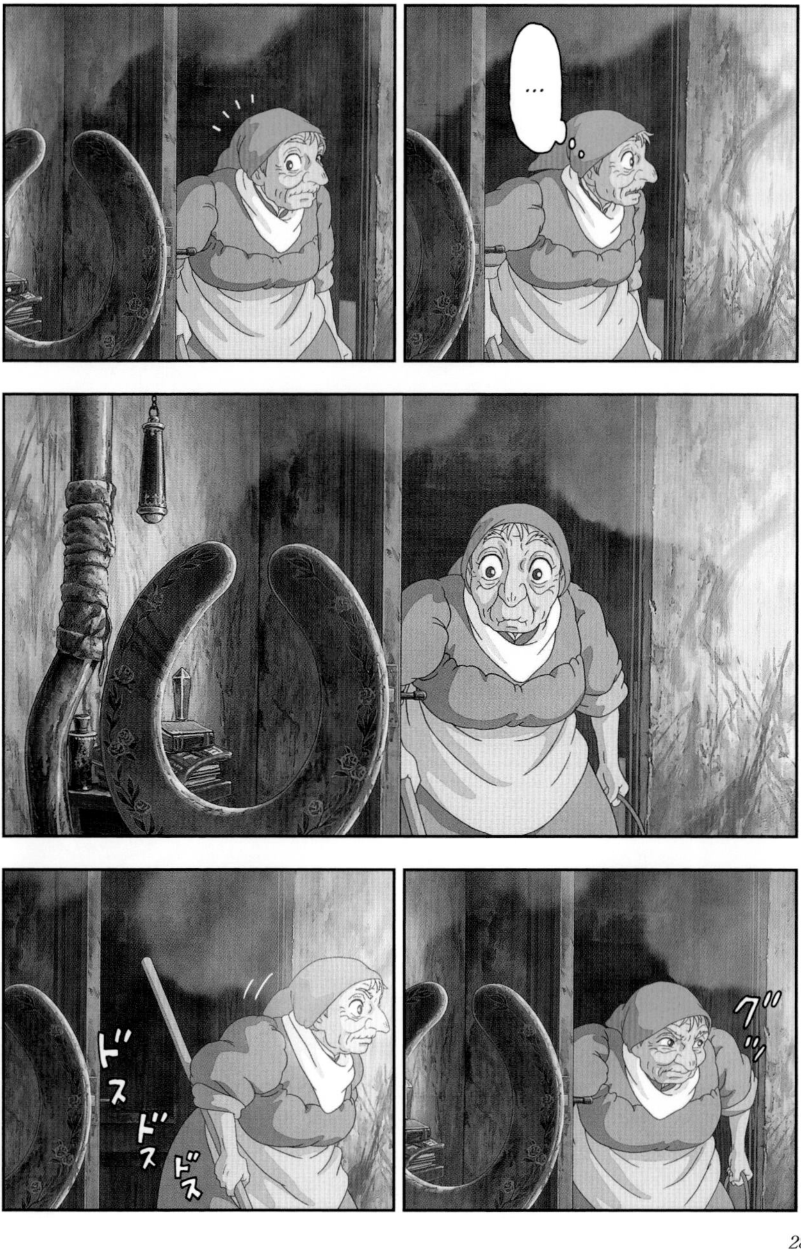
...
グッ
ドス
ドス
ドス

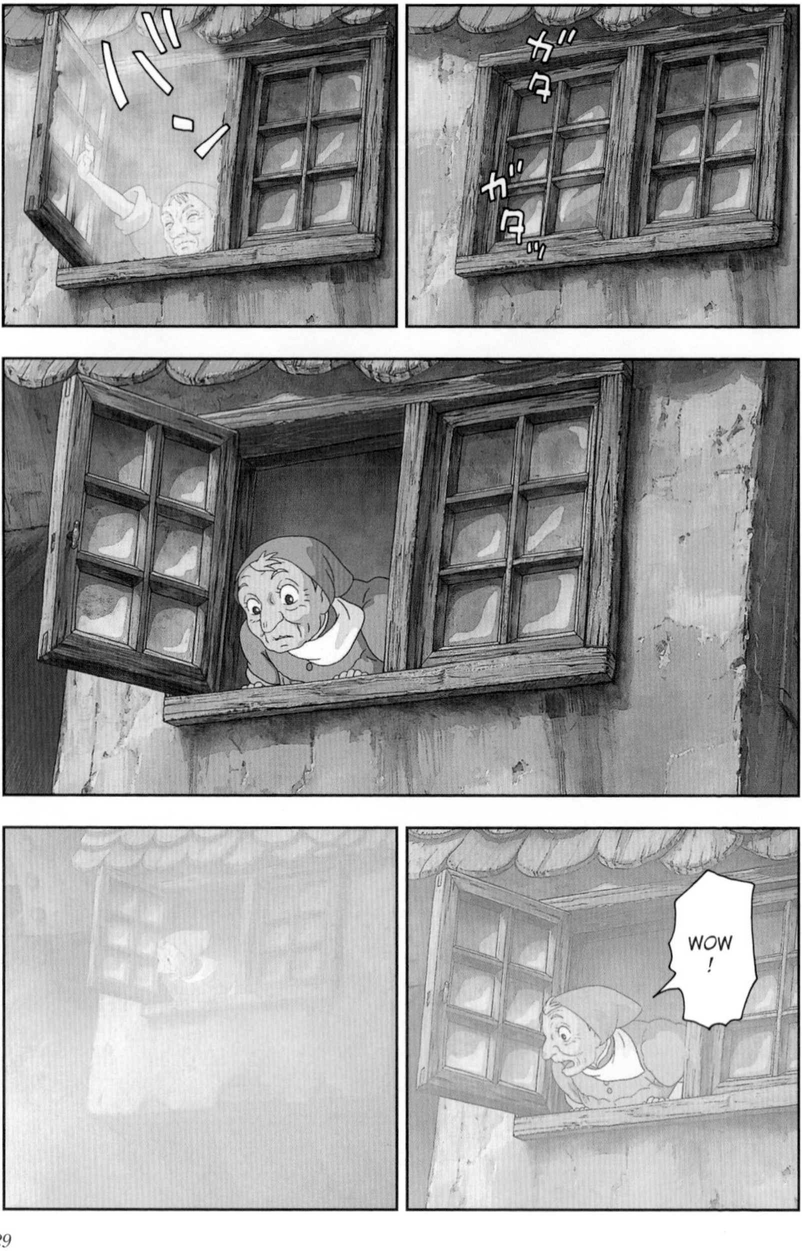
ガタ
ガタッ
バン
WOW!

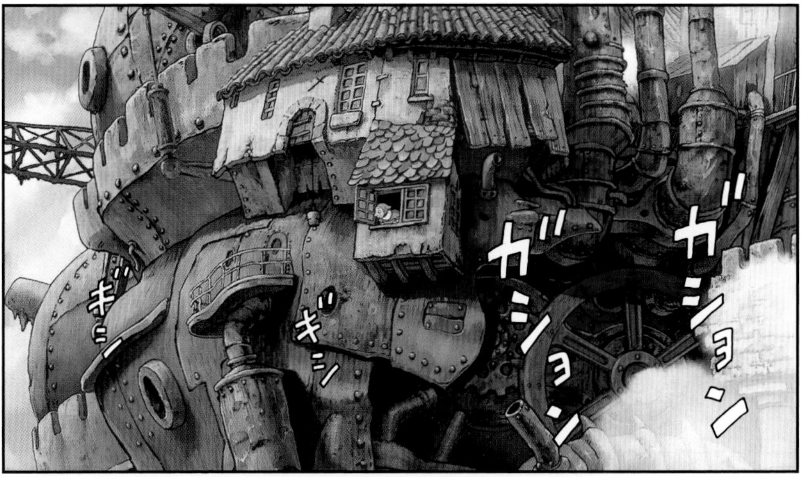
ガション
ガション
ギシン
ギシー
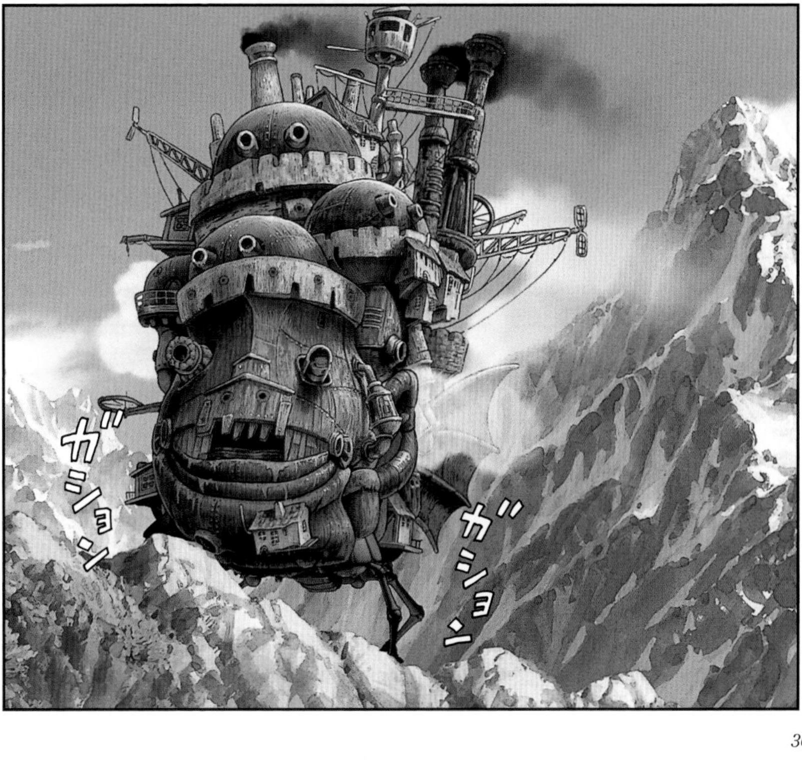
ガション
ガション

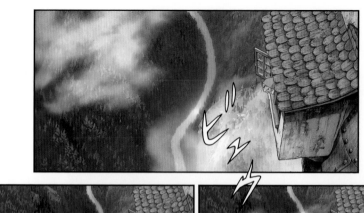

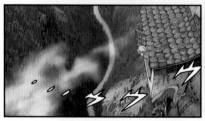

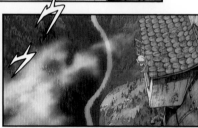

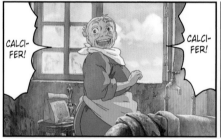

INCRED-IBLE...
CALCI-FER!
CALCI-FER!
ARE YOU THE ONE MOVING THE CASTLE?
OF COURSE I AM. NO ONE ELSE DOES ANY WORK AROUND HERE.

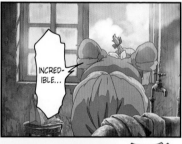

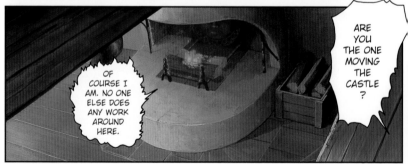

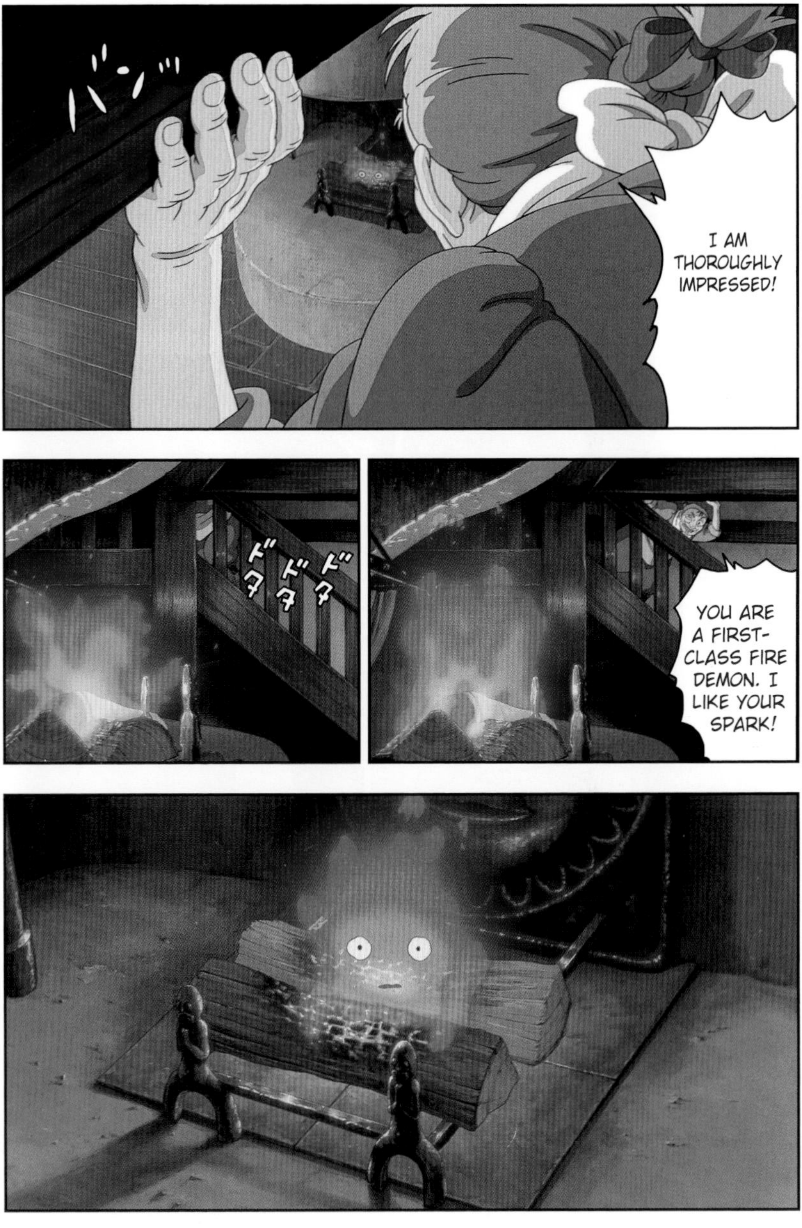
I AM THOROUGHLY IMPRESSED!
YOU ARE A FIRST-CLASS FIRE DEMON. I LIKE YOUR SPARK!
ドタドタドタ

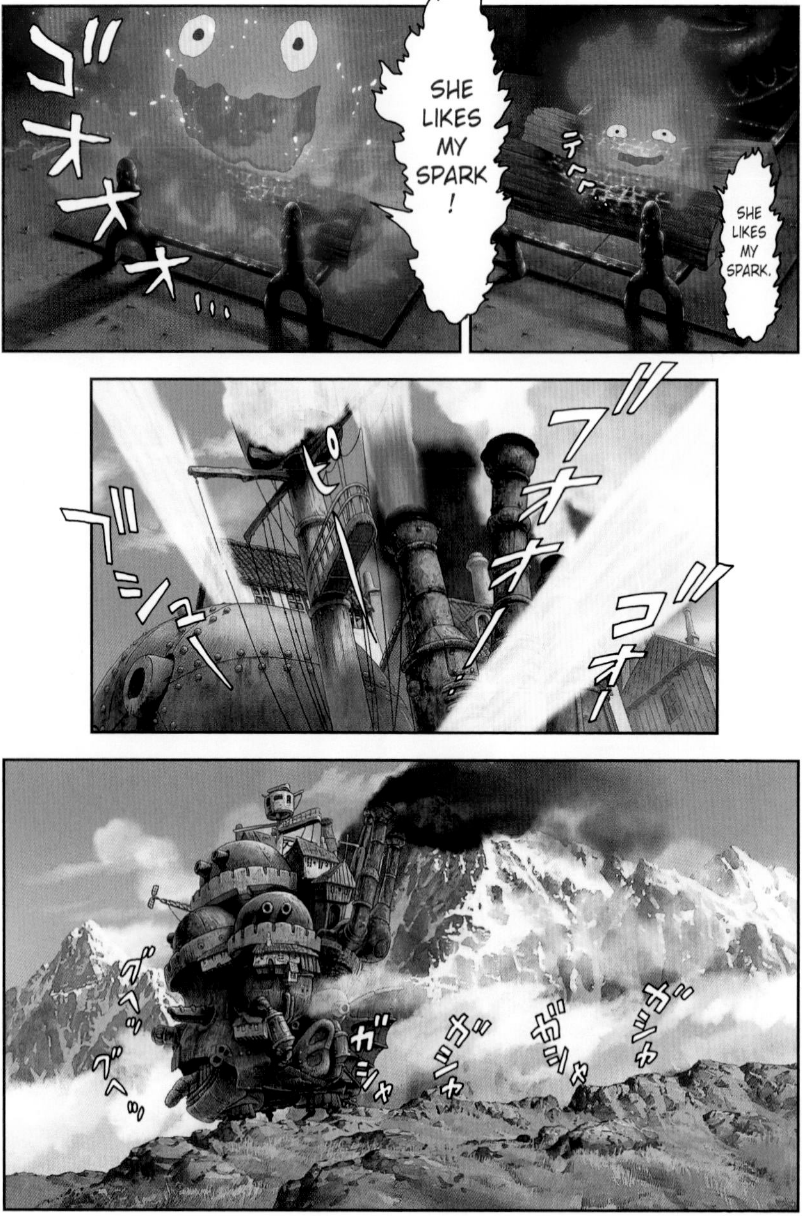
SHE LIKES MY SPARK.
SHE LIKES MY SPARK!

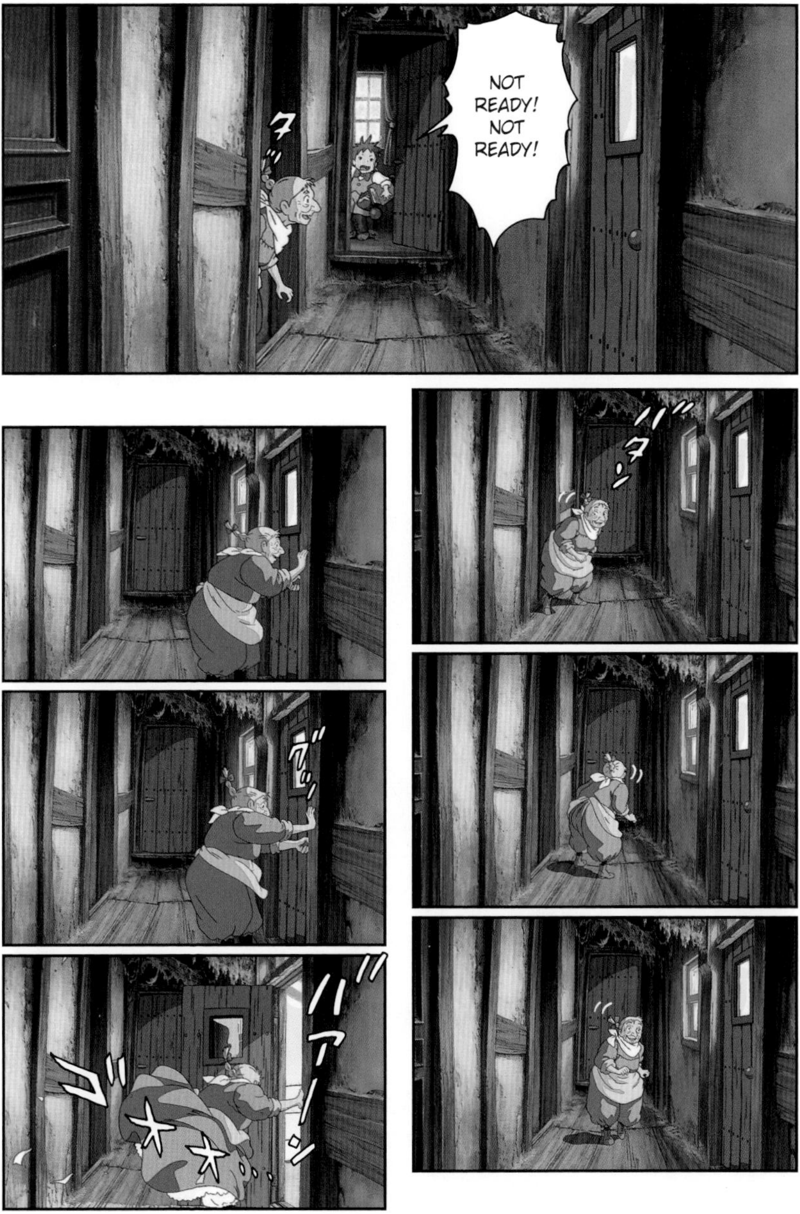
NOT READY! NOT READY!

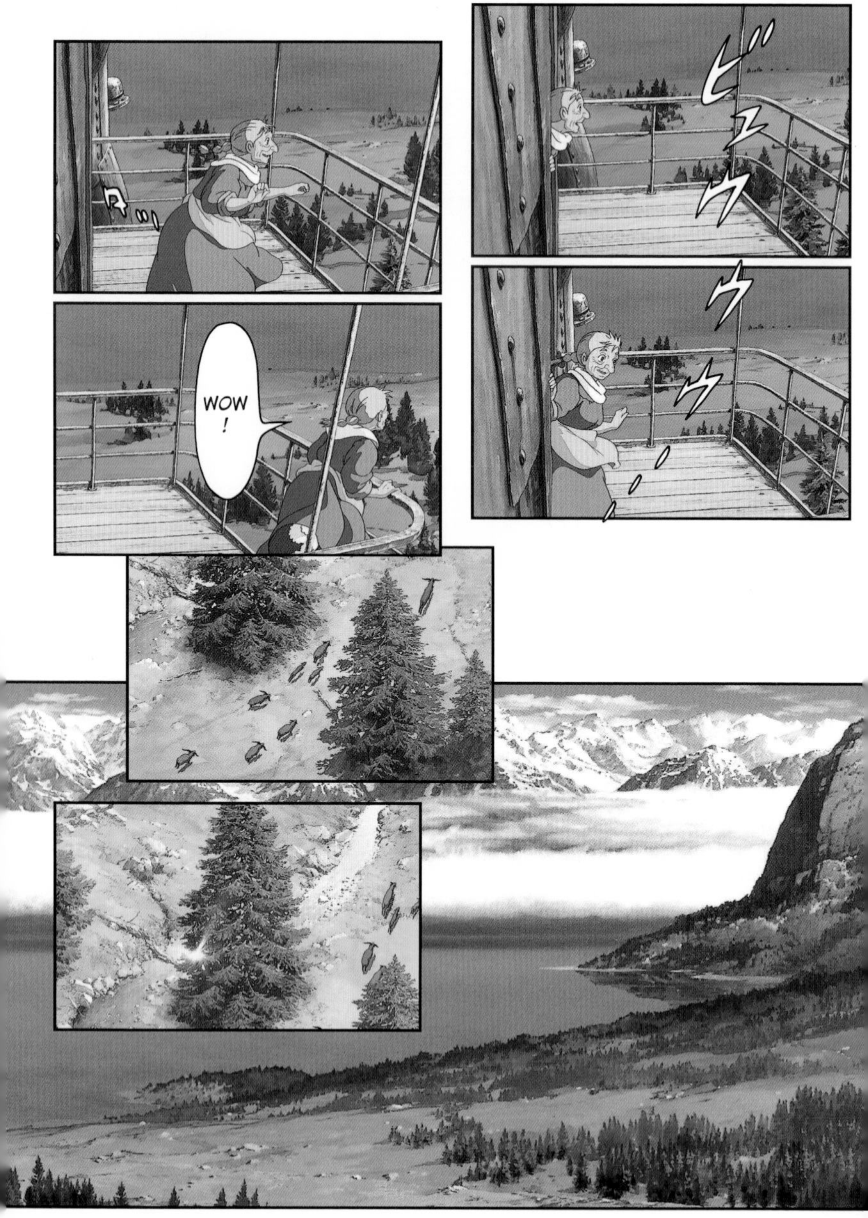
ビュウ
ウウ
ダッ
WOW !

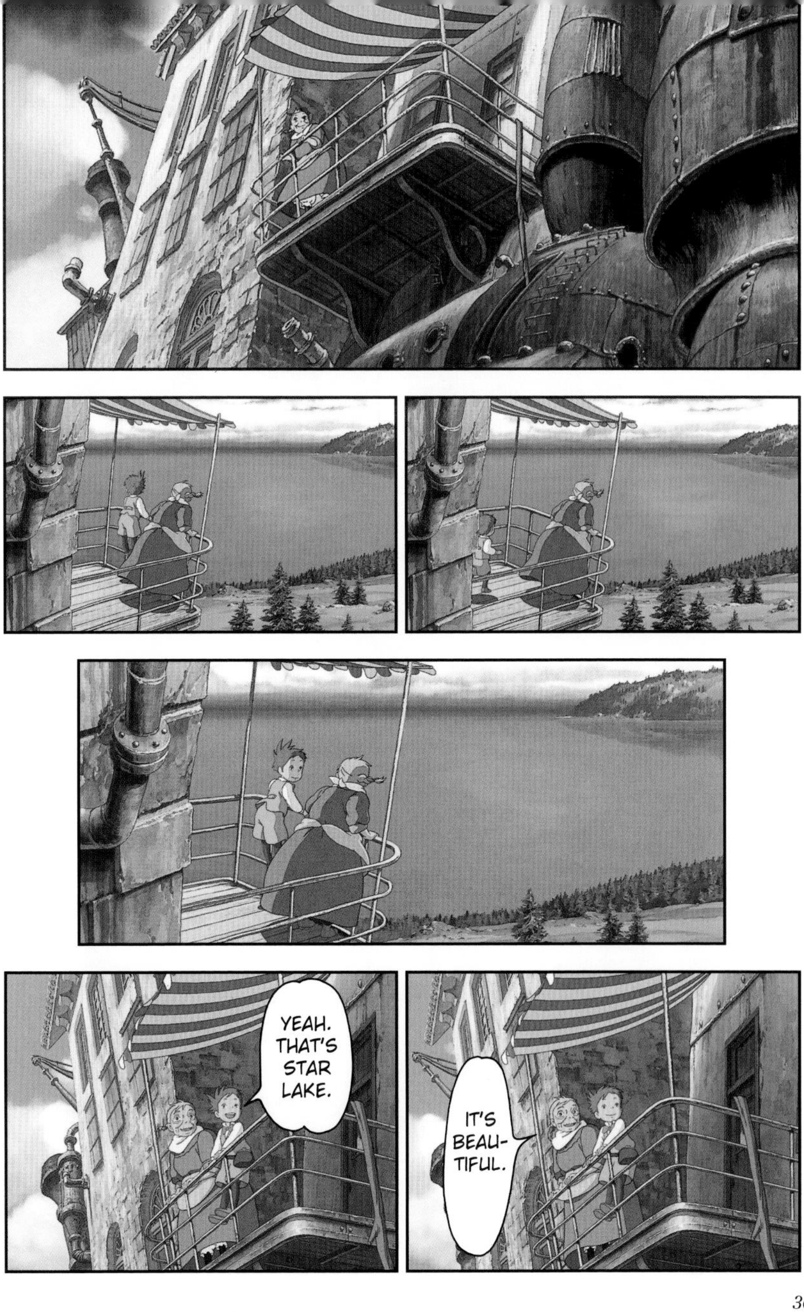
IT'S BEAU-TIFUL.
YEAH. THAT'S STAR LAKE.

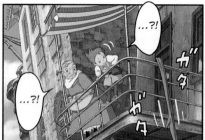

...?!

...?!

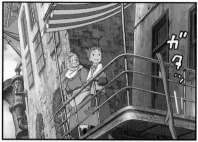

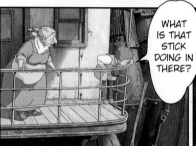

WHAT IS THAT STICK DOING IN THERE?

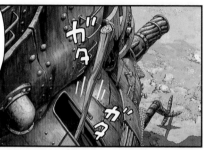

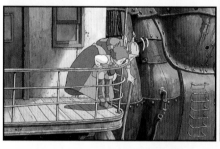

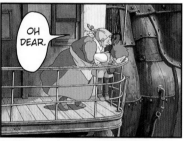

OH DEAR.

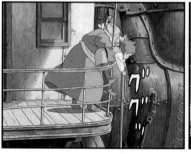

HMM.

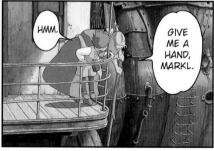

GIVE ME A HAND, MARKL.

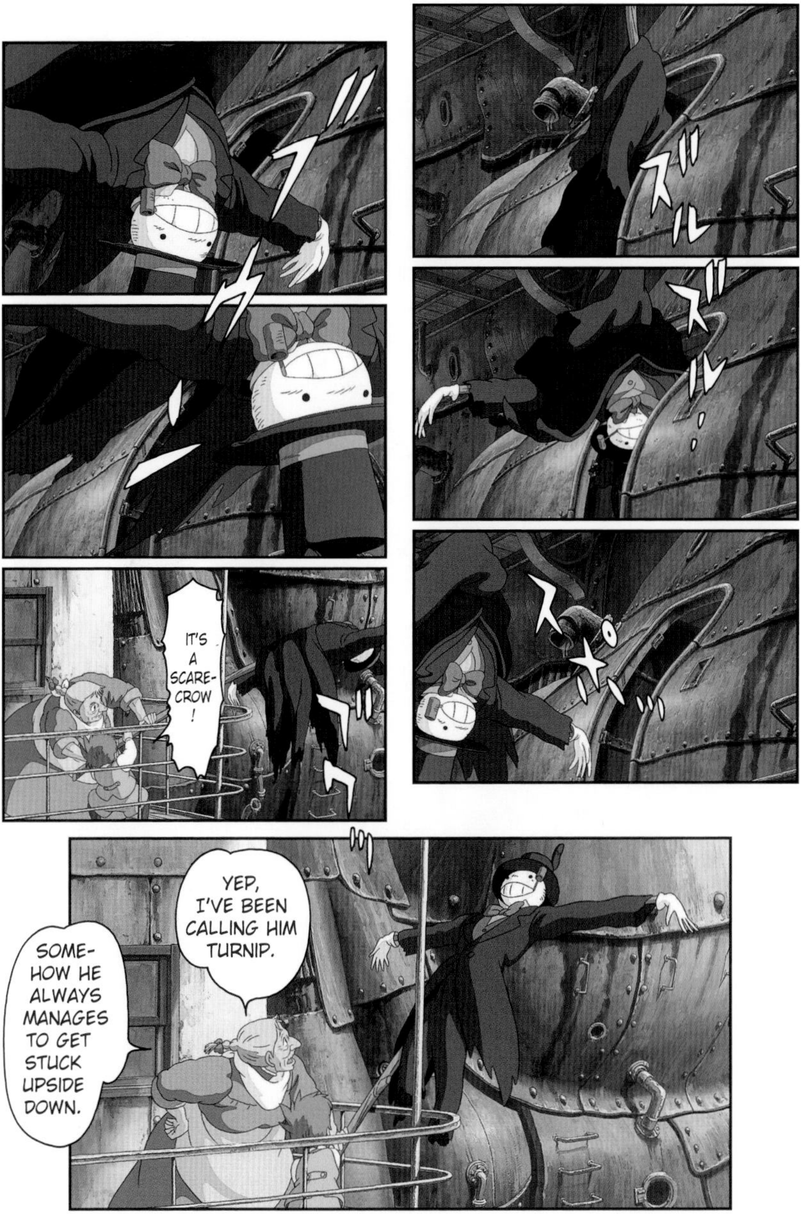
ズル
ズル
IT'S A SCARE-CROW!
YEP, I'VE BEEN CALLING HIM TURNIP.
SOME-HOW HE ALWAYS MANAGES TO GET STUCK UPSIDE DOWN.

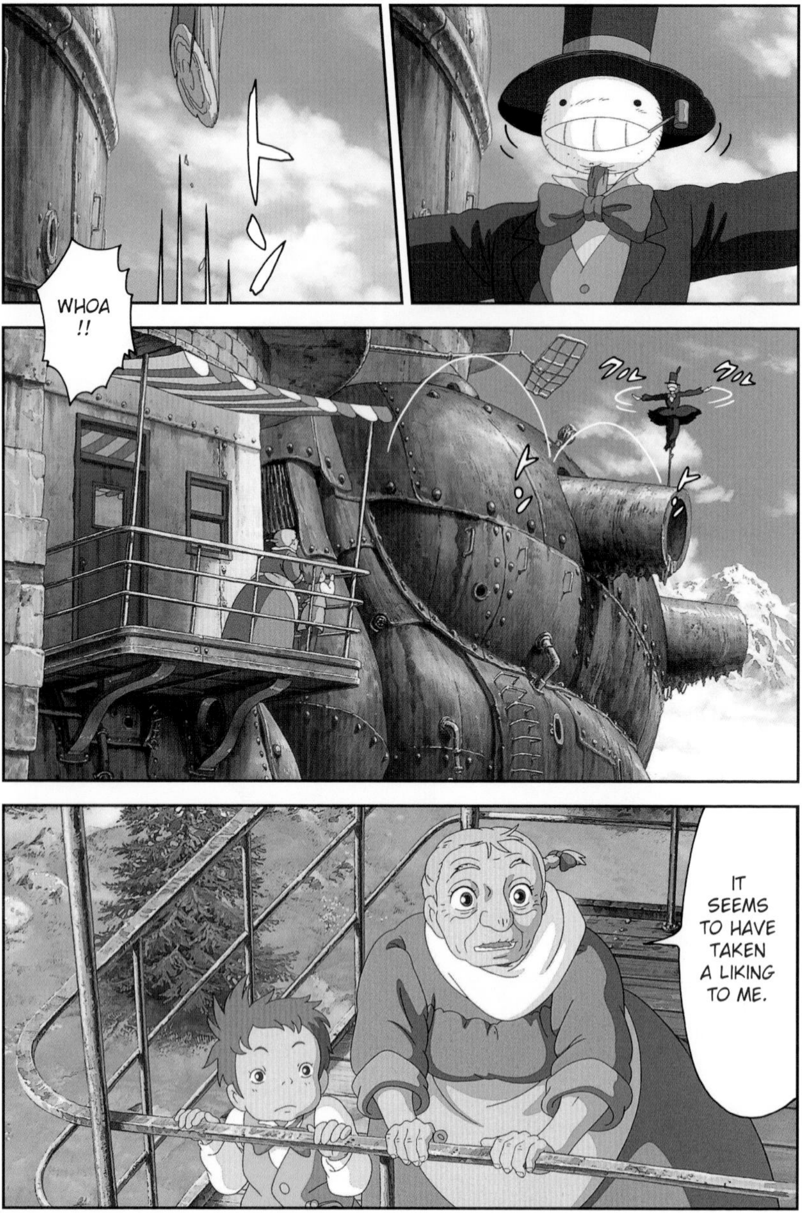
WHOA !!
IT SEEMS TO HAVE TAKEN A LIKING TO ME.

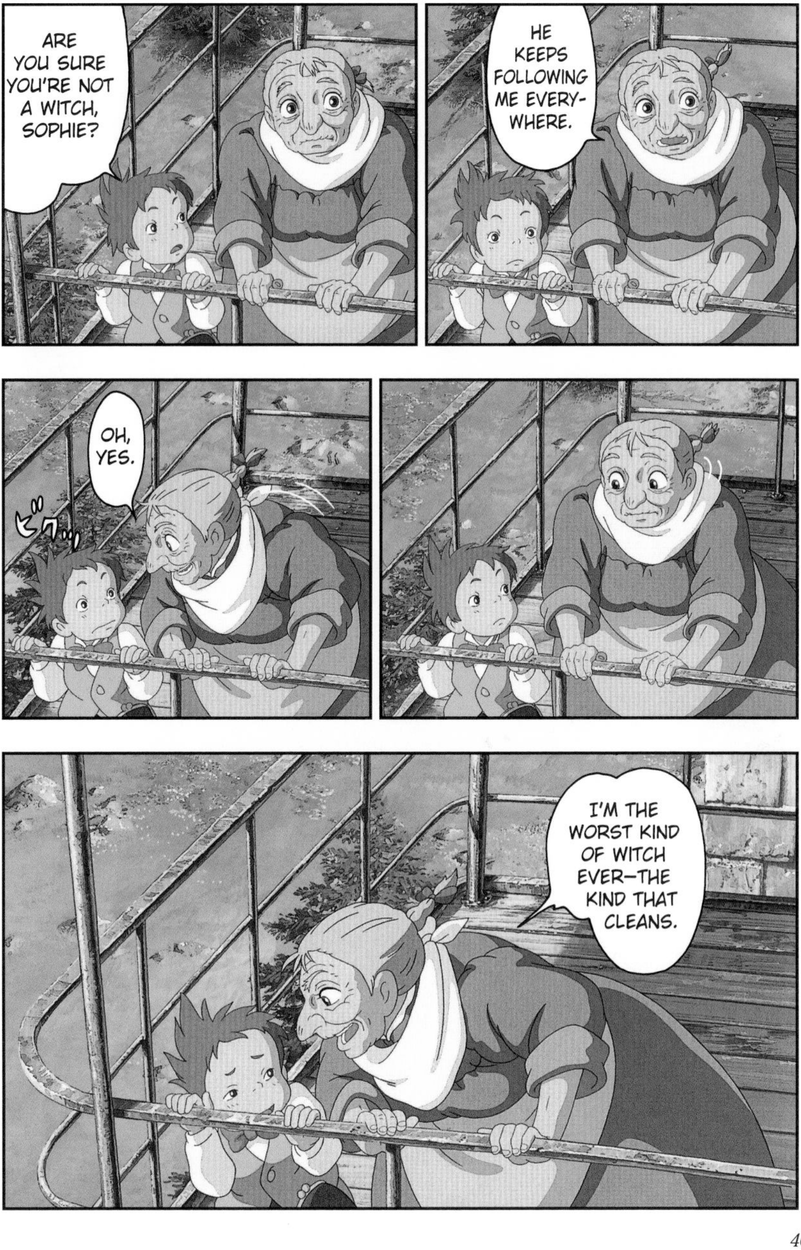
HE KEEPS FOLLOWING ME EVERY-WHERE.
ARE YOU SURE YOU'RE NOT A WITCH, SOPHIE?
OH, YES.
ビクッ…
I'M THE WORST KIND OF WITCH EVER—THE KIND THAT CLEANS.

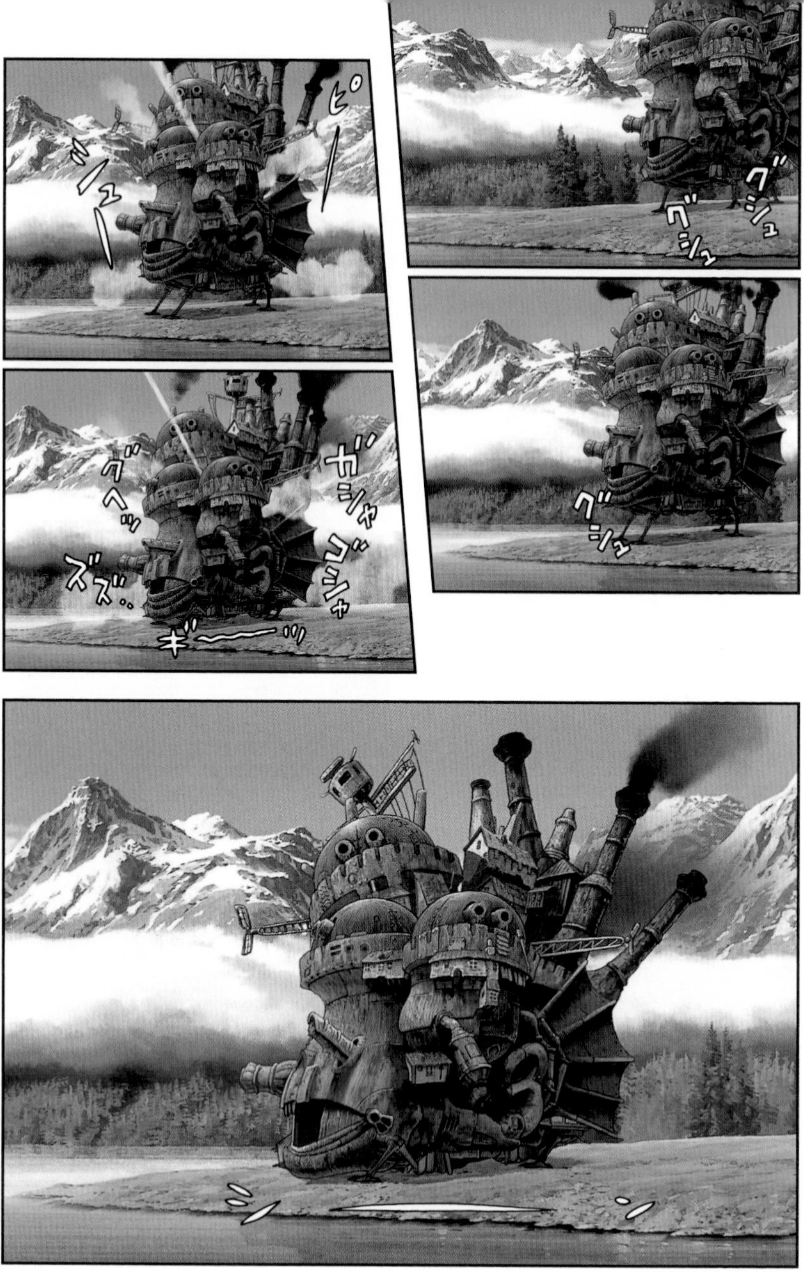
グシュ
グシュ
ピー
シュー
グシュ
ガシャ
ゴシャ
グヘッ
ズズ‥
ギ～～ッ

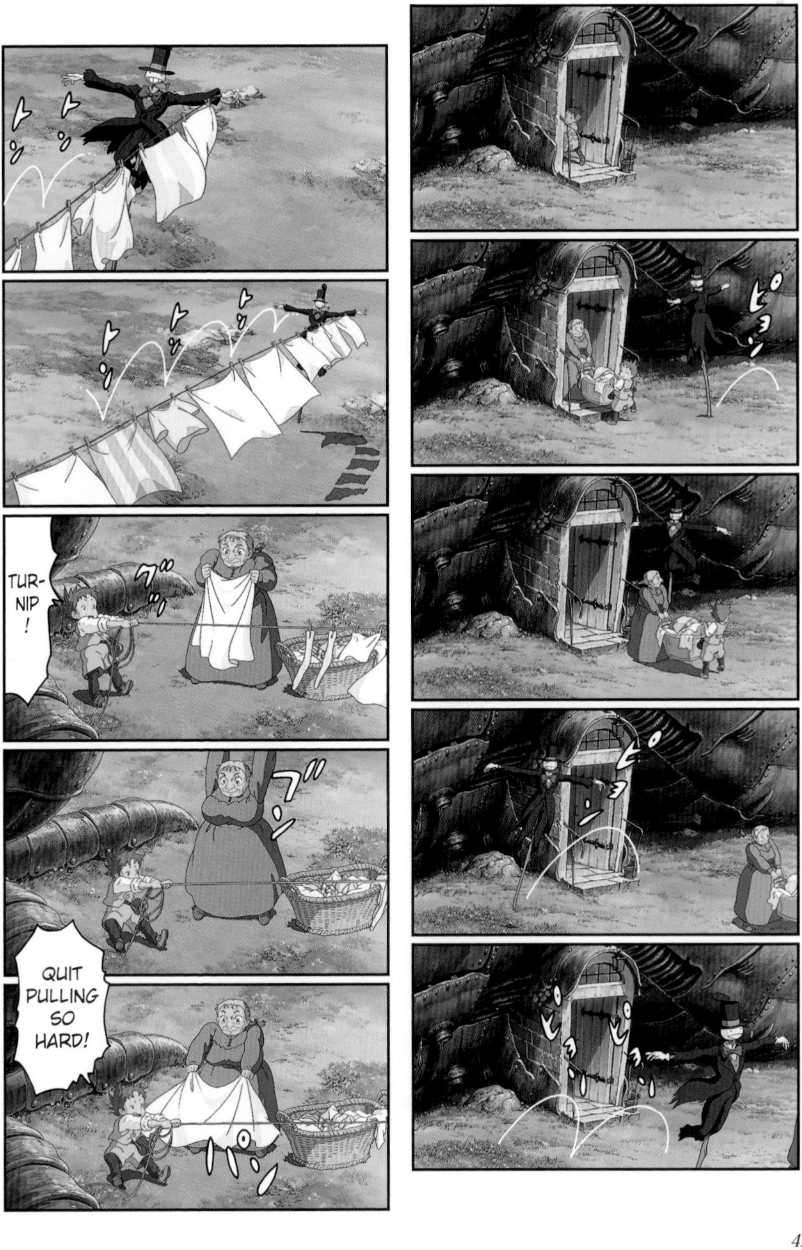
TURNIP!
QUIT PULLING SO HARD!

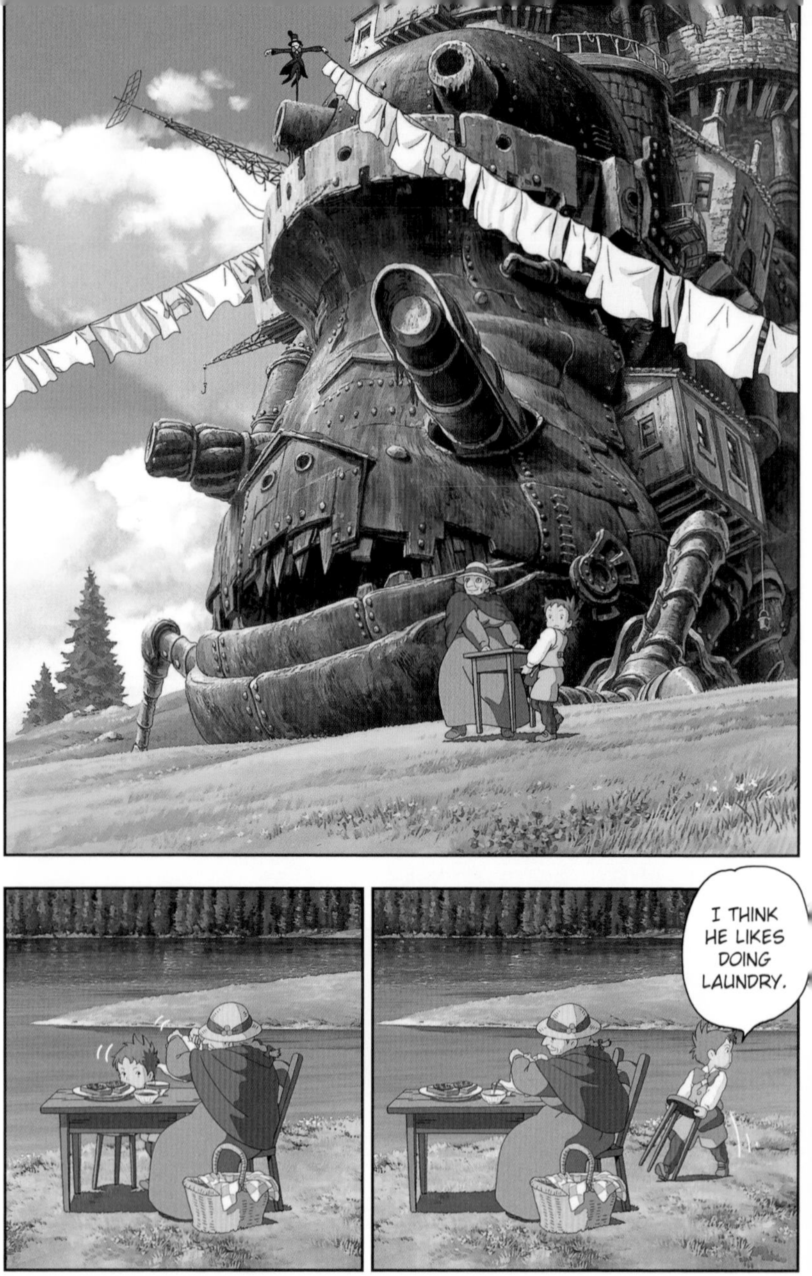
I THINK HE LIKES DOING LAUNDRY.

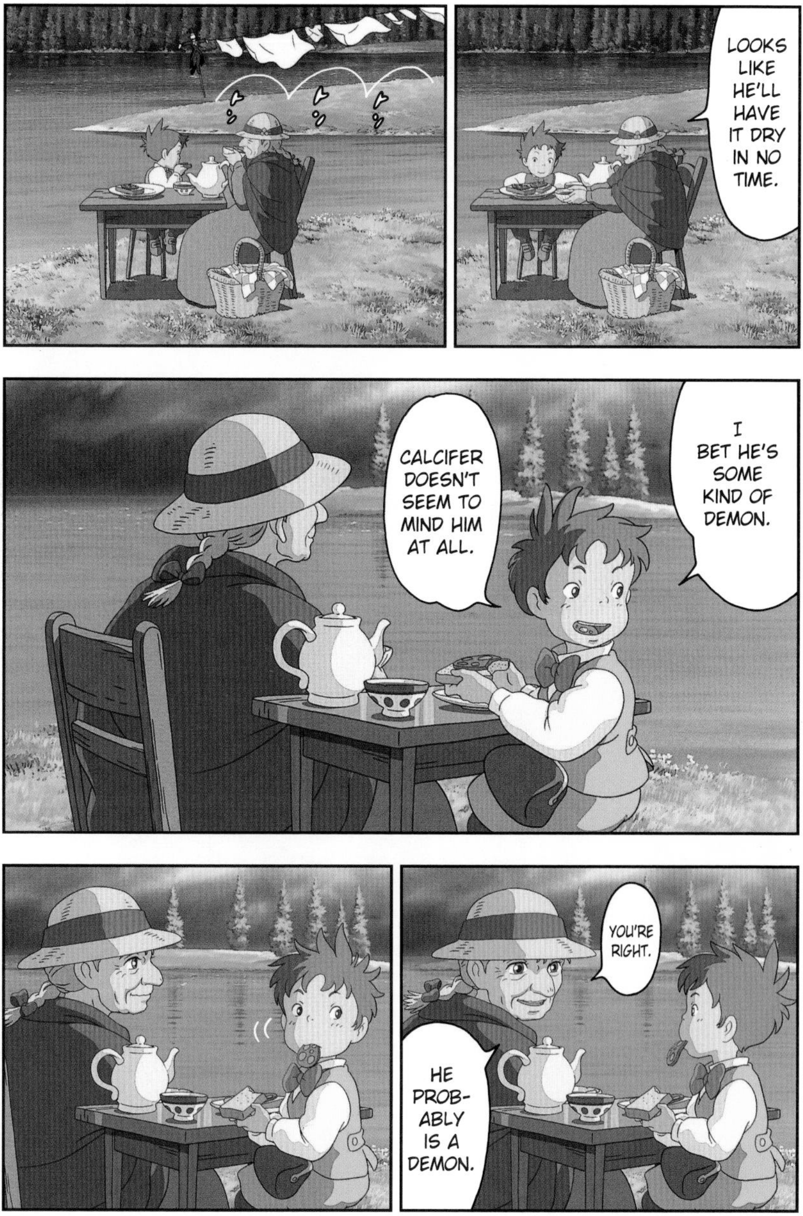
LOOKS LIKE HE'LL HAVE IT DRY IN NO TIME.
I BET HE'S SOME KIND OF DEMON.
CALCIFER DOESN'T SEEM TO MIND HIM AT ALL.
YOU'RE RIGHT.
HE PROB-ABLY IS A DEMON.

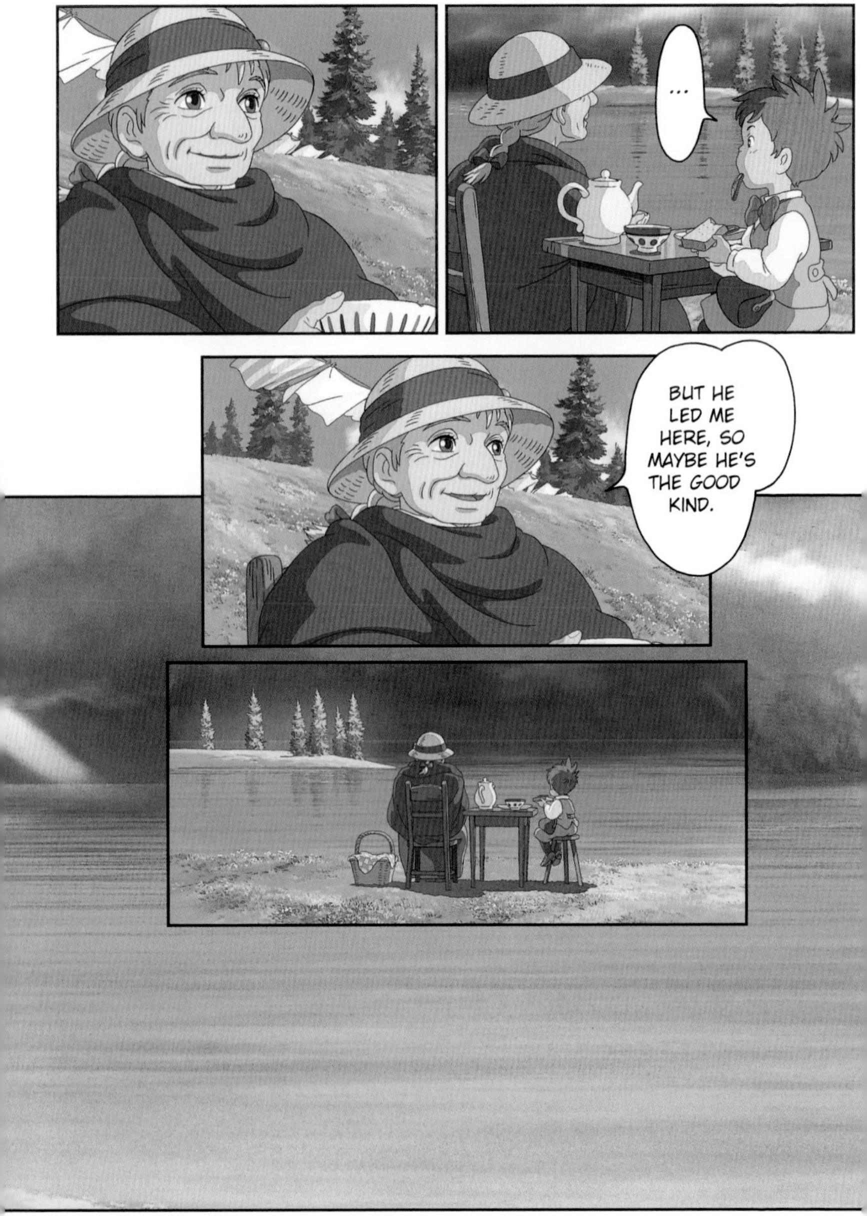
...
BUT HE LED ME HERE, SO MAYBE HE'S THE GOOD KIND.

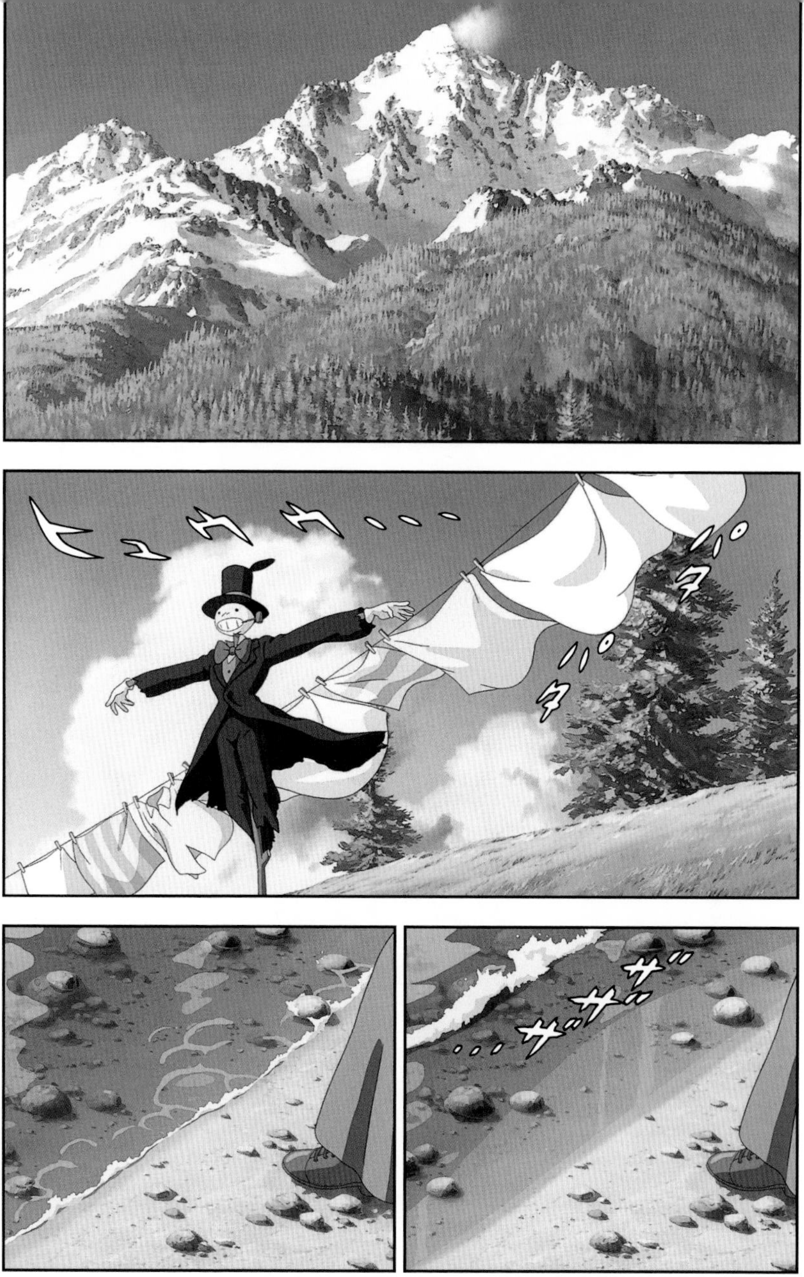
ヒュウウ…
パタパタ
ザザザ…

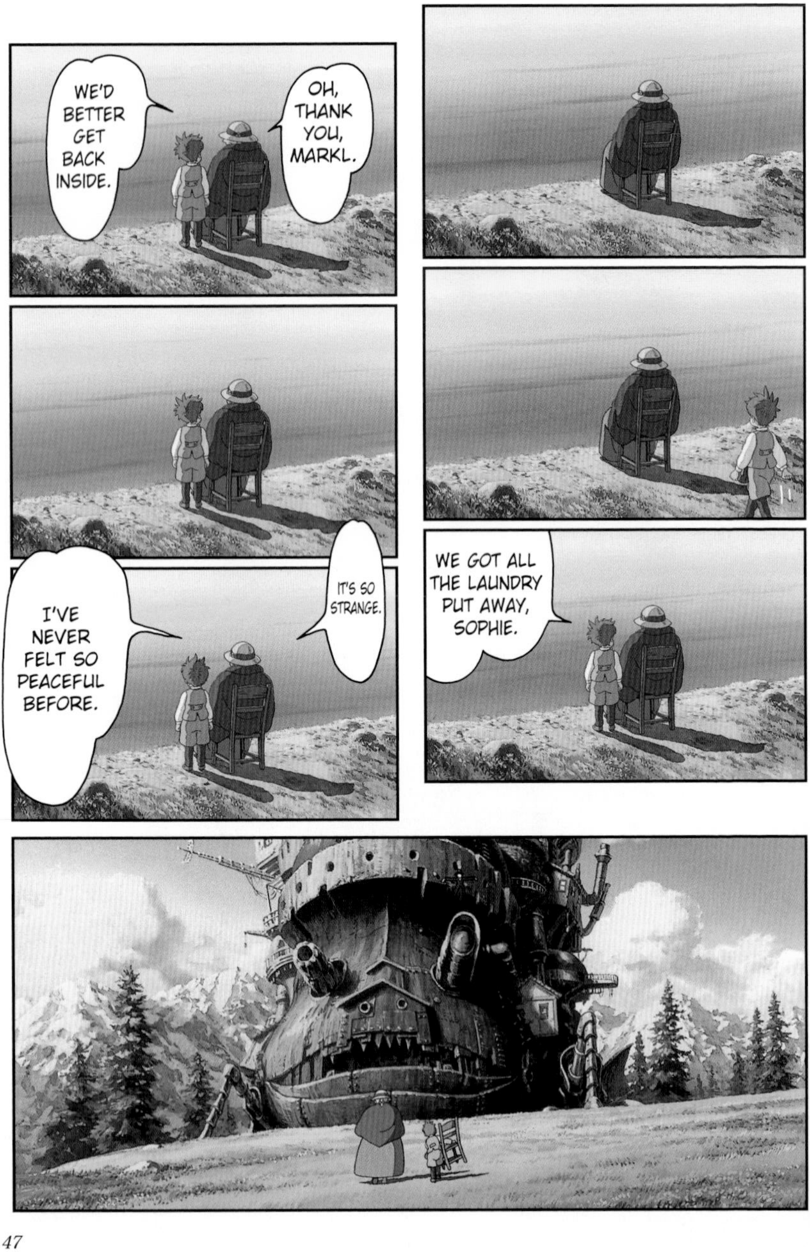
WE GOT ALL THE LAUNDRY PUT AWAY, SOPHIE.
OH, THANK YOU, MARKL.
WE'D BETTER GET BACK INSIDE.
IT'S SO STRANGE.
I'VE NEVER FELT SO PEACEFUL BEFORE.

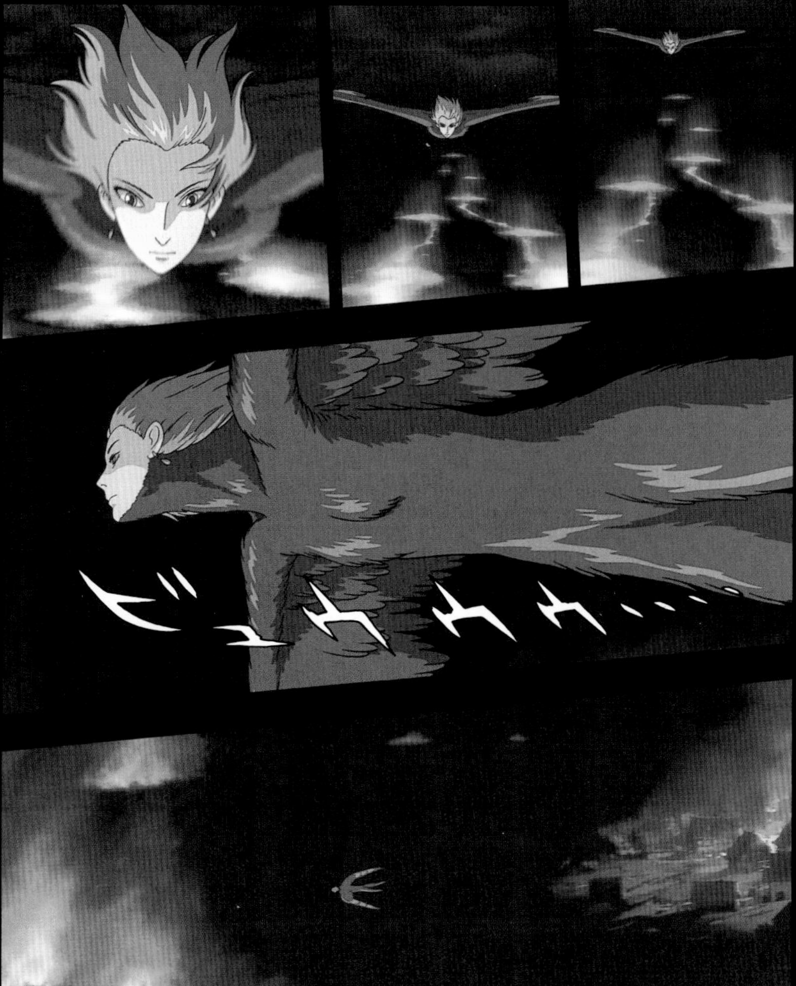
ビュオオオ…

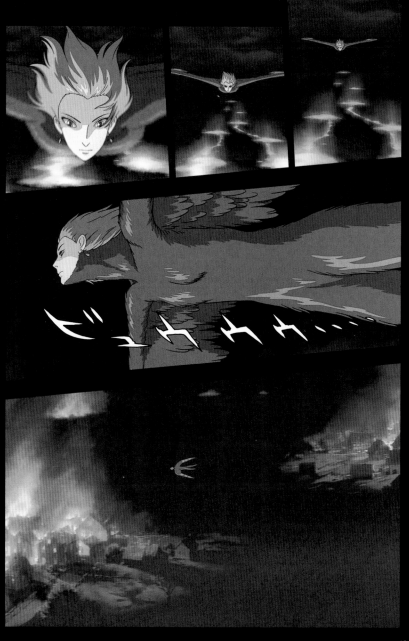

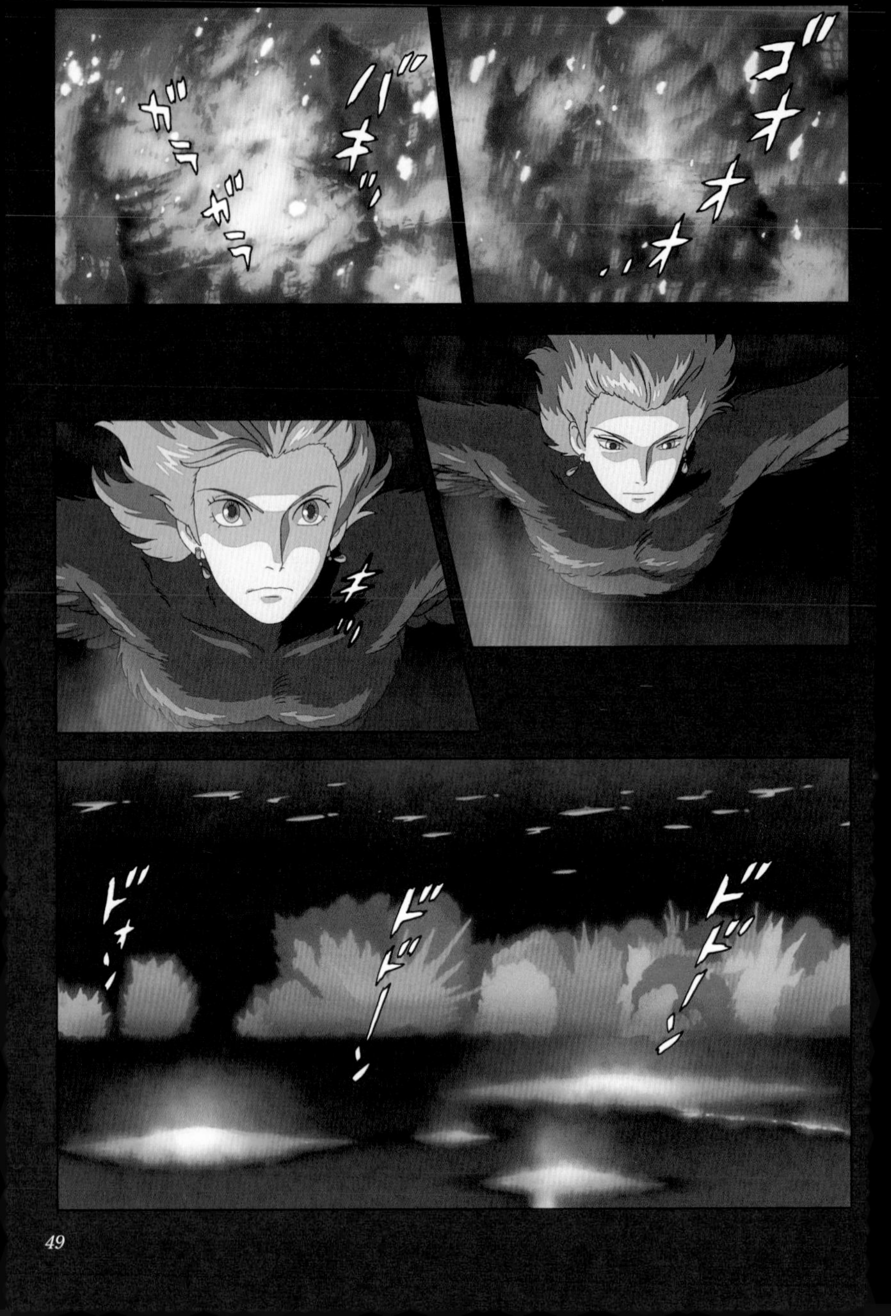
ゴオオオ…
バキッ
ガラ
ガラ
キッ
ドドーン
ドドーン
ドォン

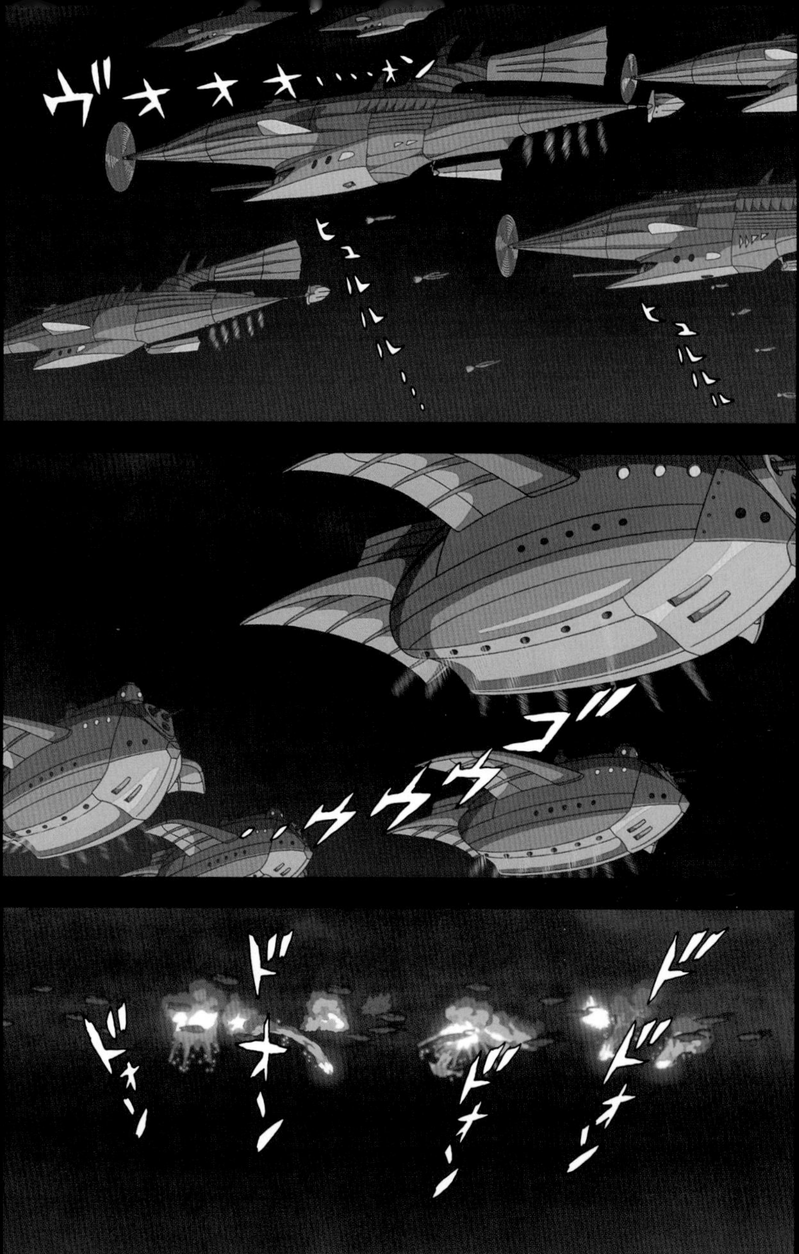

ヴォオオ…ォン
ヒュルルル
ヒュルルル…
ゴゴゴゴ…
ドドォーン
ドォーン
ドォーン
ドォン

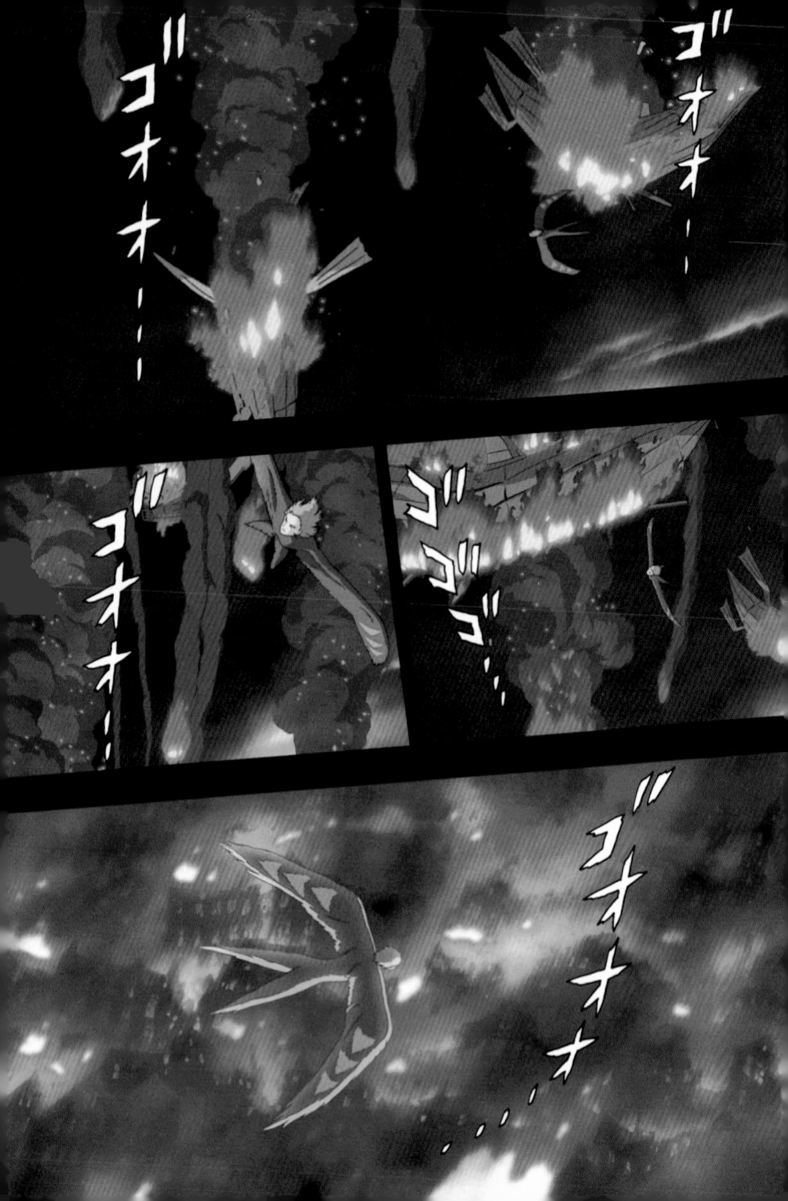
ゴオオーー
ゴオオーーー
ゴゴゴ…
ゴオオオーー
ゴオオオオ……

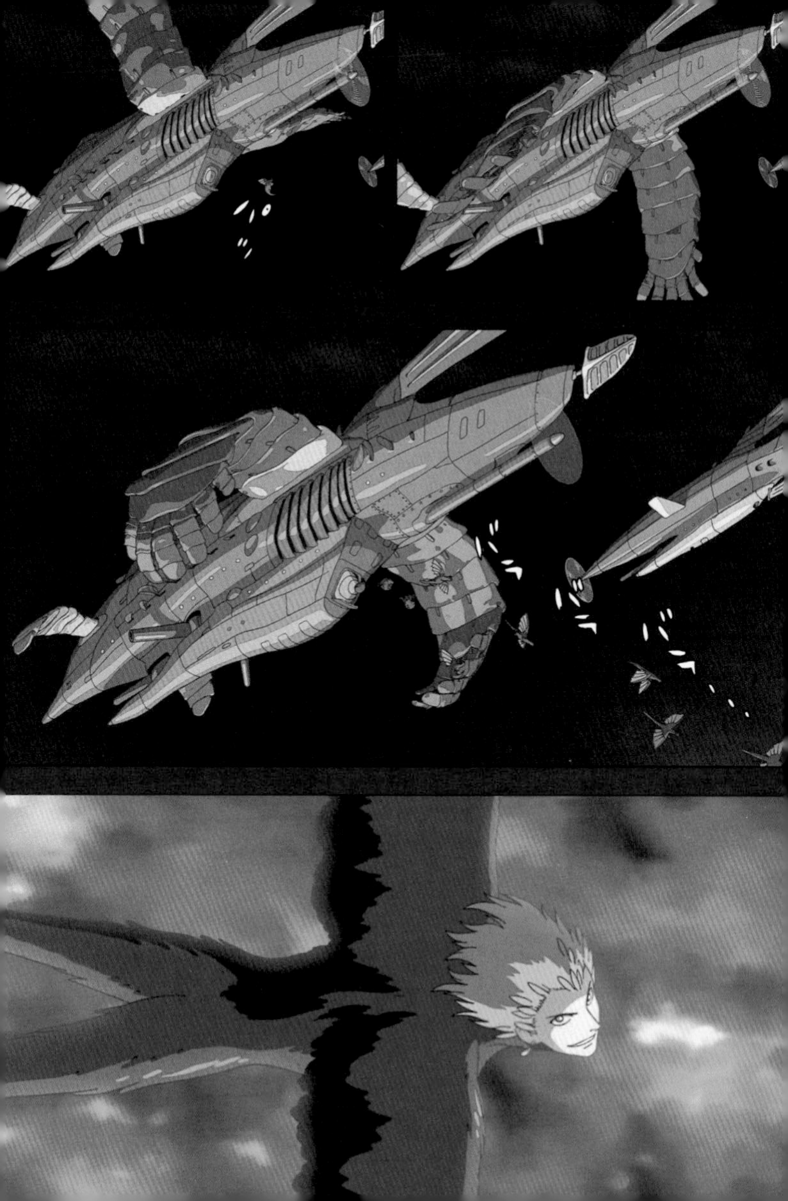

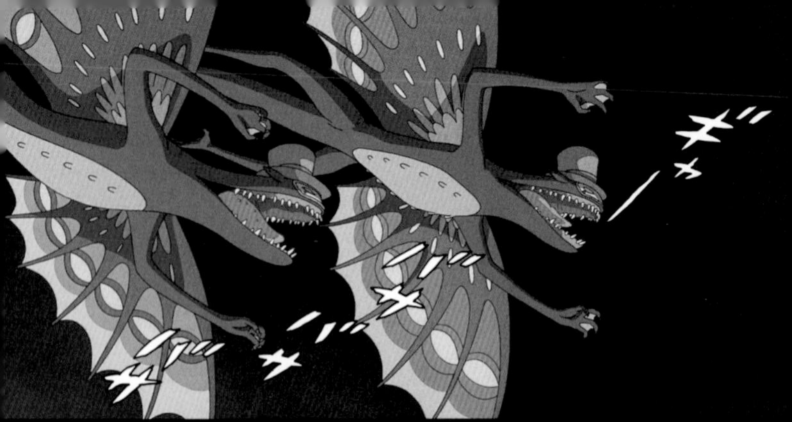
ギャー
ギャ
ギャ
ギャ
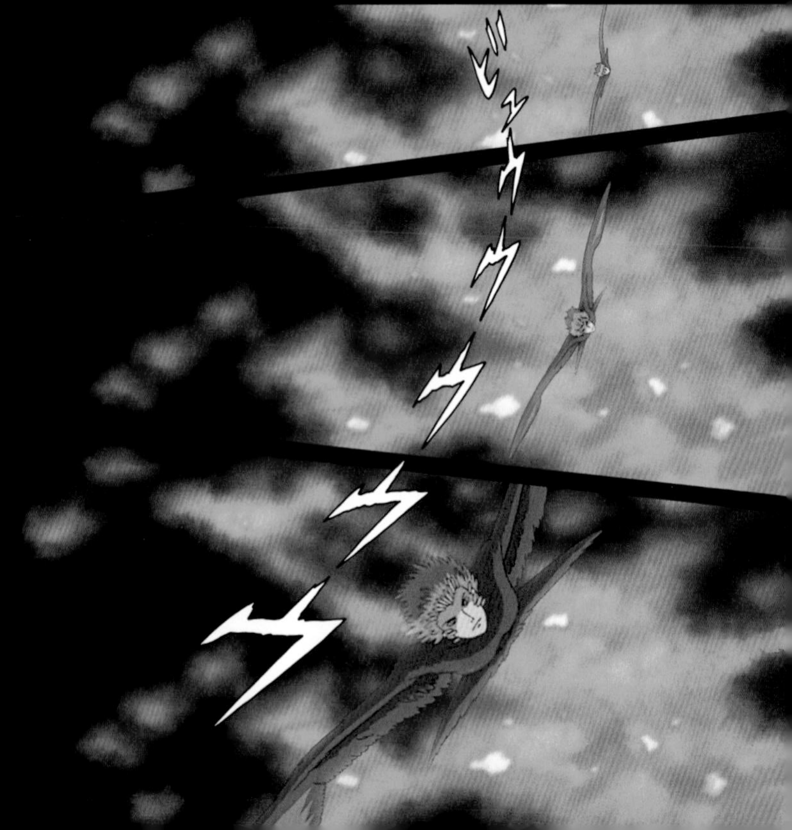
ビュウウウウウ

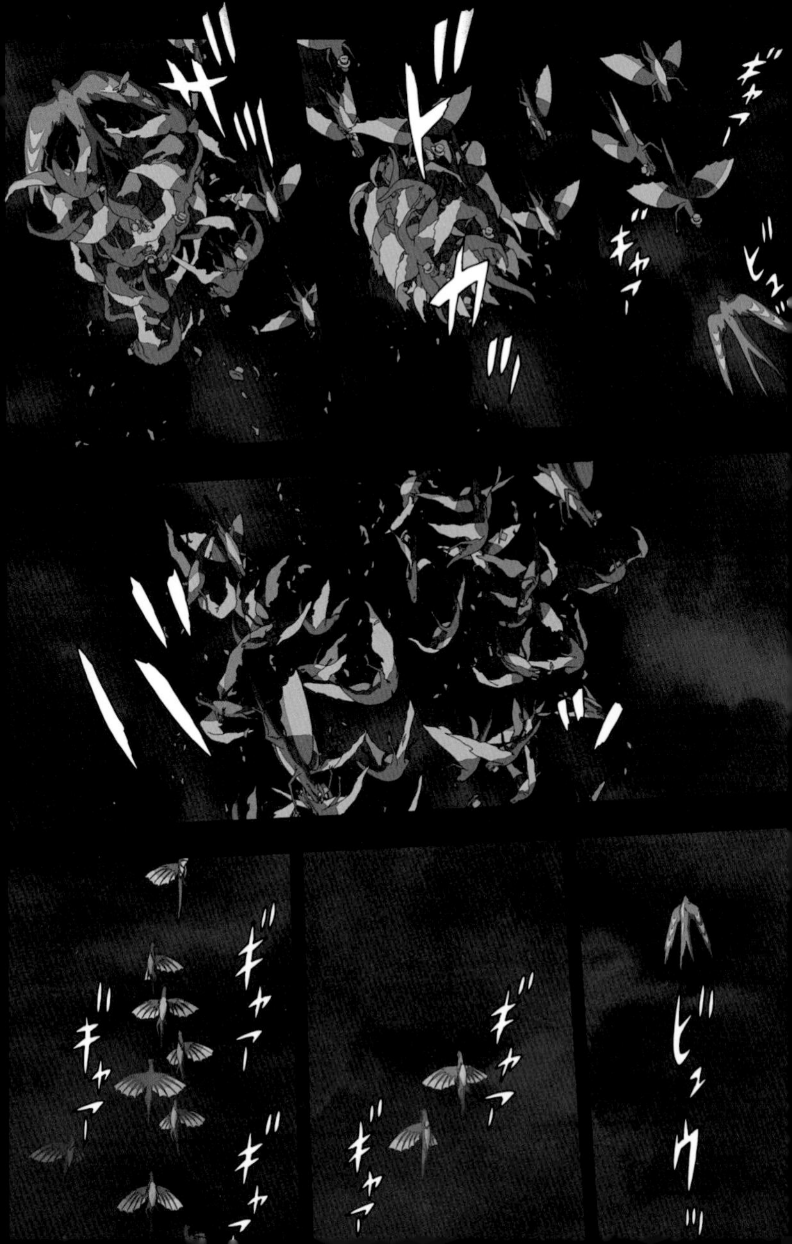
ギャァー
ギャァー
ビュゥ
ドカッ
ザッ
ビュウッ
ギャァー
ギャァ
ギャァー
ギャァー
ギャァ

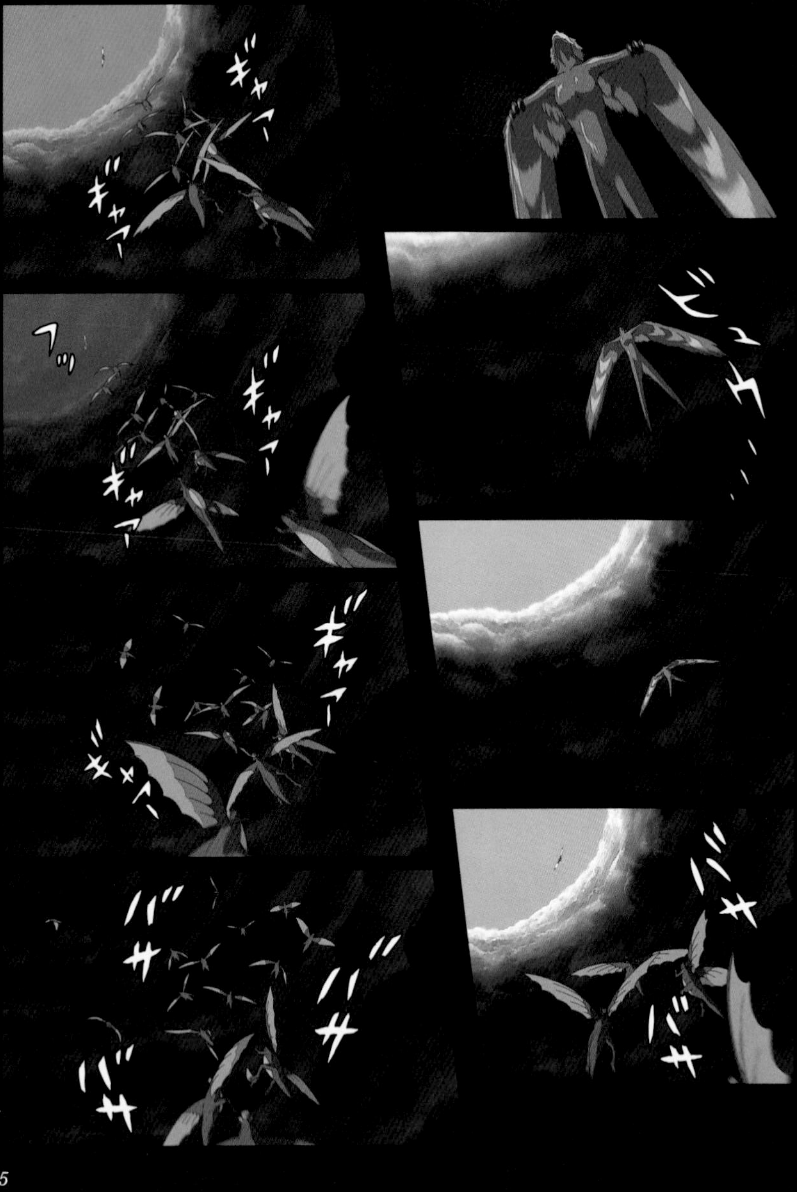
ギャァー
ギャァー
ビュウゥ…
フッ
ギャァー
ギャァー
ギャァー
ギャァー
バサ
バサ
バサ
バサ
バサ

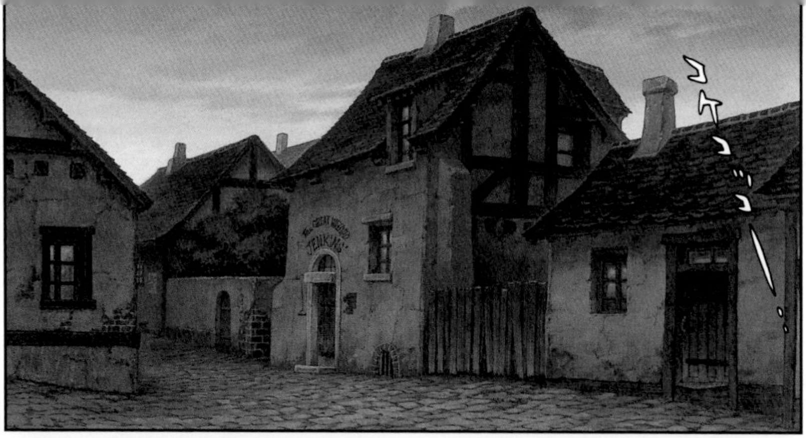
JENKINS
コケコッコー‥
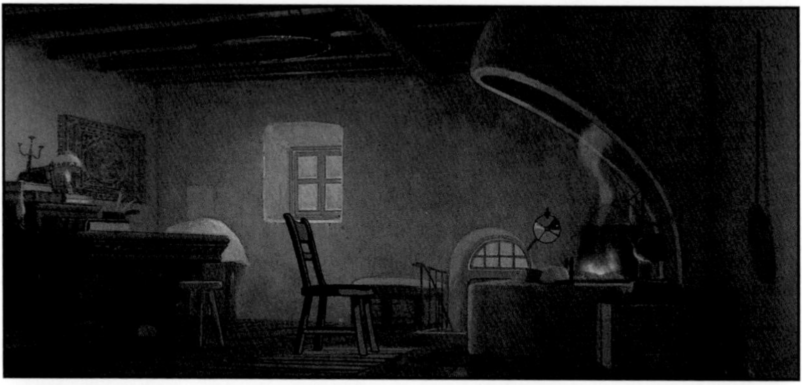
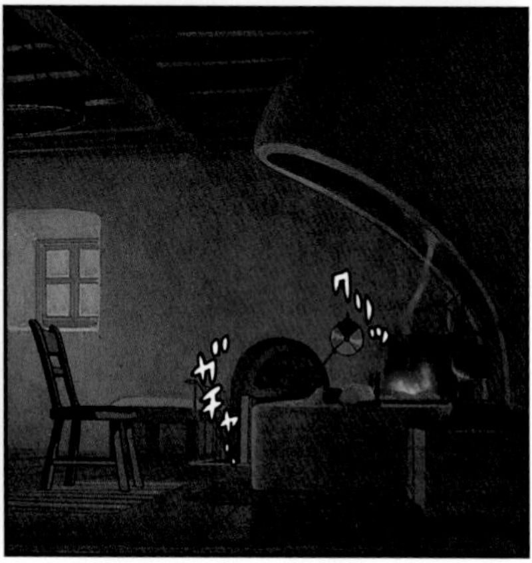
ヘッッ
ガチャ‥
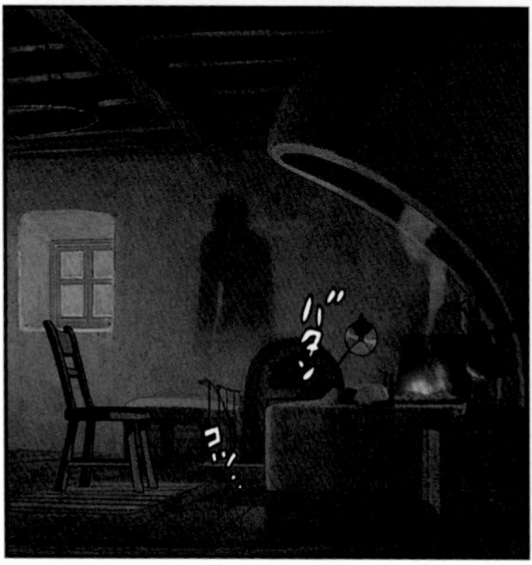
バタン
コッ‥

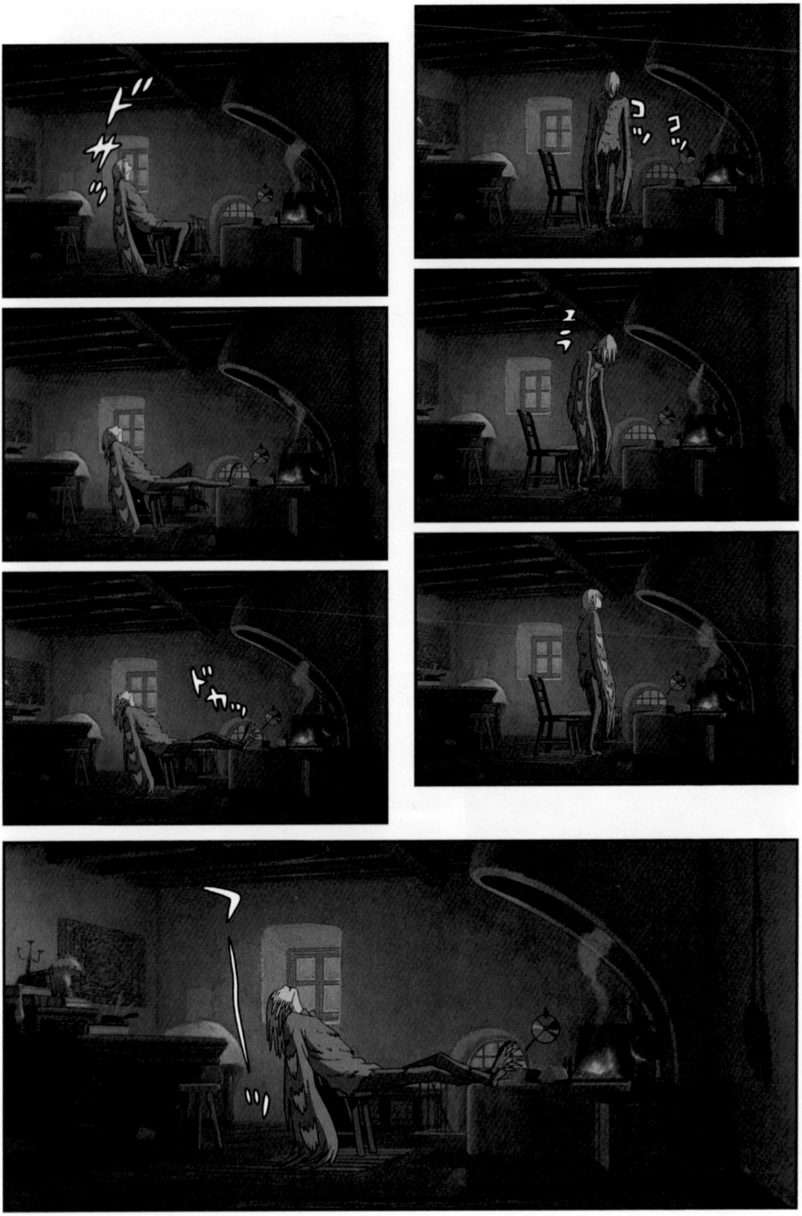

コツ
コツ
ユラ
ドサッ
ドカッ
フーッ

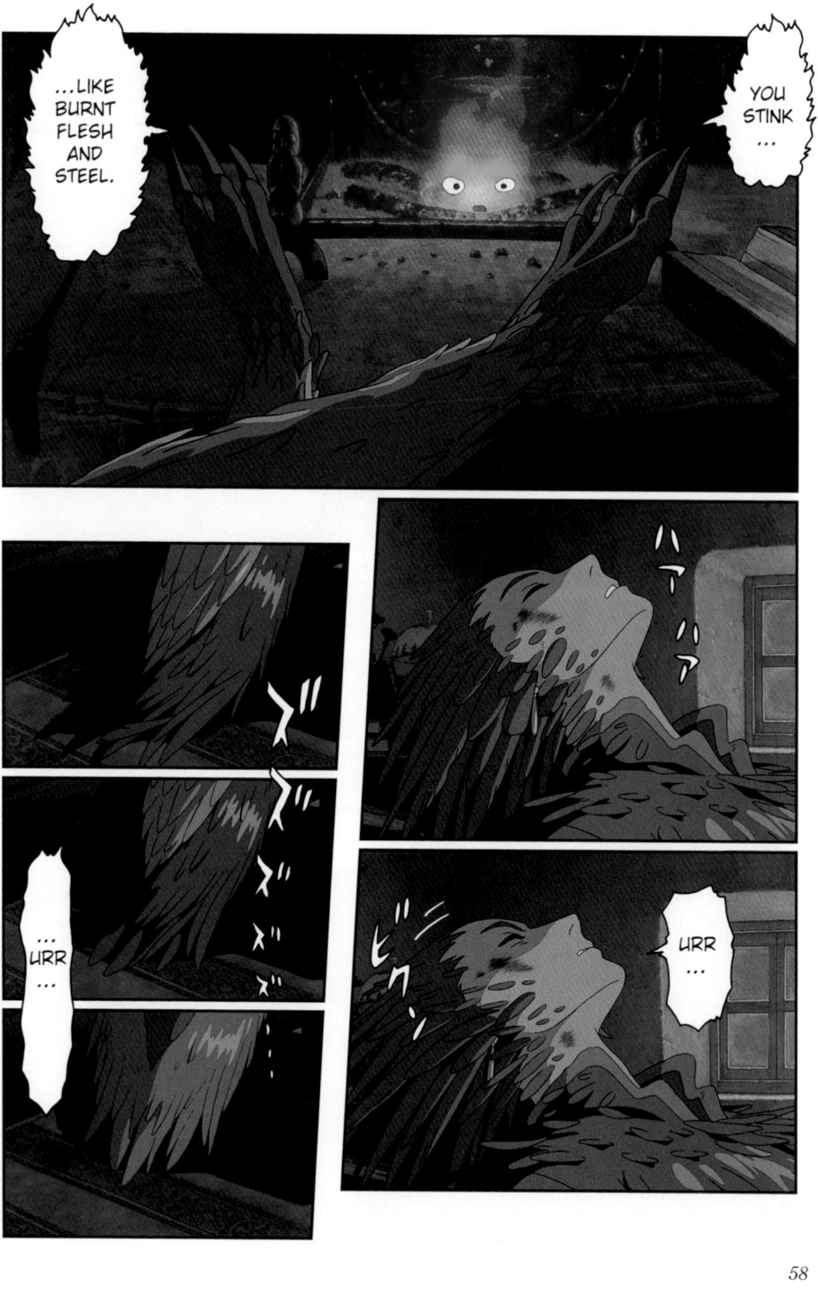
YOU STINK ...
...LIKE BURNT FLESH AND STEEL.
ハァハァ
ビクッ
URR ...
ズズズズズ
... URR ...

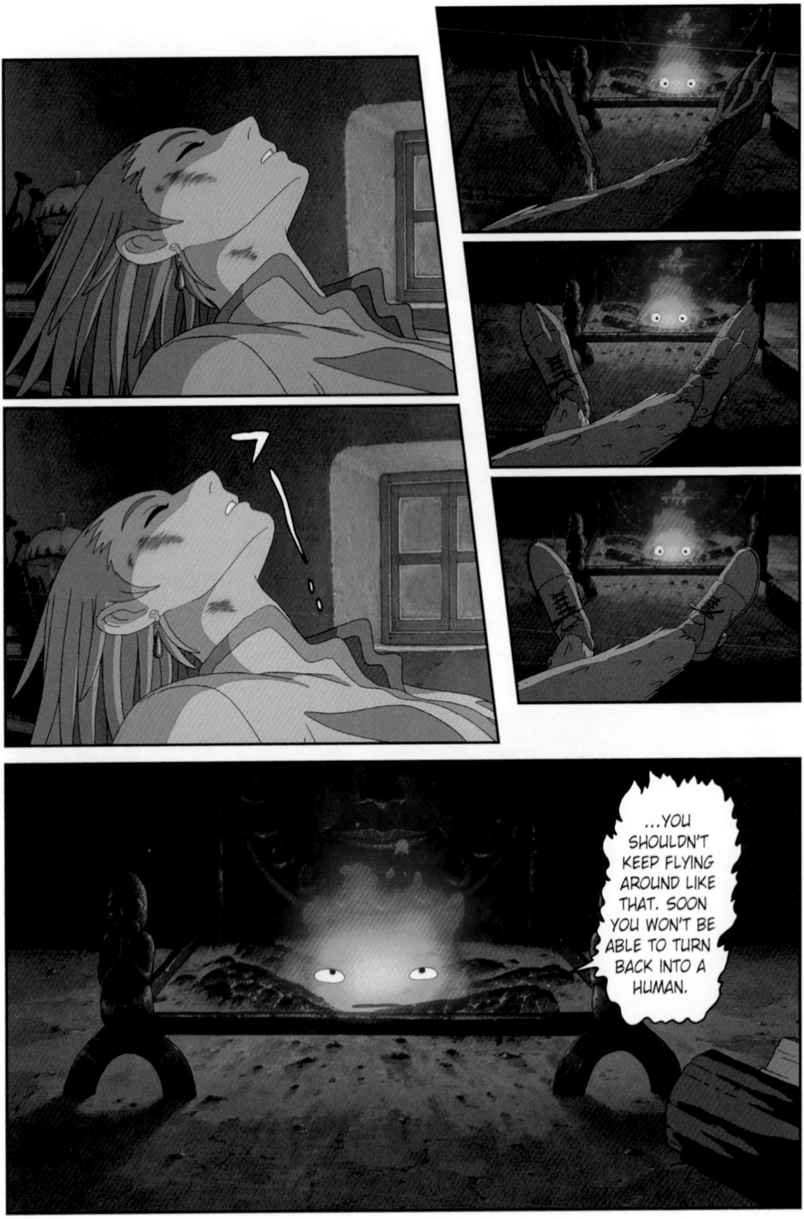
...YOU SHOULDN'T KEEP FLYING AROUND LIKE THAT. SOON YOU WON'T BE ABLE TO TURN BACK INTO A HUMAN.

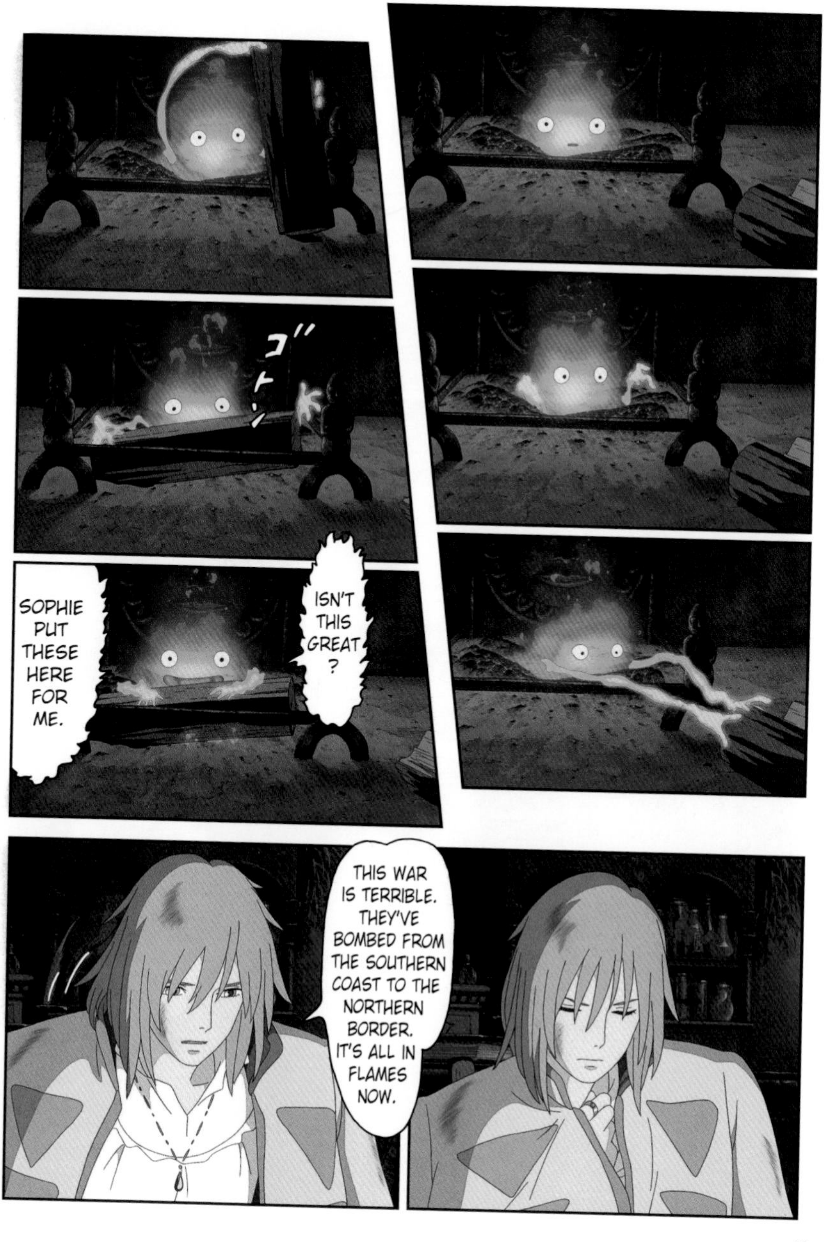
ゴト
ISN'T THIS GREAT?
SOPHIE PUT THESE HERE FOR ME.
THIS WAR IS TERRIBLE. THEY'VE BOMBED FROM THE SOUTHERN COAST TO THE NORTHERN BORDER. IT'S ALL IN FLAMES NOW.

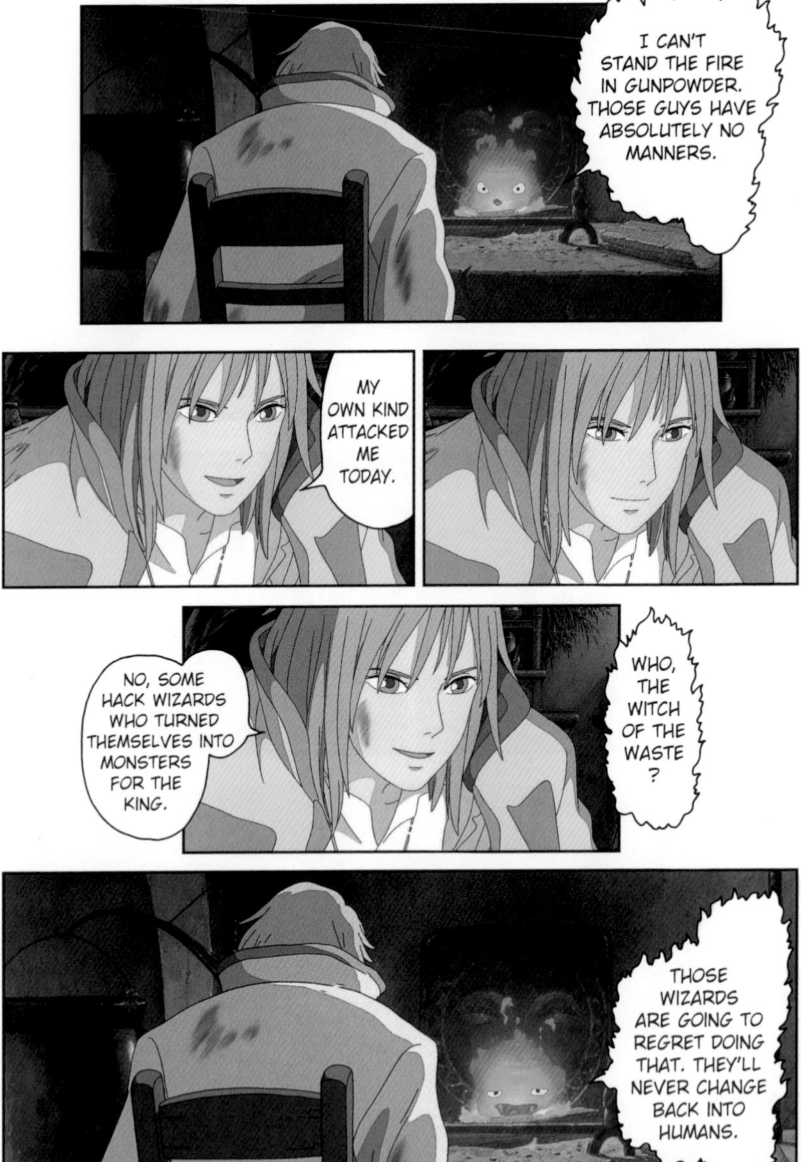
I CAN'T STAND THE FIRE IN GUNPOWDER. THOSE GUYS HAVE ABSOLUTELY NO MANNERS.
MY OWN KIND ATTACKED ME TODAY.
WHO, THE WITCH OF THE WASTE ?
NO, SOME HACK WIZARDS WHO TURNED THEMSELVES INTO MONSTERS FOR THE KING.
THOSE WIZARDS ARE GOING TO REGRET DOING THAT. THEY'LL NEVER CHANGE BACK INTO HUMANS.

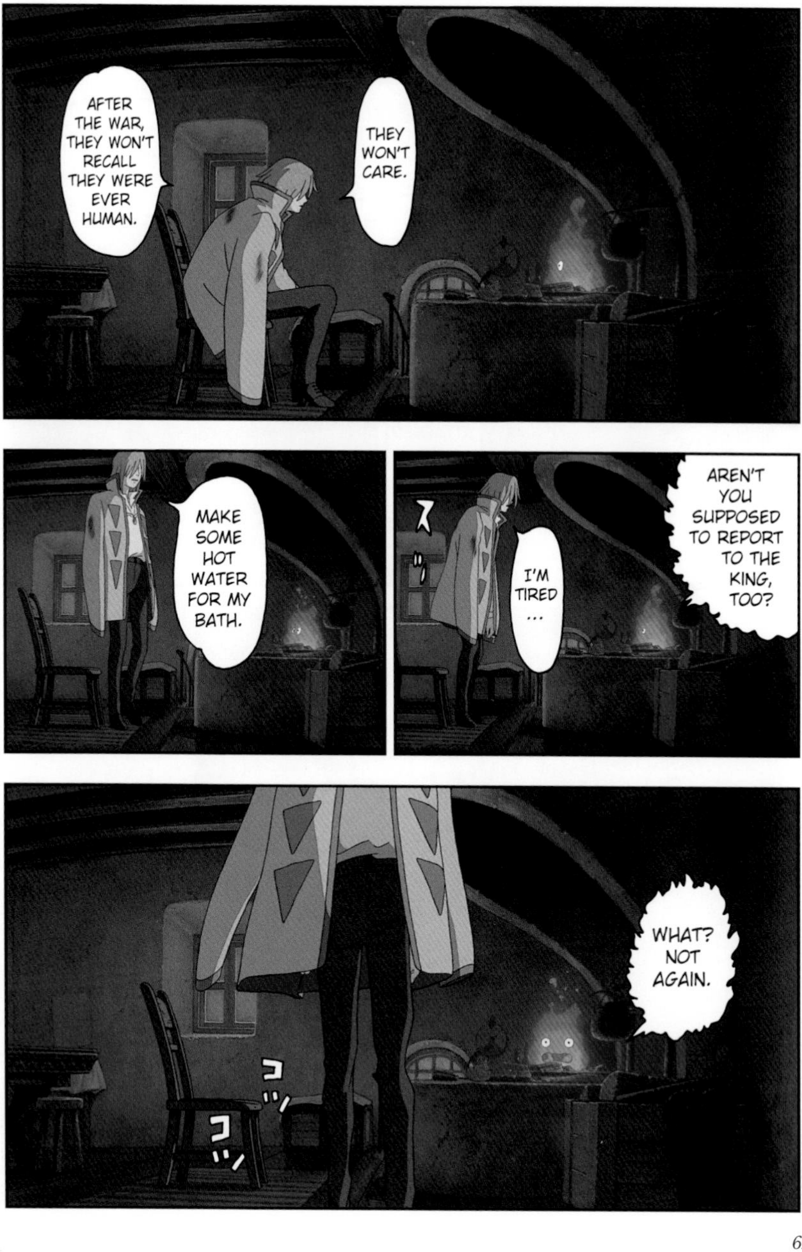
THEY WON'T CARE.
AFTER THE WAR, THEY WON'T RECALL THEY WERE EVER HUMAN.
AREN'T YOU SUPPOSED TO REPORT TO THE KING, TOO?
I'M TIRED ...
ス
MAKE SOME HOT WATER FOR MY BATH.
WHAT? NOT AGAIN.
コツ
コツ

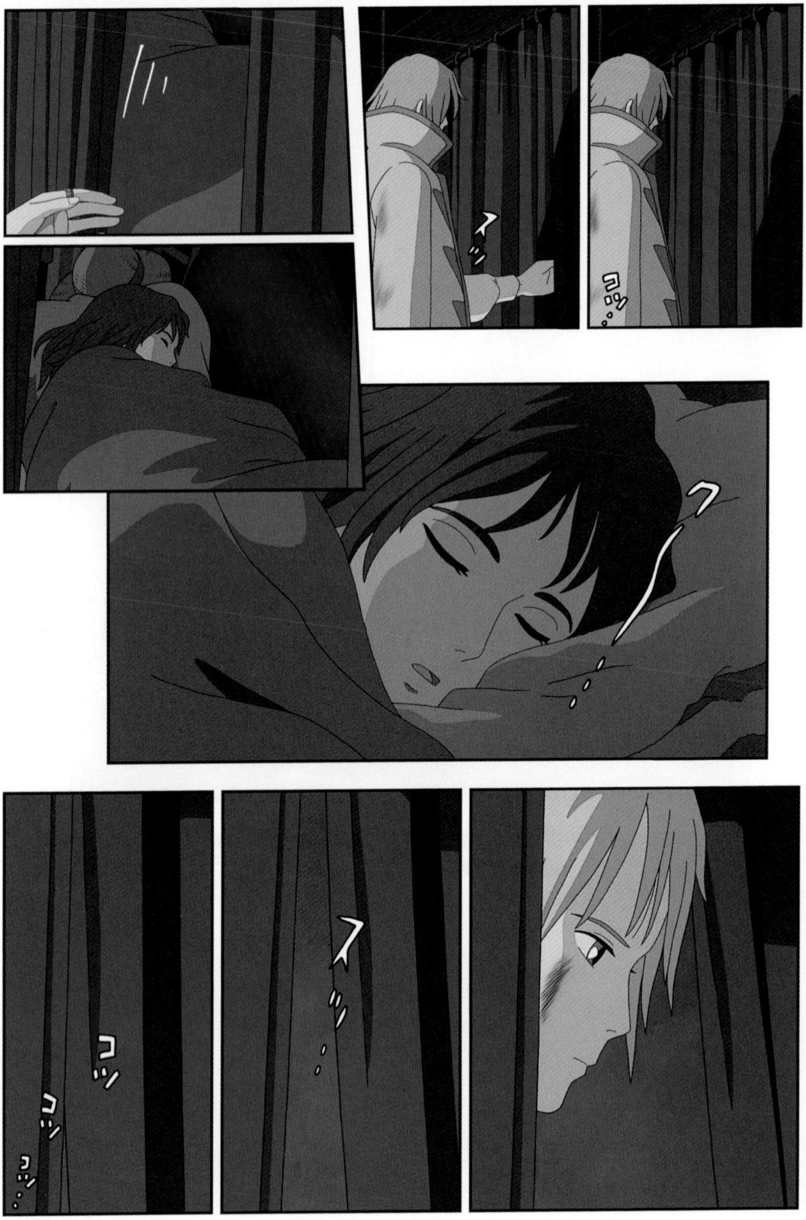
コッ…
スッ
ク…
スッ…
コッ
コッ
コッ…

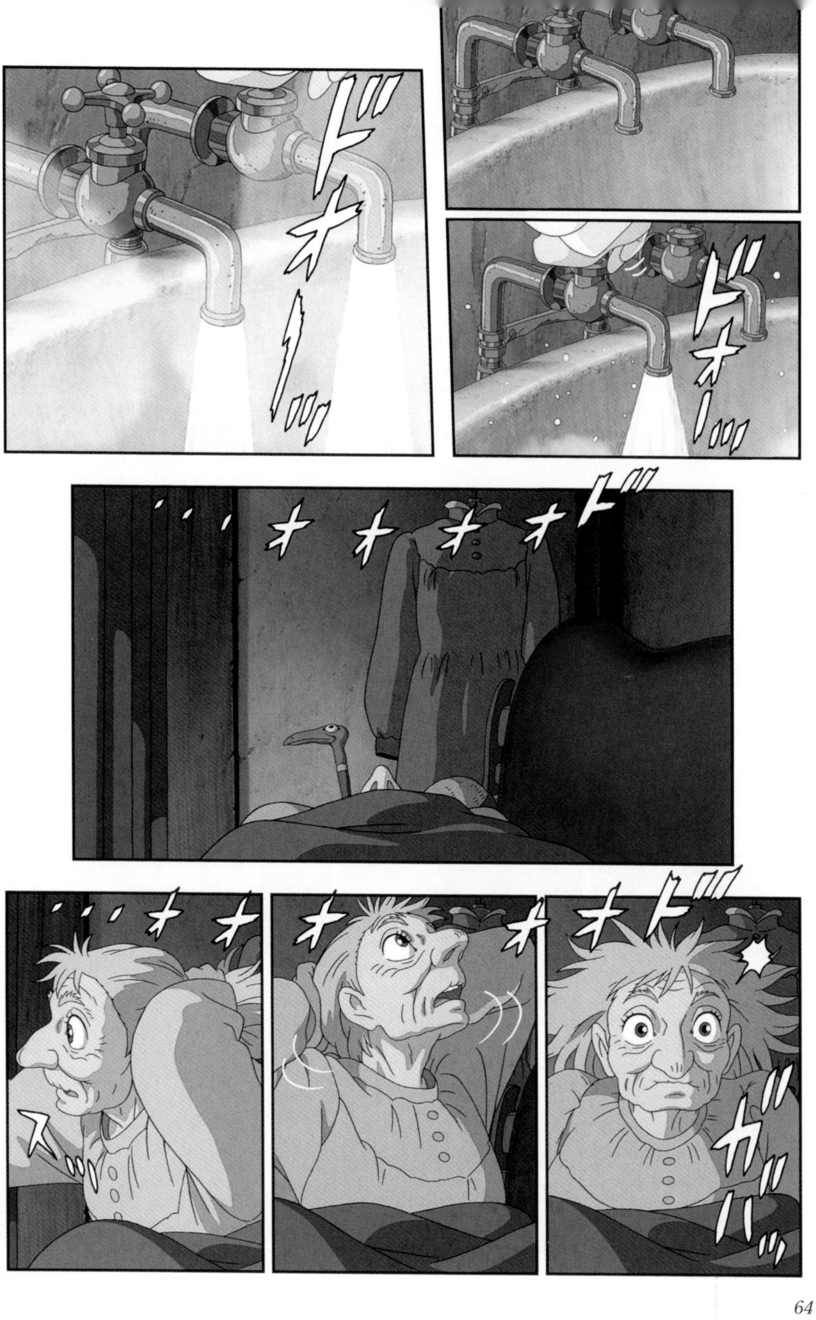
ドドオー…
ドドオー…
ドドオオオオ…
ドドオオオオ…
ガバッ
スッ

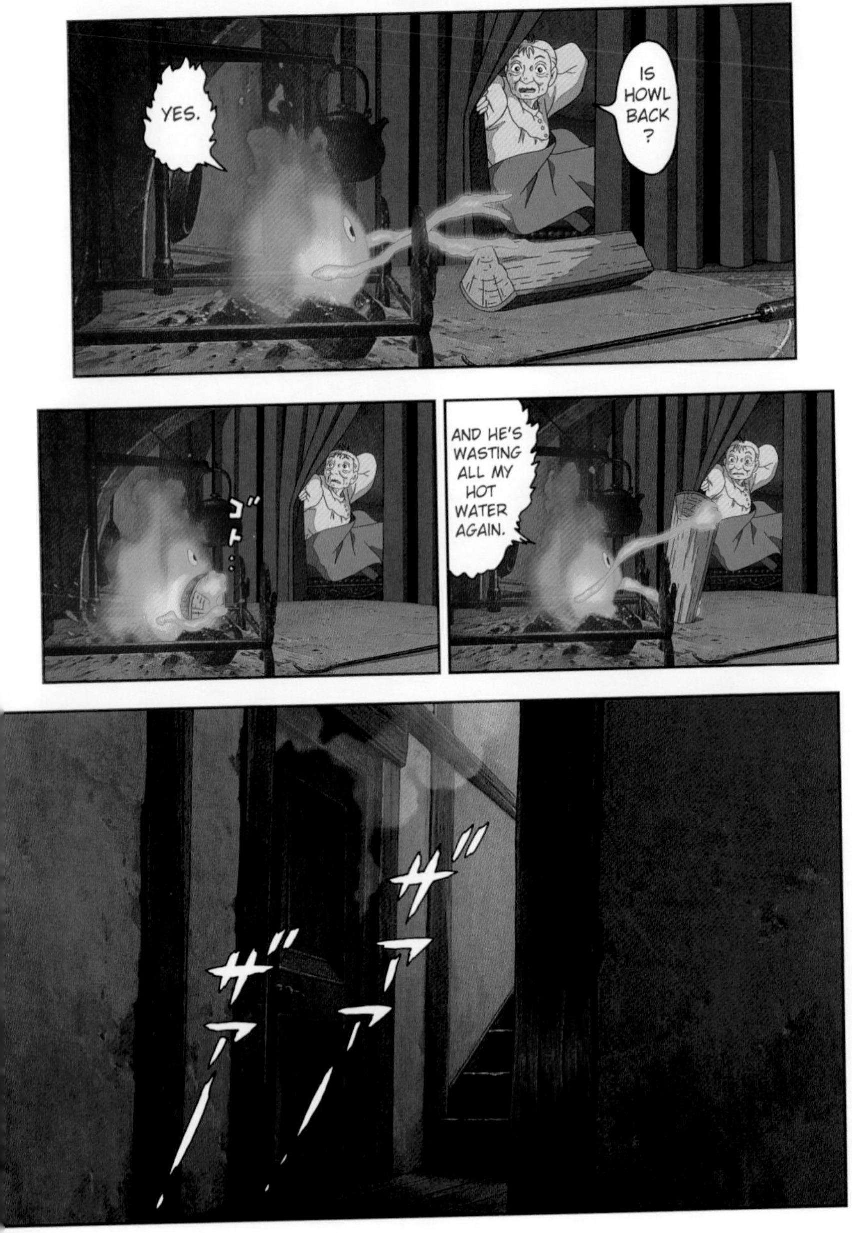
IS HOWL BACK?
YES.
AND HE'S WASTING ALL MY HOT WATER AGAIN.
ゴト‥
ザァァ
ザァァ

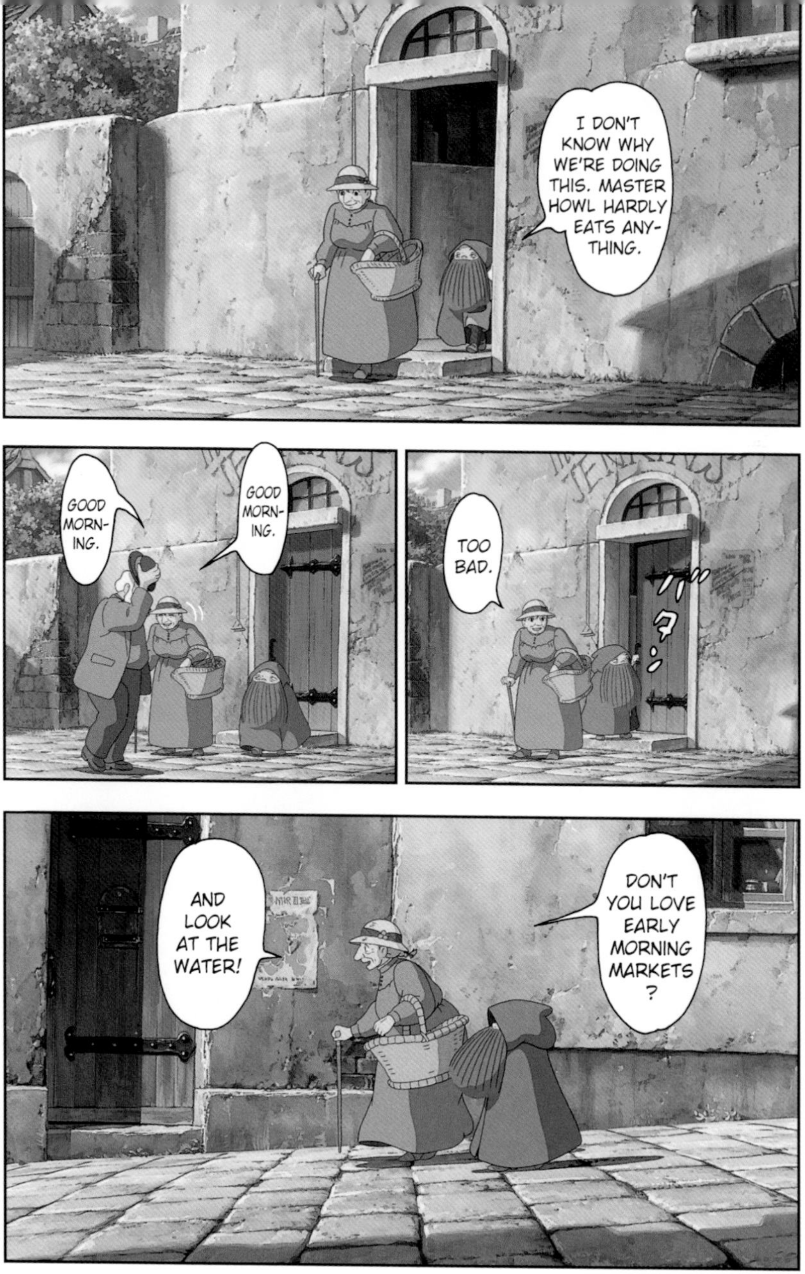
I DON'T KNOW WHY WE'RE DOING THIS. MASTER HOWL HARDLY EATS ANY-THING.
TOO BAD.
GOOD MORN-ING.
GOOD MORN-ING.
DON'T YOU LOVE EARLY MORNING MARKETS?
AND LOOK AT THE WATER!

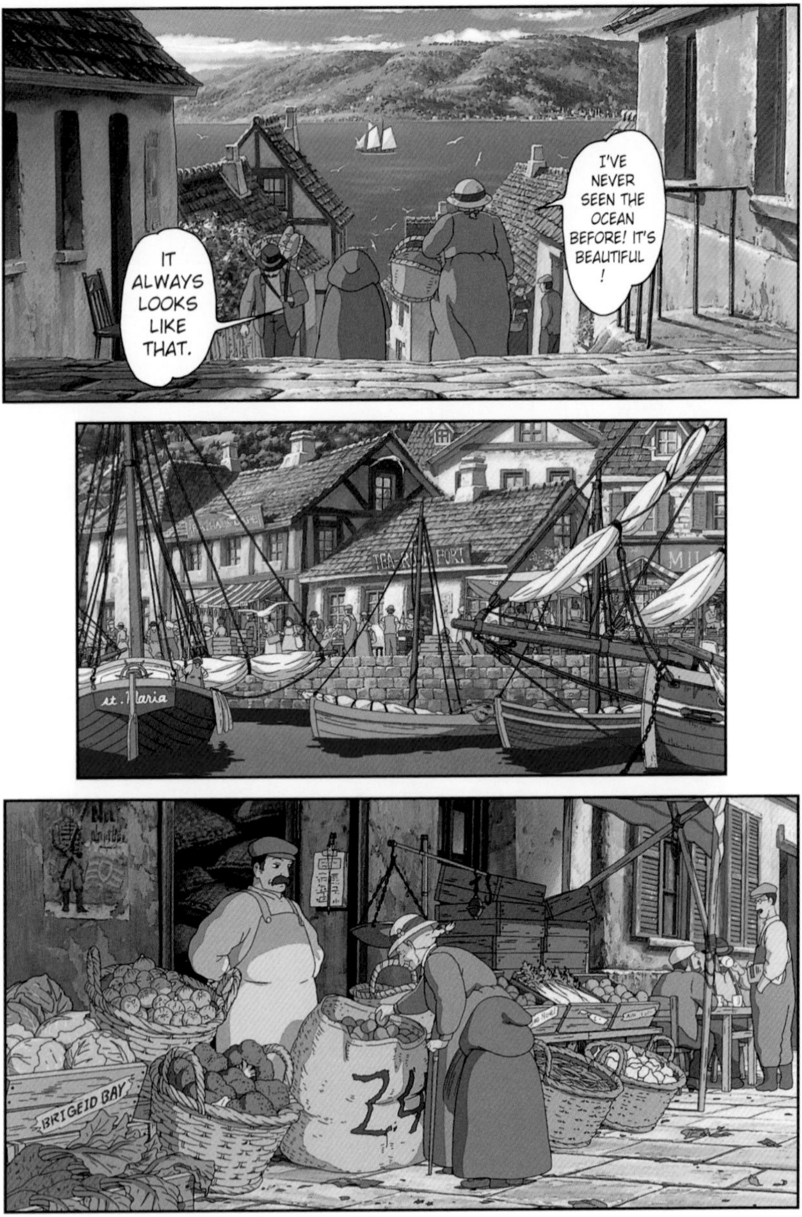
I'VE NEVER SEEN THE OCEAN BEFORE! IT'S BEAUTIFUL!
IT ALWAYS LOOKS LIKE THAT.
st. Maria
BRIGEID BAY

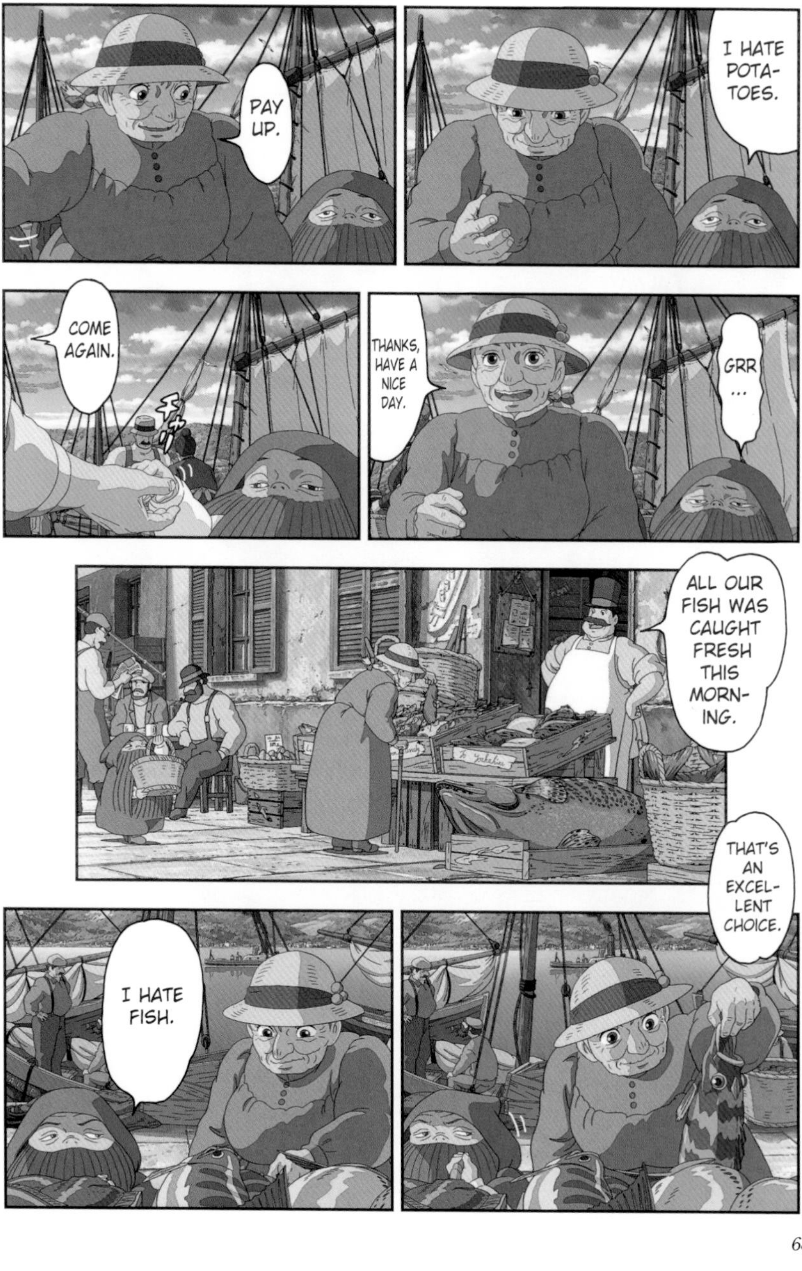
I HATE POTA-TOES.
PAY UP.
GRR ...
THANKS, HAVE A NICE DAY.
COME AGAIN.
ALL OUR FISH WAS CAUGHT FRESH THIS MORN-ING.
THAT'S AN EXCEL-LENT CHOICE.
I HATE FISH.

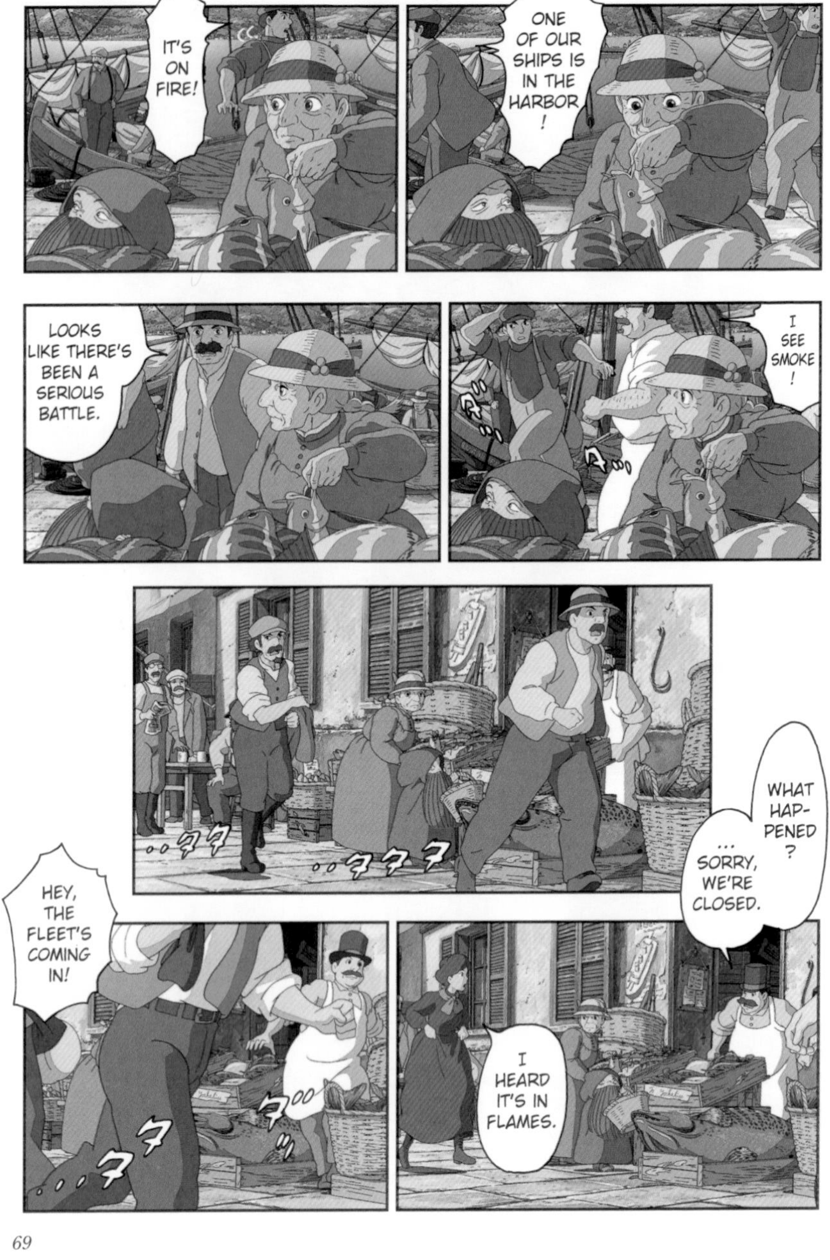

ONE OF OUR SHIPS IS IN THE HARBOR!
IT'S ON FIRE!
I SEE SMOKE!
LOOKS LIKE THERE'S BEEN A SERIOUS BATTLE.
WHAT HAP-PENED? ... SORRY, WE'RE CLOSED.
I HEARD IT'S IN FLAMES.
HEY, THE FLEET'S COMING IN!

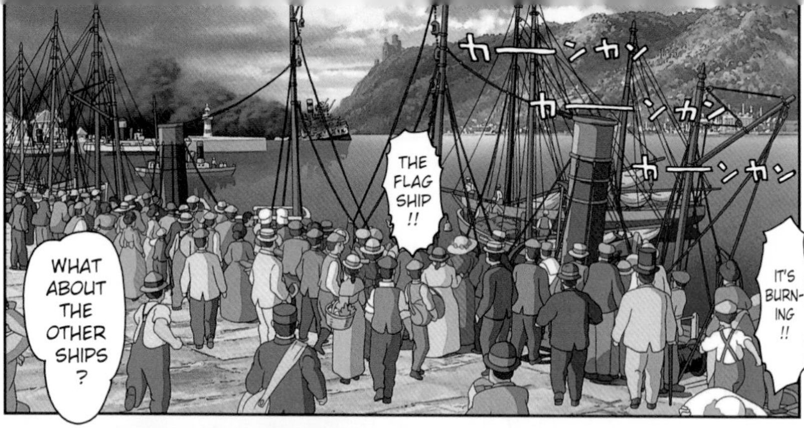
カーンカン
カーンカン
カーンカン
IT'S BURN-ING!!
THE FLAG SHIP!!
WHAT ABOUT THE OTHER SHIPS?
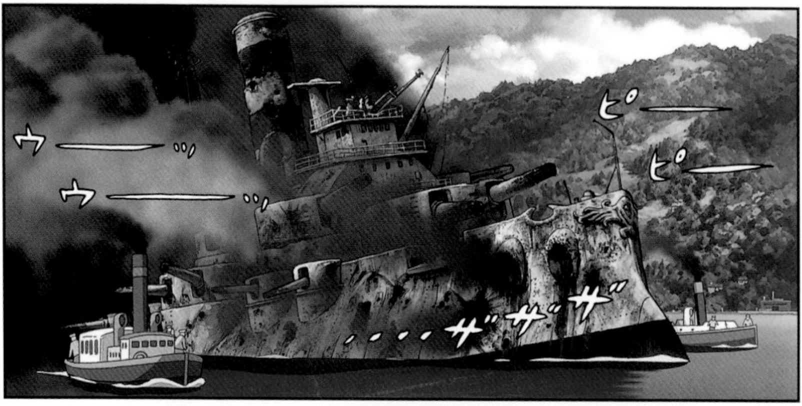
ピー
ピー
ザザザ
ウーッ
ウーッ
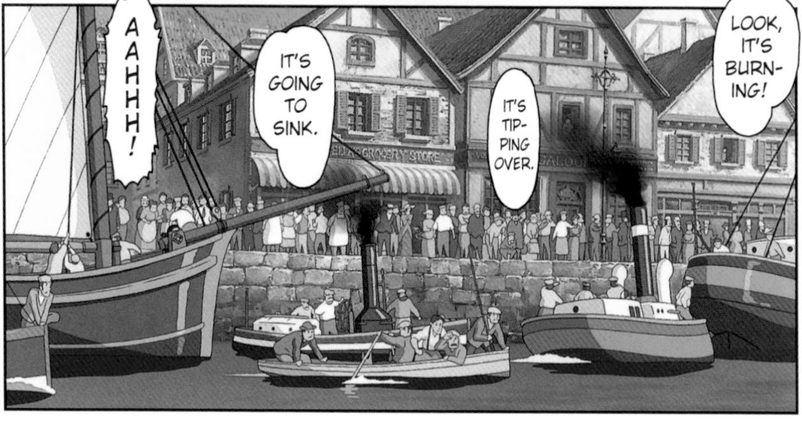
LOOK, IT'S BURN-ING!
IT'S TIP-PING OVER.
IT'S GOING TO SINK.
AAHHH!

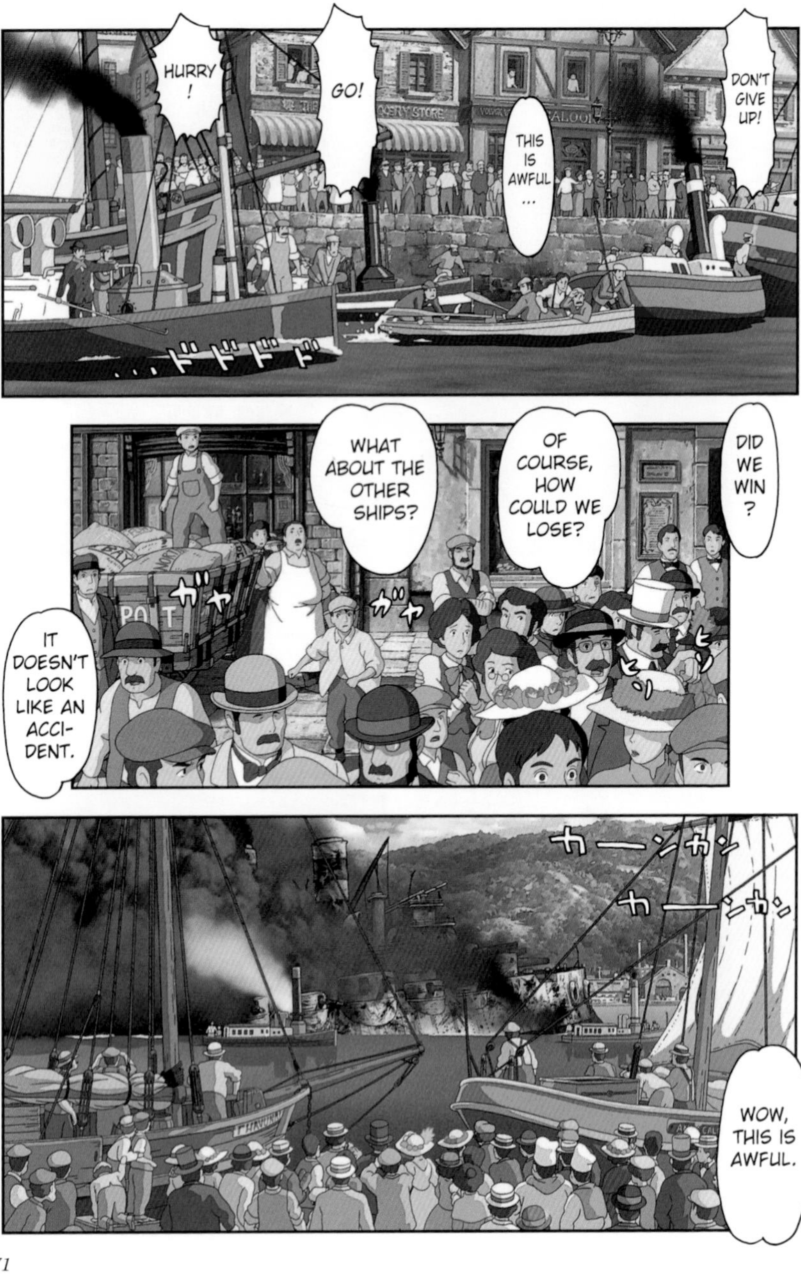
DON'T GIVE UP!
THIS IS AWFUL...
GO!
HURRY!
ドドドド…
DID WE WIN?
OF COURSE, HOW COULD WE LOSE?
WHAT ABOUT THE OTHER SHIPS?
ヒソヒソ
ガヤガヤ
IT DOESN'T LOOK LIKE AN ACCI-DENT.
カーンカン
カーンカン
WOW, THIS IS AWFUL.

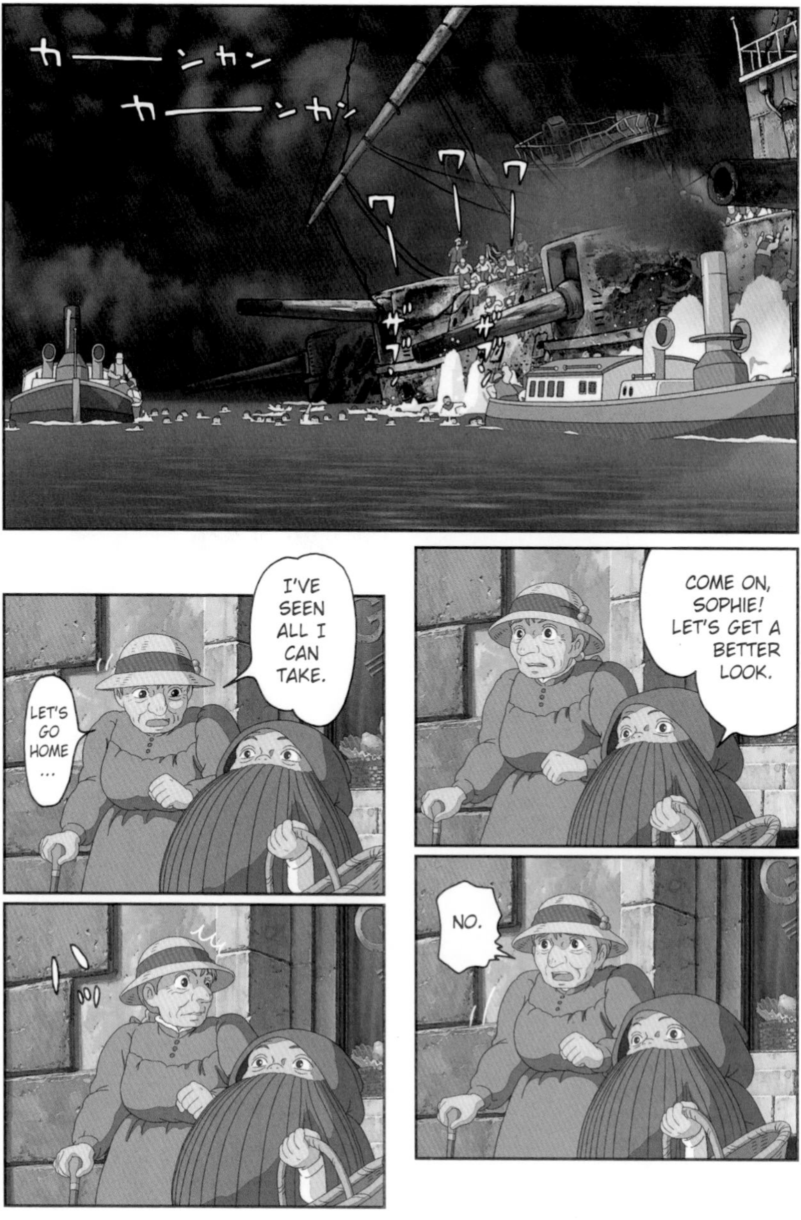

カーーンカン
カーーンカン
ワー
ワー
ワー
ザブ
ザブ
COME ON, SOPHIE! LET'S GET A BETTER LOOK.
I'VE SEEN ALL I CAN TAKE.
LET'S GO HOME ...
NO.

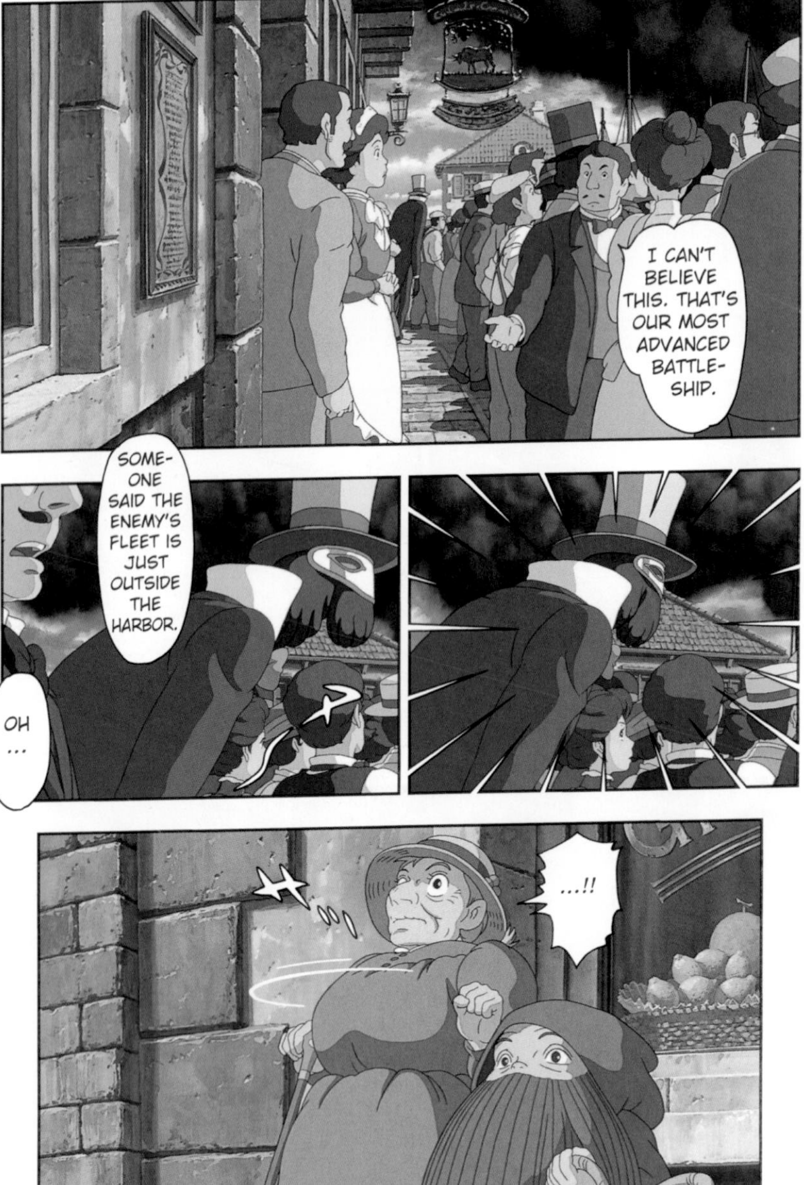
I CAN'T BELIEVE THIS. THAT'S OUR MOST ADVANCED BATTLE-SHIP.
SOME-ONE SAID THE ENEMY'S FLEET IS JUST OUTSIDE THE HARBOR.
OH ...
...!!

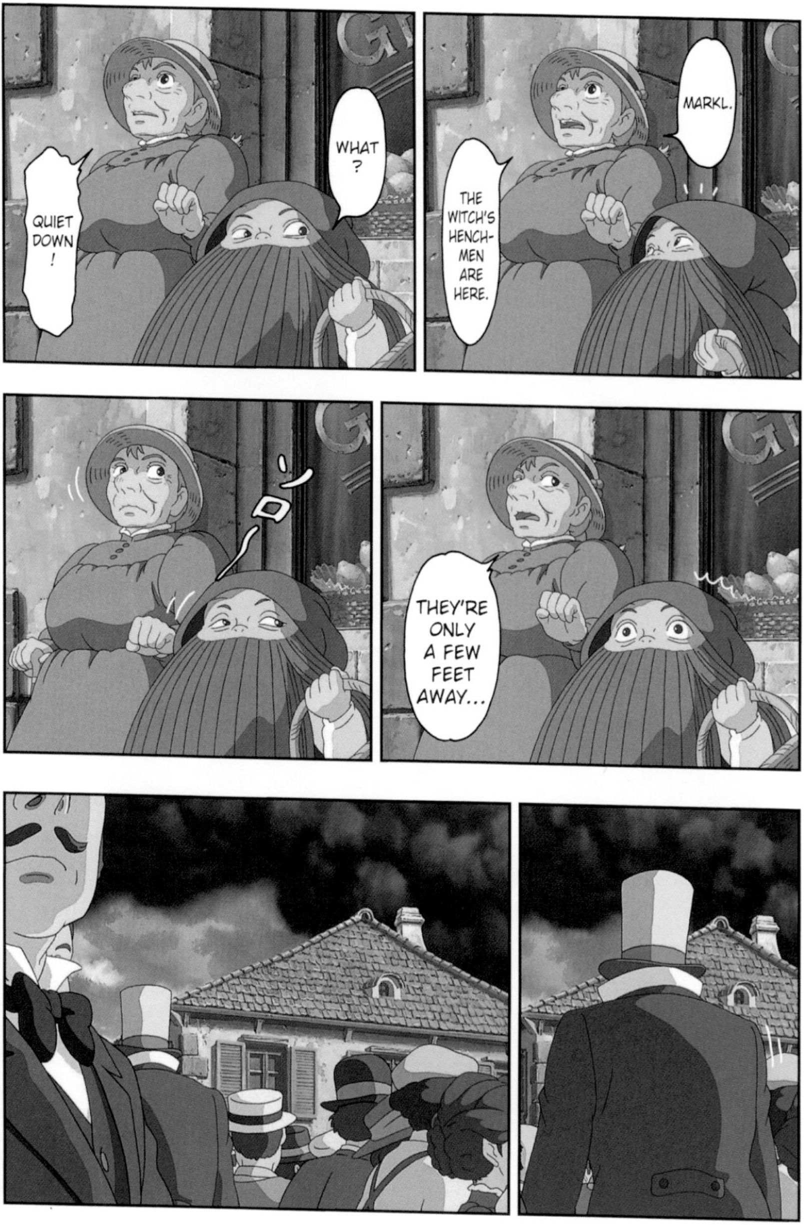
MARKL.
THE WITCH'S HENCH-MEN ARE HERE.
WHAT?
QUIET DOWN!
THEY'RE ONLY A FEW FEET AWAY...

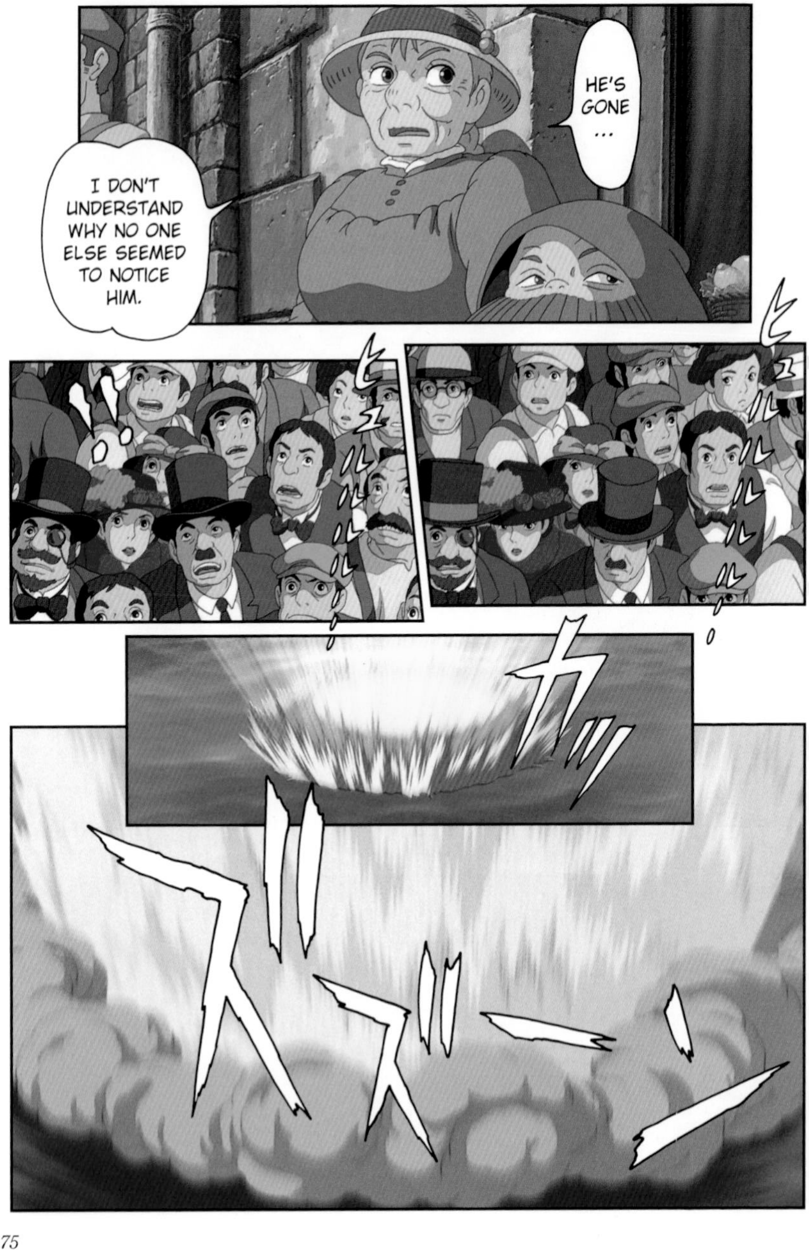
HE'S GONE ...
I DON'T UNDERSTAND WHY NO ONE ELSE SEEMED TO NOTICE HIM.
カッ
ズズーン

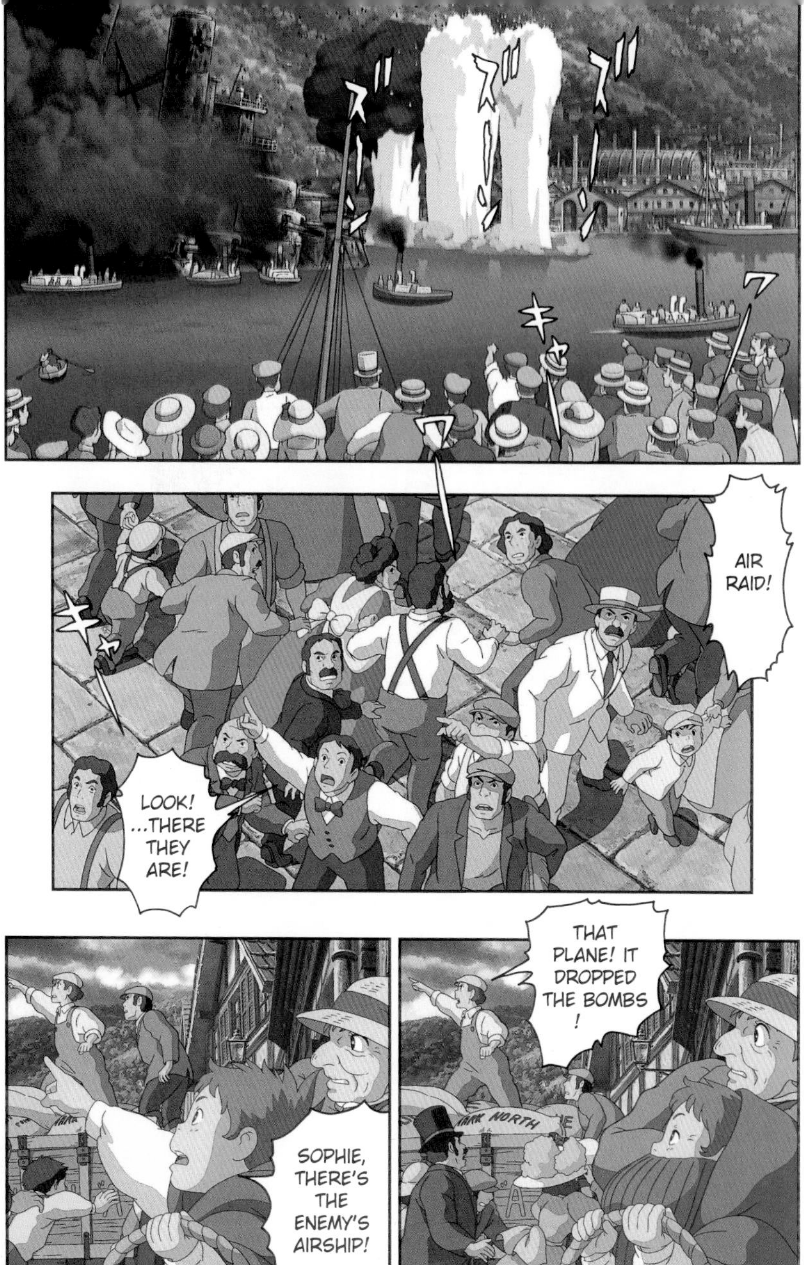
AIR RAID!
LOOK! ...THERE THEY ARE!
THAT PLANE! IT DROPPED THE BOMBS!
SOPHIE, THERE'S THE ENEMY'S AIRSHIP!

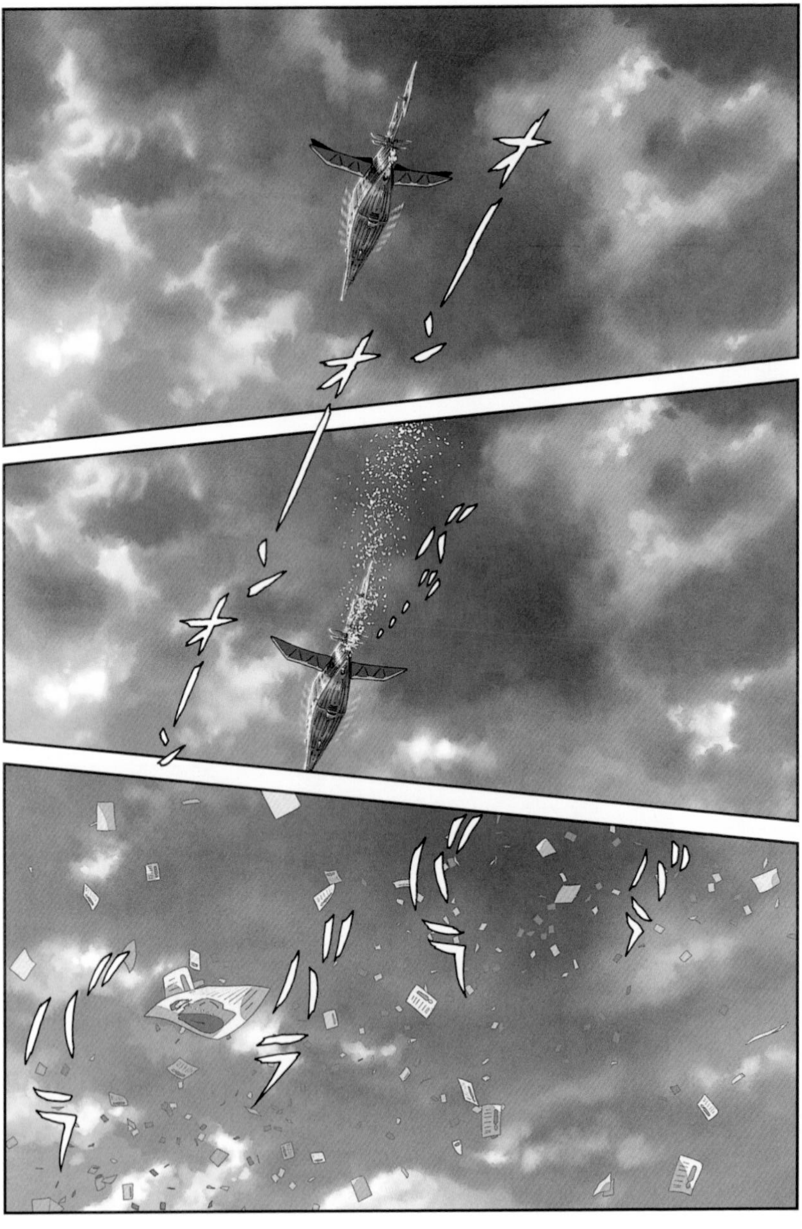
オーン
オーン
オーン
バラ
バラ
バラ

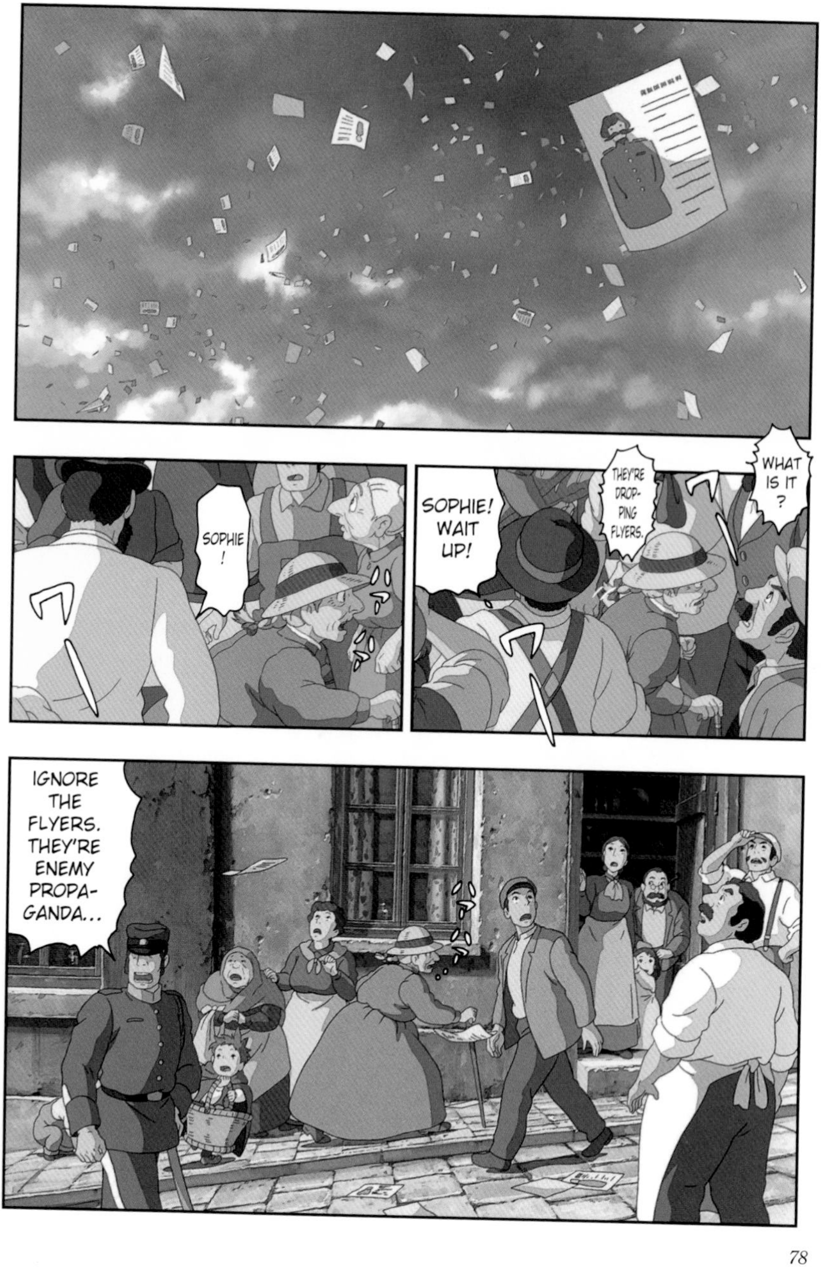
WHAT IS IT?
THEY'RE DROPPING FLYERS.
SOPHIE! WAIT UP!
SOPHIE!
IGNORE THE FLYERS. THEY'RE ENEMY PROPAGANDA...

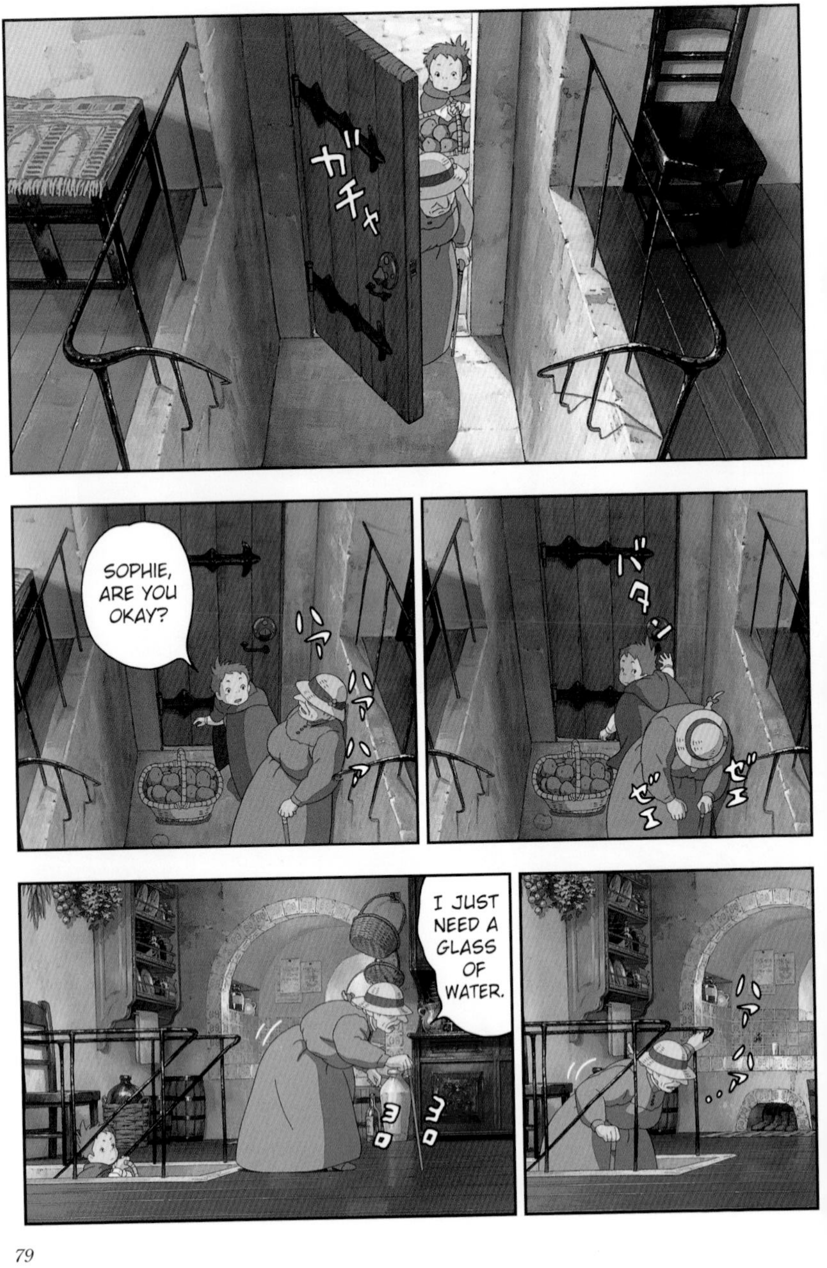
ガチャ
ゼェ ゼェ
SOPHIE, ARE YOU OKAY?
ハァ ハァ ハァ
ハァ ハァ
I JUST NEED A GLASS OF WATER.
ヨロ ヨロ

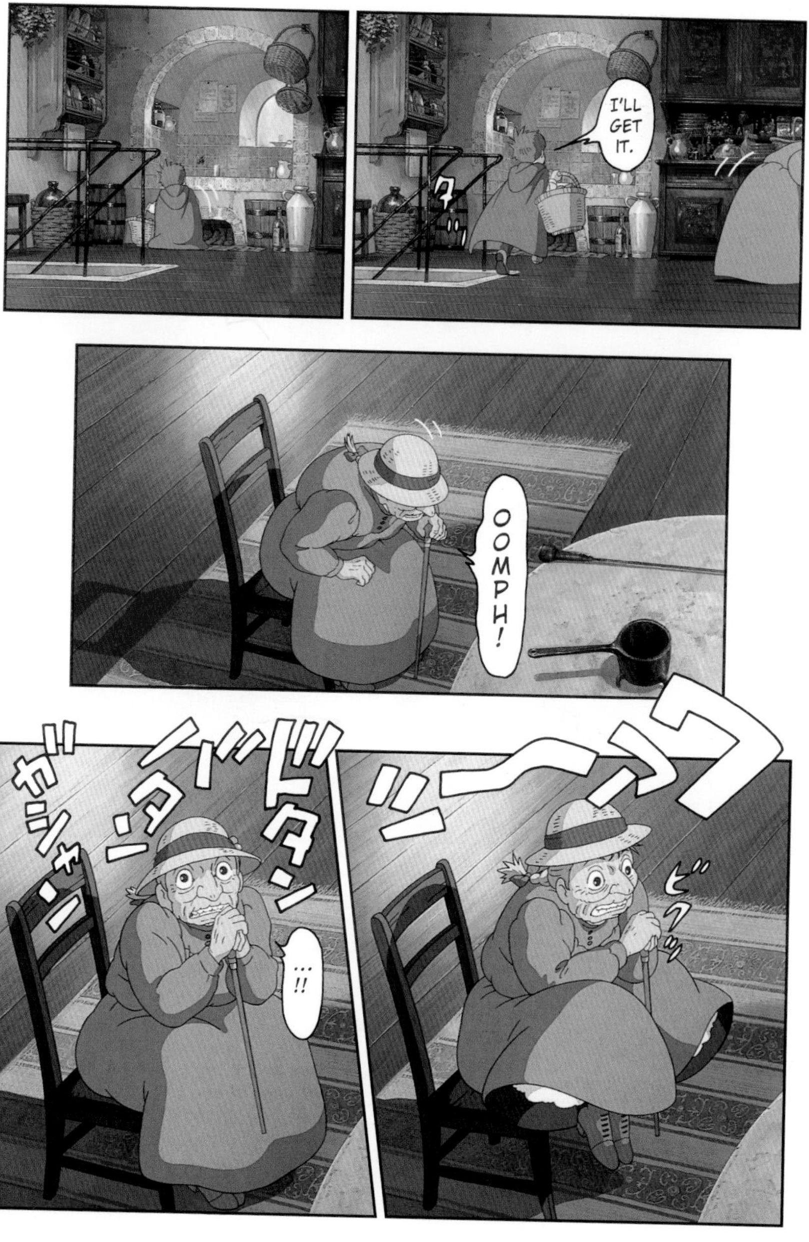
I'LL GET IT.
OOMPH!
...!!

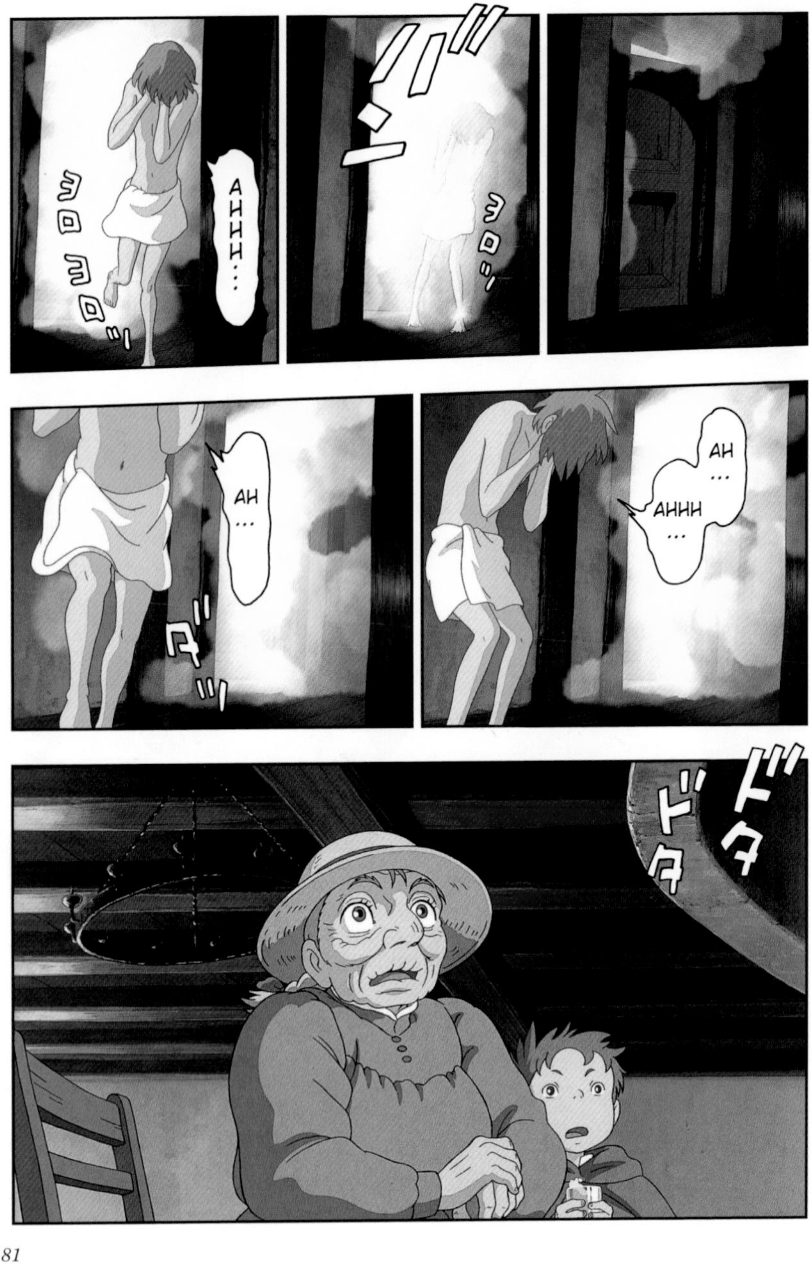
ヨロッ
AHHH...
ヨロヨロッ
AH... AHHH...
AH...
ダッ
ドタドタ

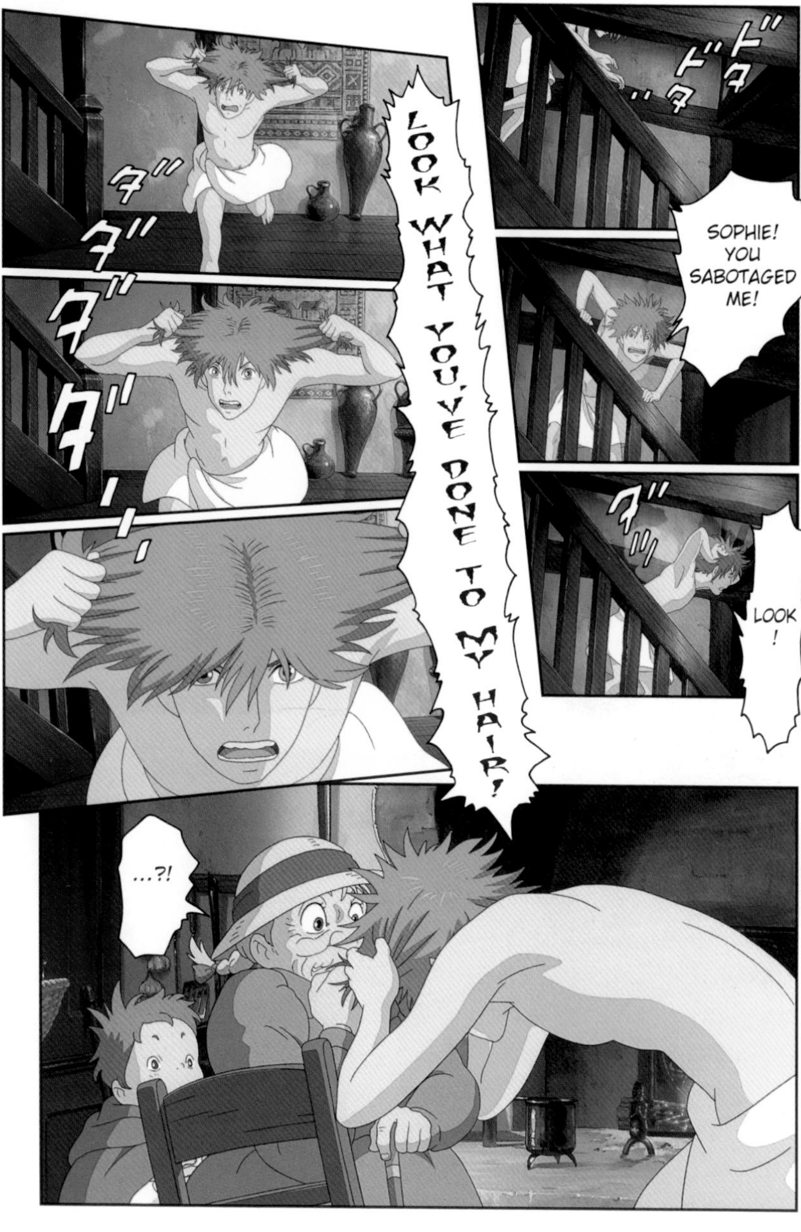
SOPHIE! YOU SABOTAGED ME!
LOOK!
LOOK WHAT YOU'VE DONE TO MY HAIR!
...?!

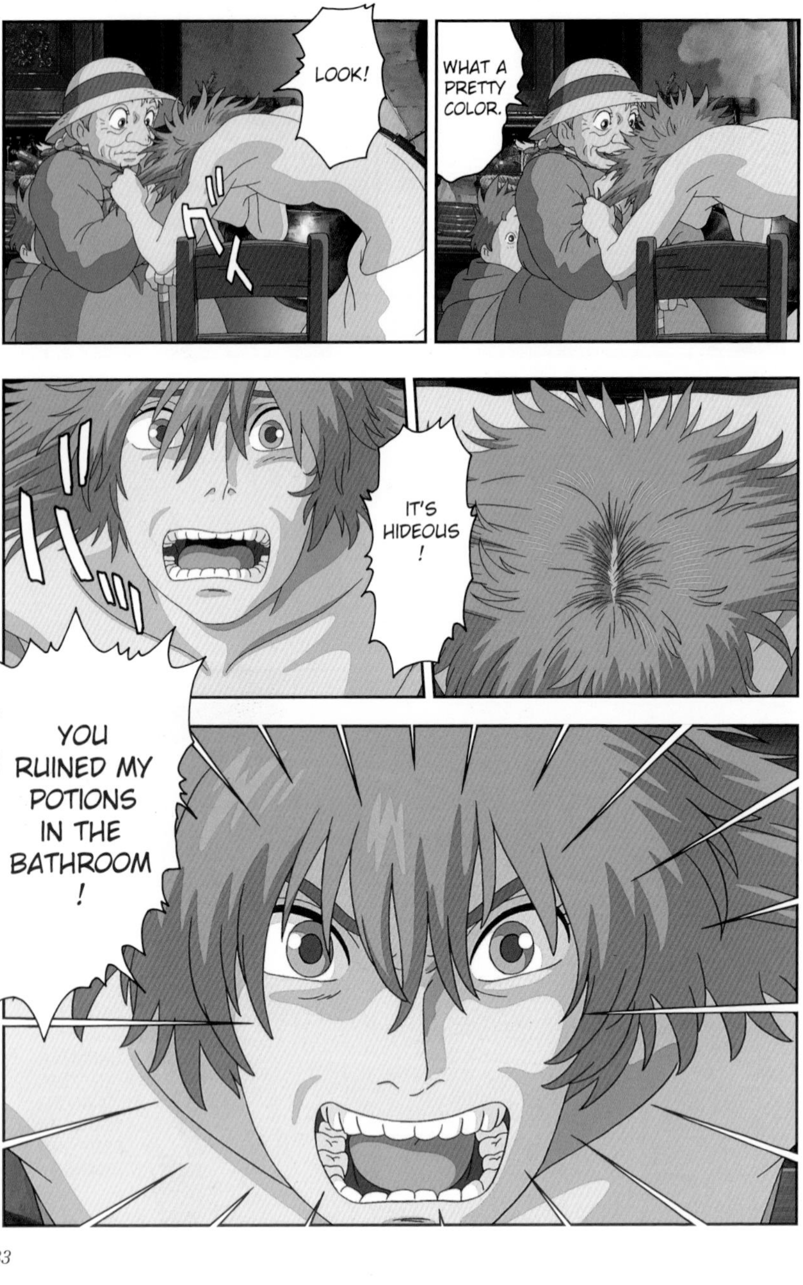
WHAT A PRETTY COLOR.
LOOK!
グイ
IT'S HIDEOUS!
YOU RUINED MY POTIONS IN THE BATHROOM!

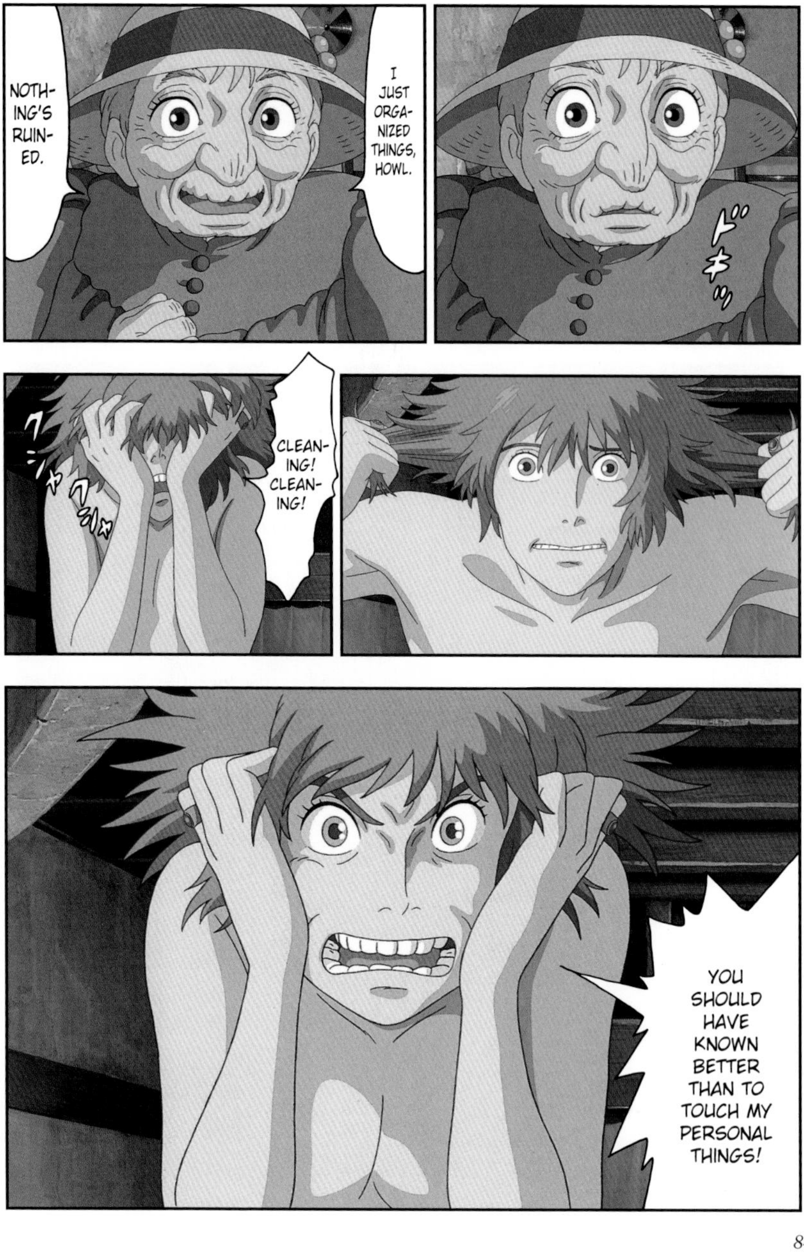
ドキッ
I JUST ORGANIZED THINGS, HOWL.
NOTHING'S RUINED.
CLEANING! CLEANING!
YOU SHOULD HAVE KNOWN BETTER THAN TO TOUCH MY PERSONAL THINGS!

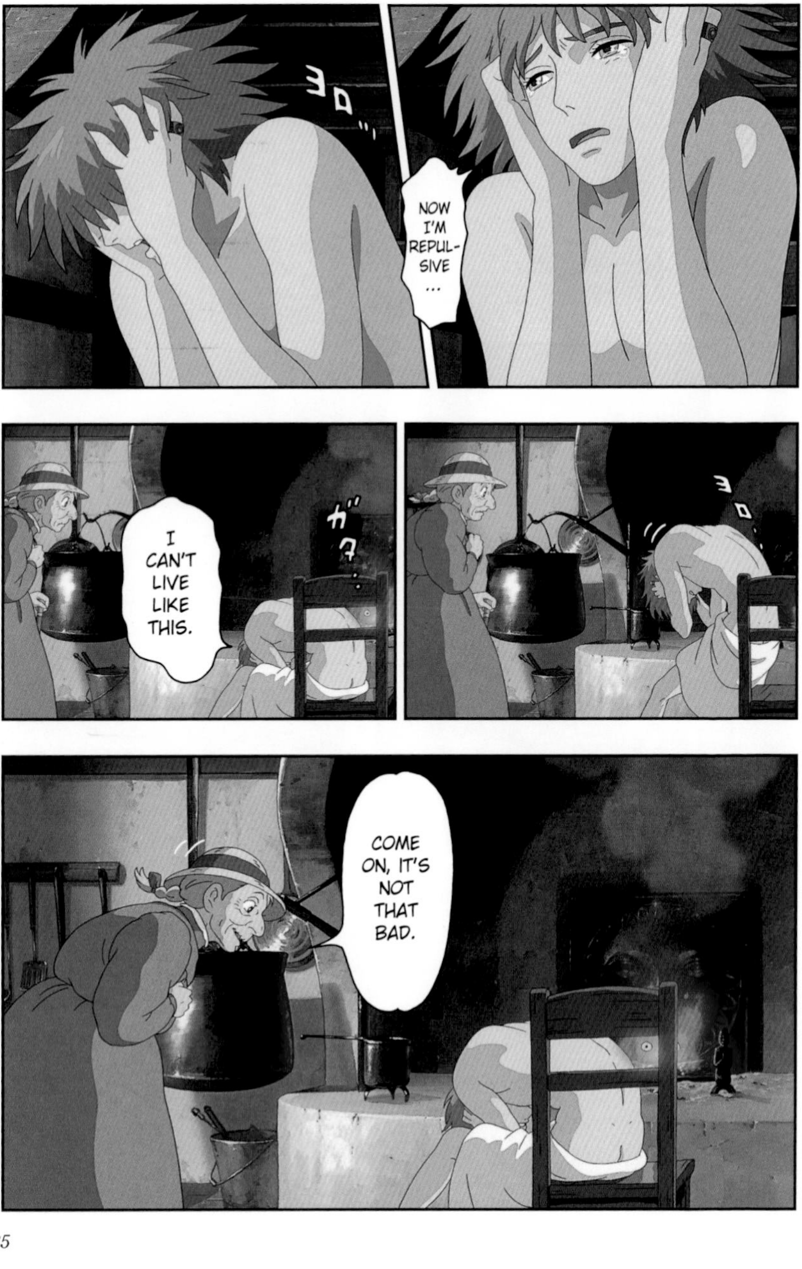
NOW I'M REPULSIVE...
ヨロ
ヨロ
I CAN'T LIVE LIKE THIS.
ガタ
COME ON, IT'S NOT THAT BAD.

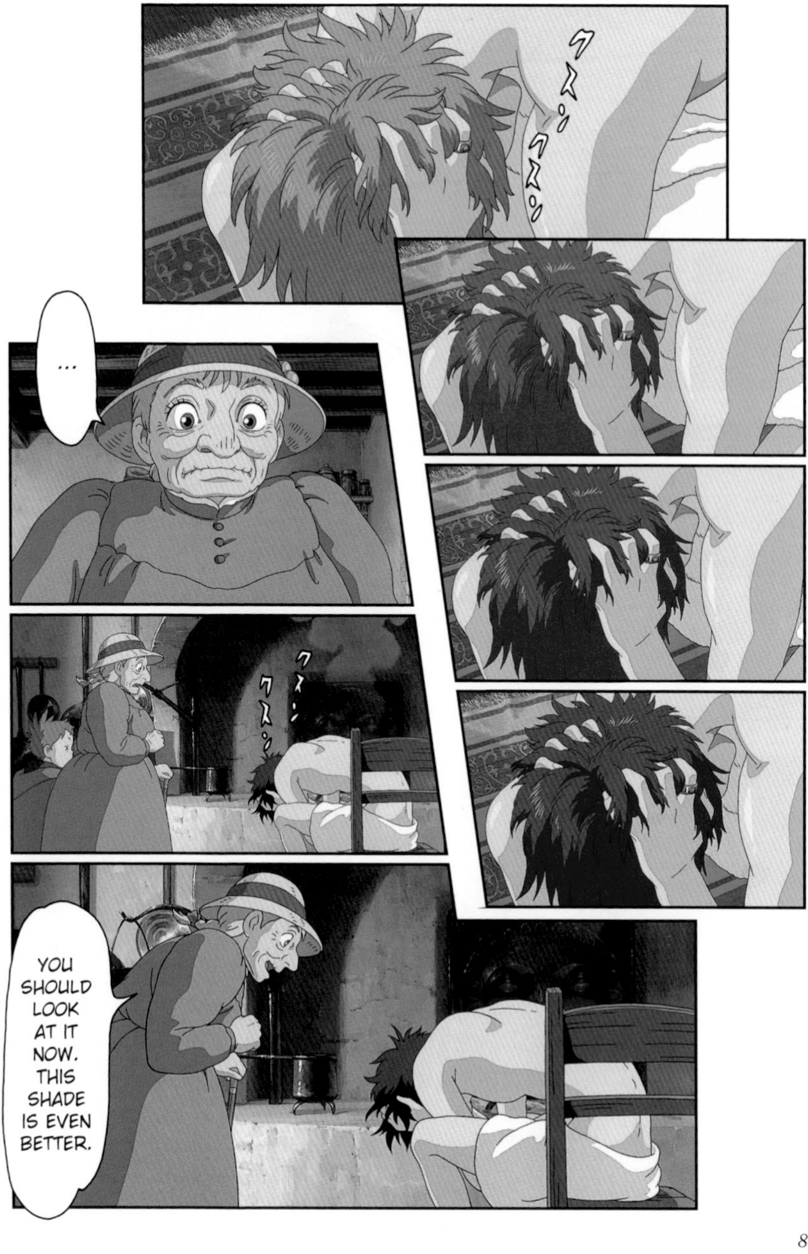
クスン クスン
...
クスン クスン
YOU SHOULD LOOK AT IT NOW. THIS SHADE IS EVEN BETTER.

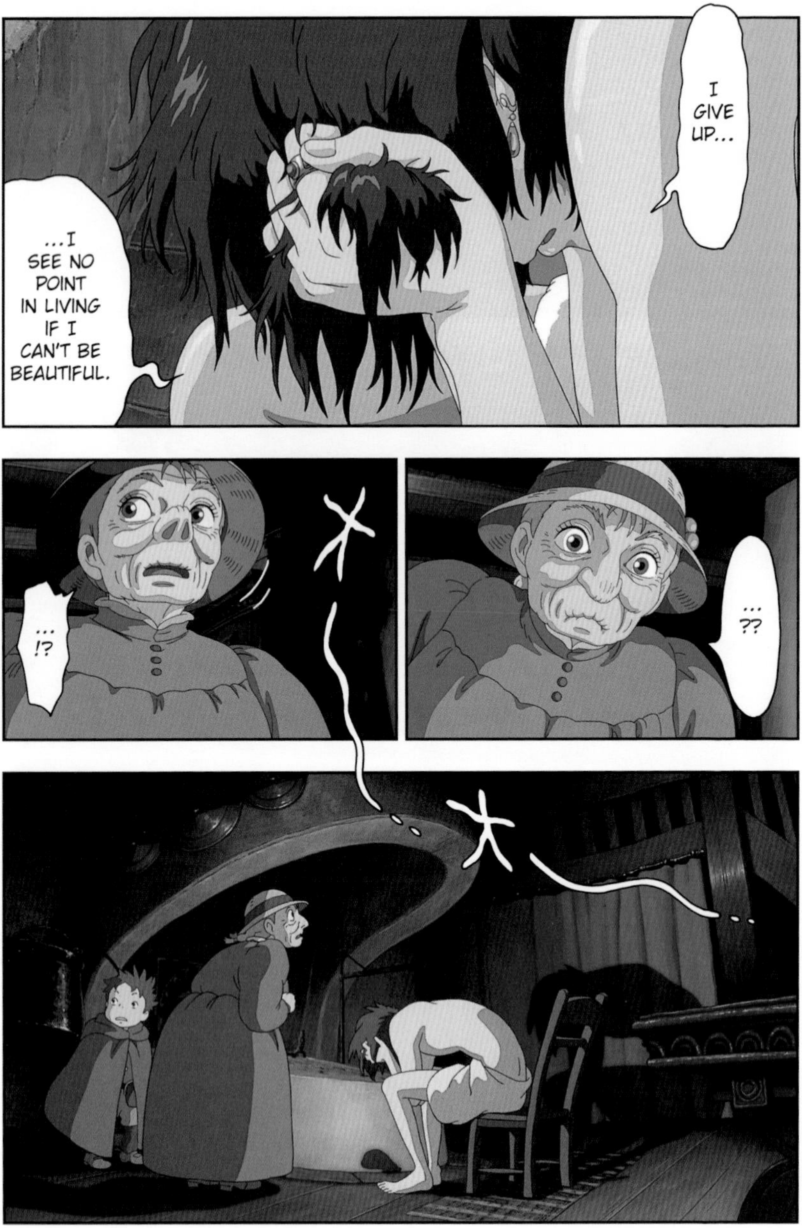
I GIVE UP...
...I SEE NO POINT IN LIVING IF I CAN'T BE BEAUTIFUL.
...??
...!?

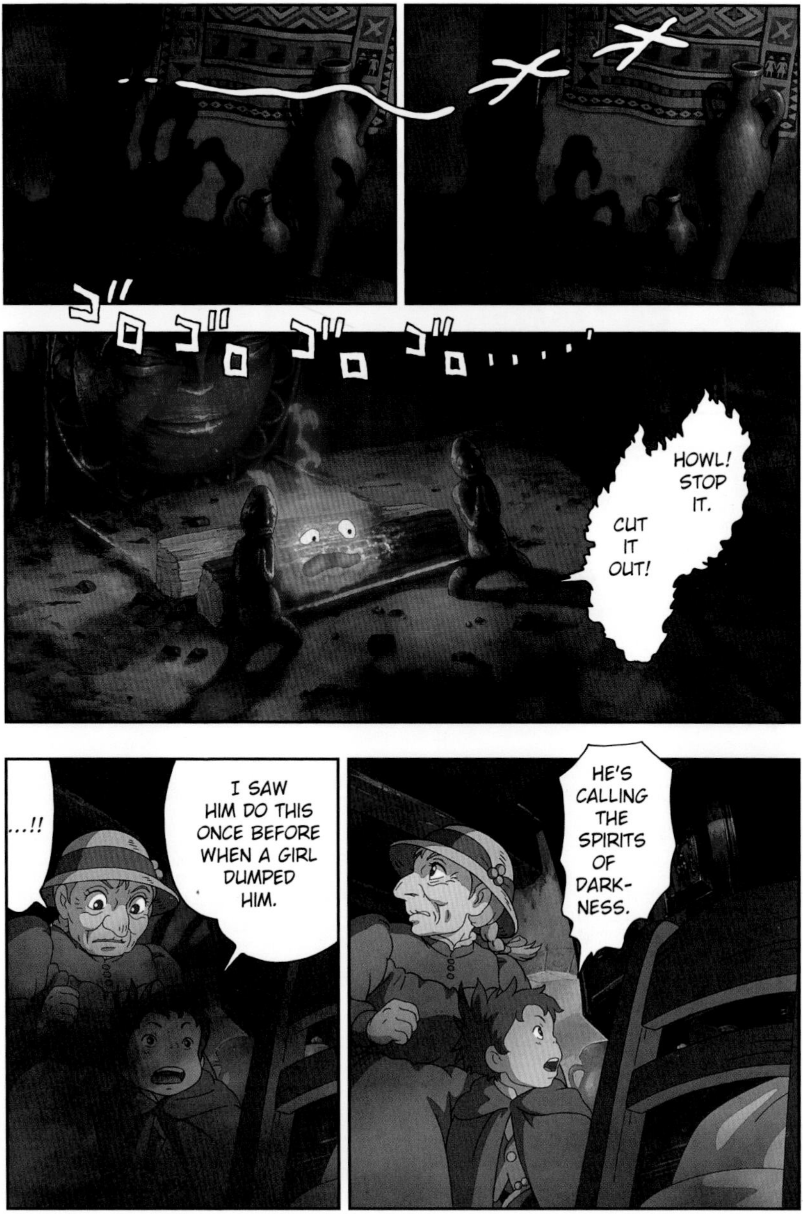
ゴロゴロゴロゴロ・・・・
HOWL! STOP IT.
CUT IT OUT!
HE'S CALLING THE SPIRITS OF DARK-NESS.
I SAW HIM DO THIS ONCE BEFORE WHEN A GIRL DUMPED HIM.
...!!

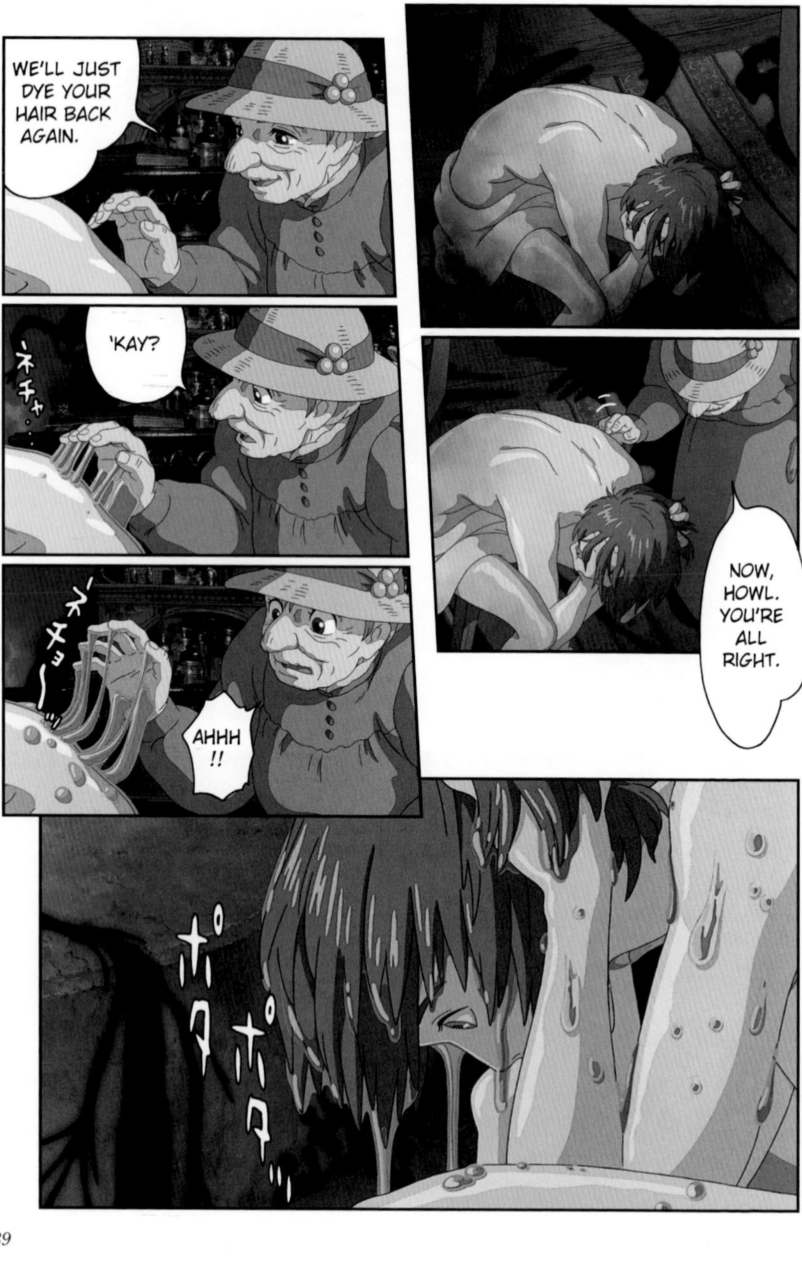
NOW, HOWL. YOU'RE ALL RIGHT.
WE'LL JUST DYE YOUR HAIR BACK AGAIN.
'KAY?
ネチャ...
ネチョ~
AHHH !!
ポタ
ポタ...

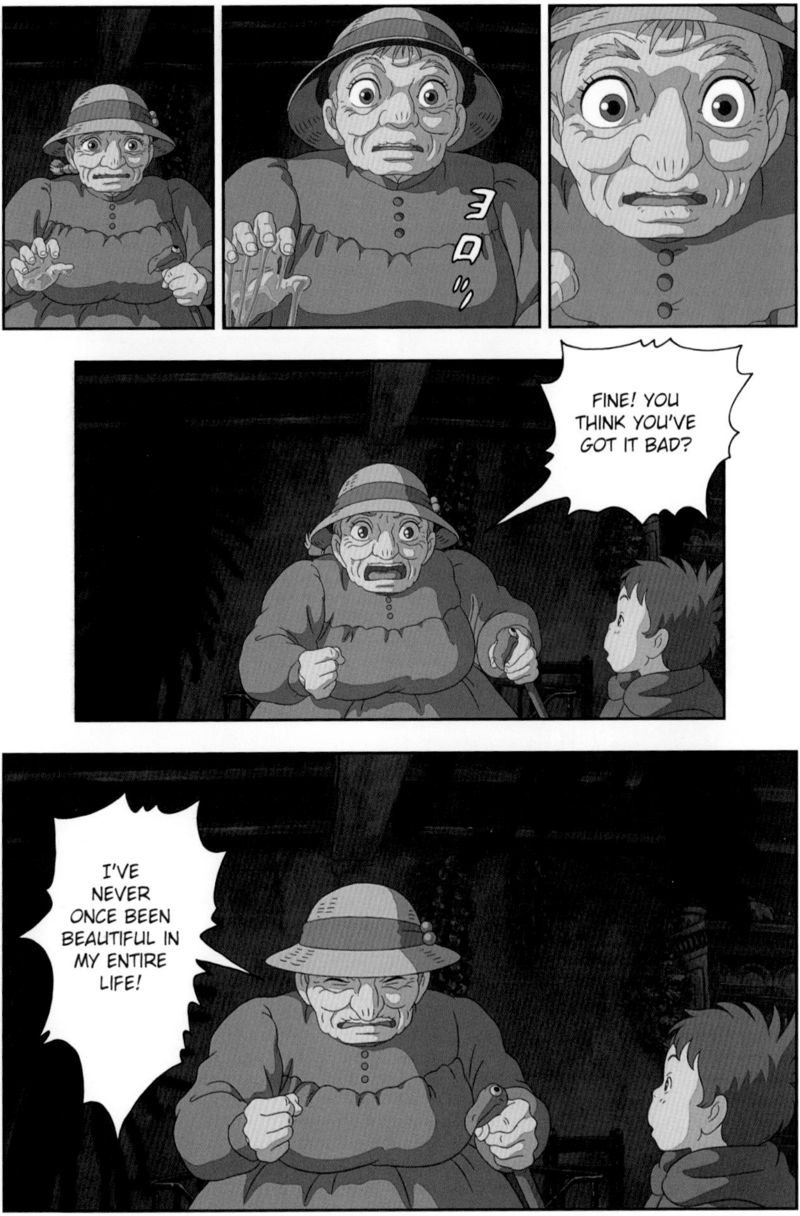
ヨロッ
FINE! YOU THINK YOU'VE GOT IT BAD?
I'VE NEVER ONCE BEEN BEAUTIFUL IN MY ENTIRE LIFE!

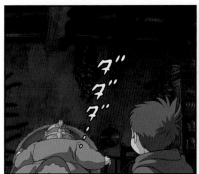

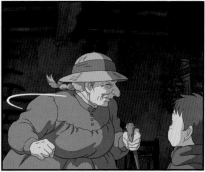

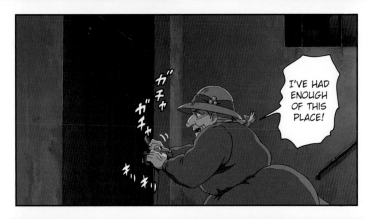

I'VE HAD ENOUGH OF THIS PLACE!

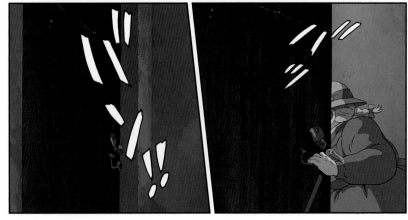

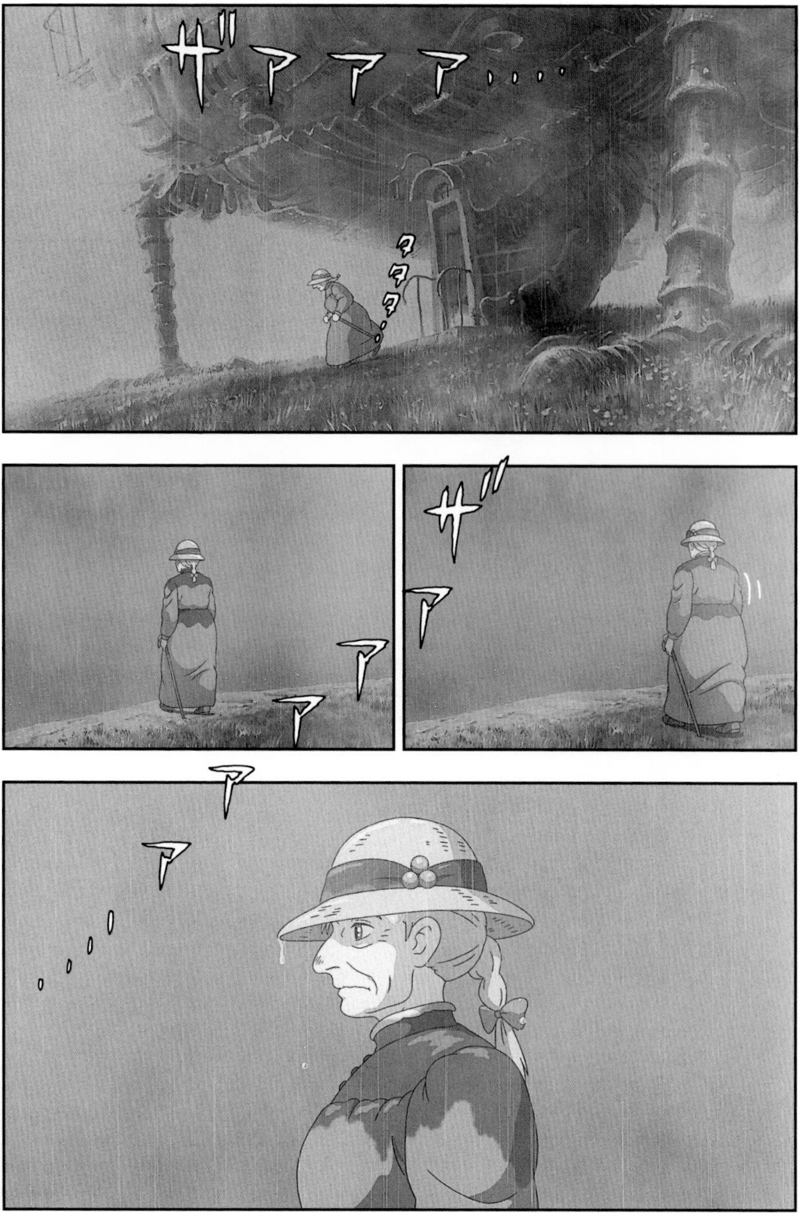
ザァァァ……
タタタ
ザァ
ァァ
ァァ……

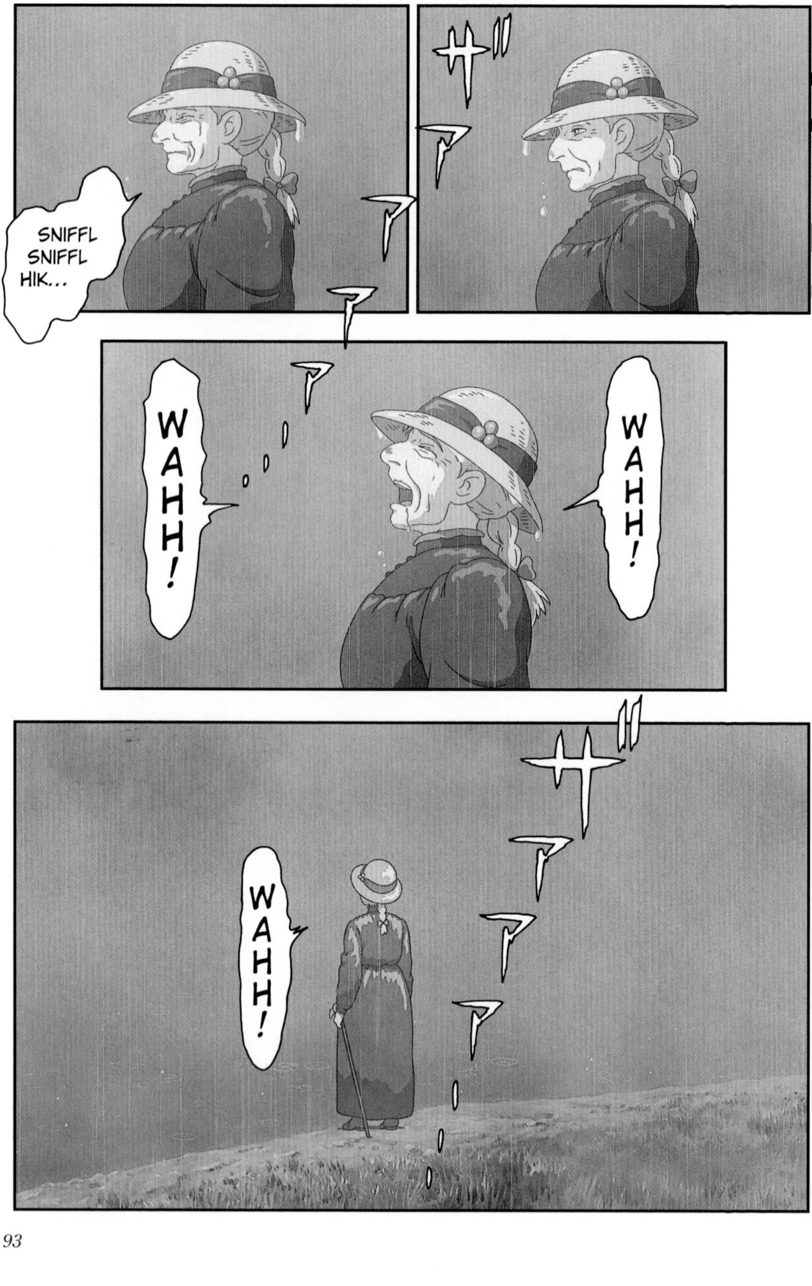
ザァアアア
SNIFFL SNIFFL HIK...
WAHH!
WAHH!
ザァアア
WAHH!

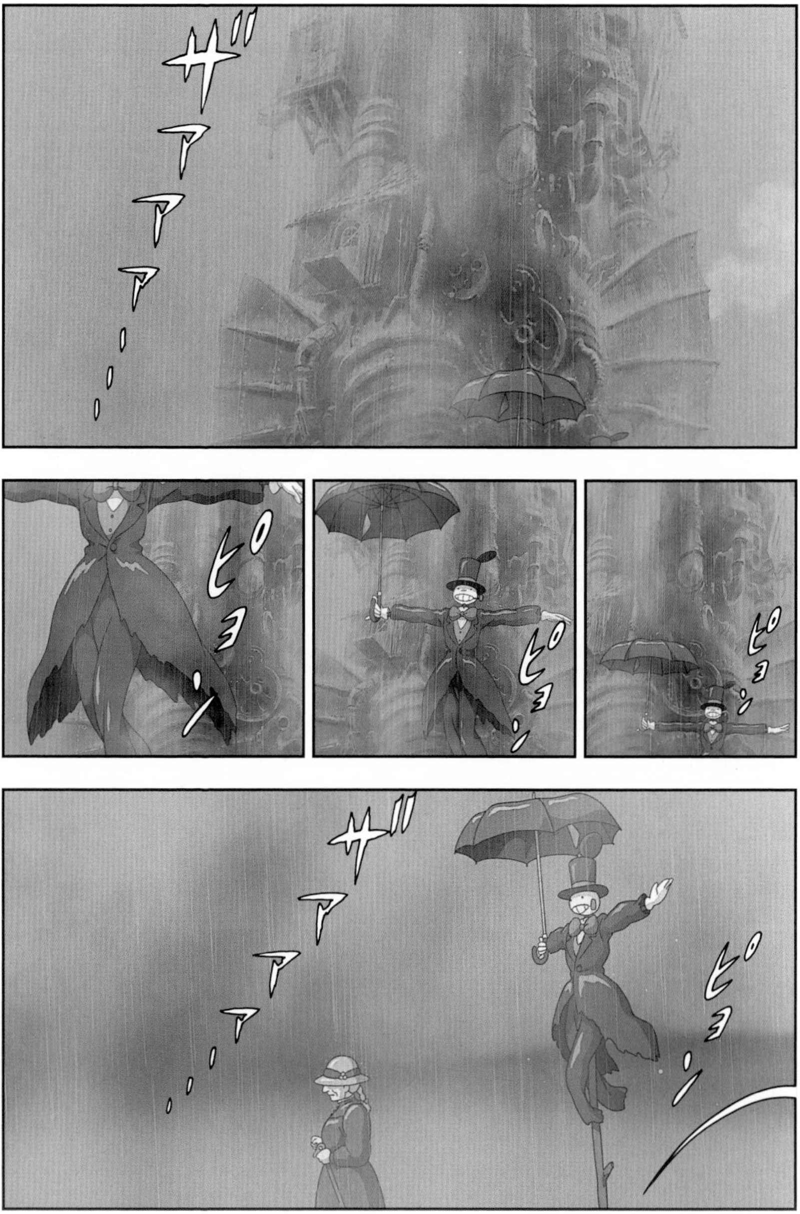
ザアアア…
ピョン
ピョン
ピョン
ザアアア…
ピョン

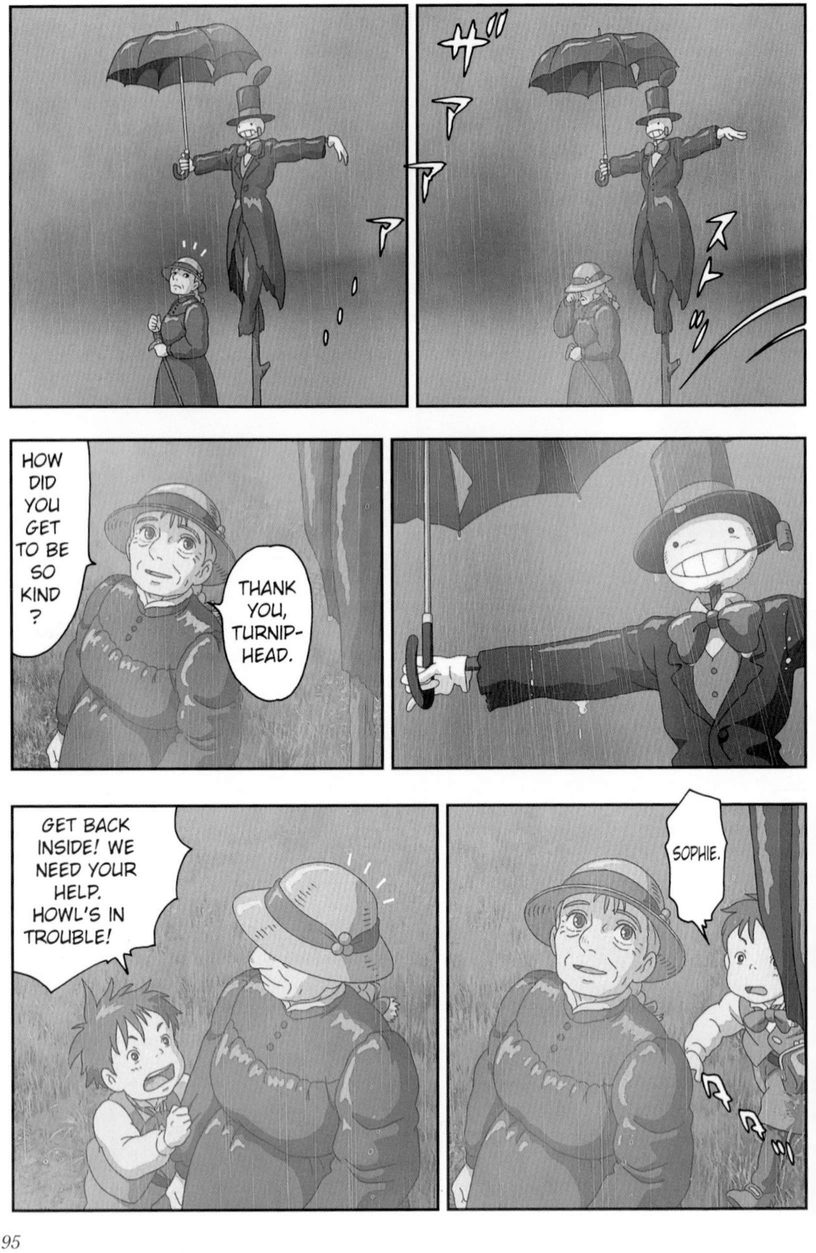
ザァァァ
THANK YOU, TURNIP-HEAD.
HOW DID YOU GET TO BE SO KIND?
SOPHIE.
GET BACK INSIDE! WE NEED YOUR HELP. HOWL'S IN TROUBLE!

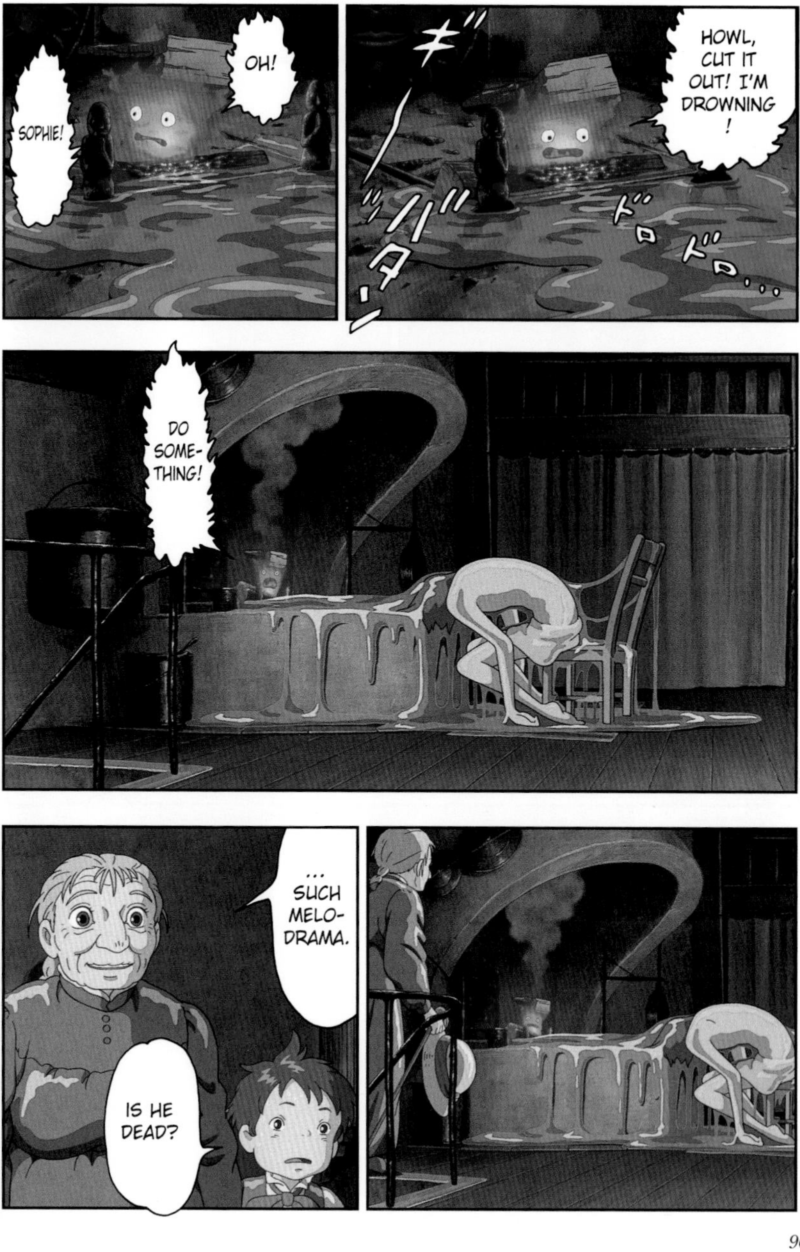
HOWL, CUT IT OUT! I'M DROWNING!
ギーッ
バタン
ドロドロ...
OH!
SOPHIE!
DO SOME-THING!
...SUCH MELO-DRAMA.
IS HE DEAD?

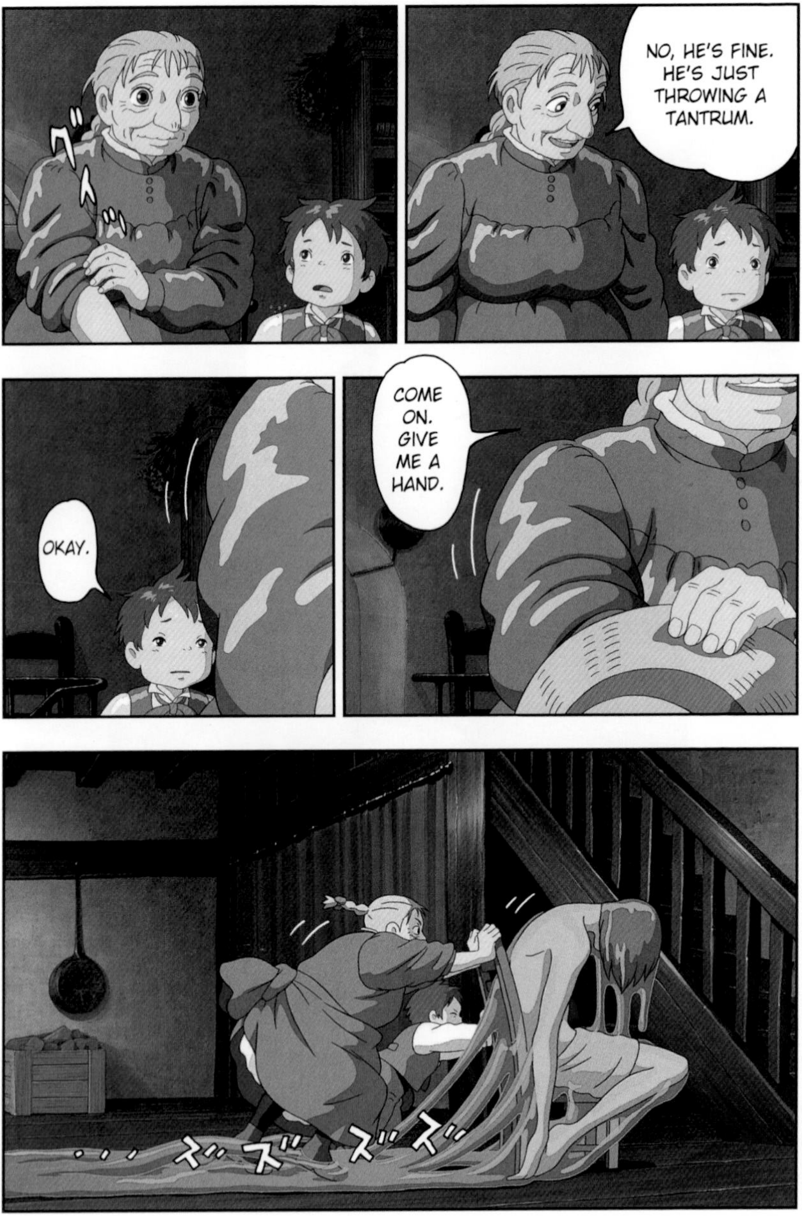
NO, HE'S FINE. HE'S JUST THROWING A TANTRUM.
COME ON. GIVE ME A HAND.
OKAY.

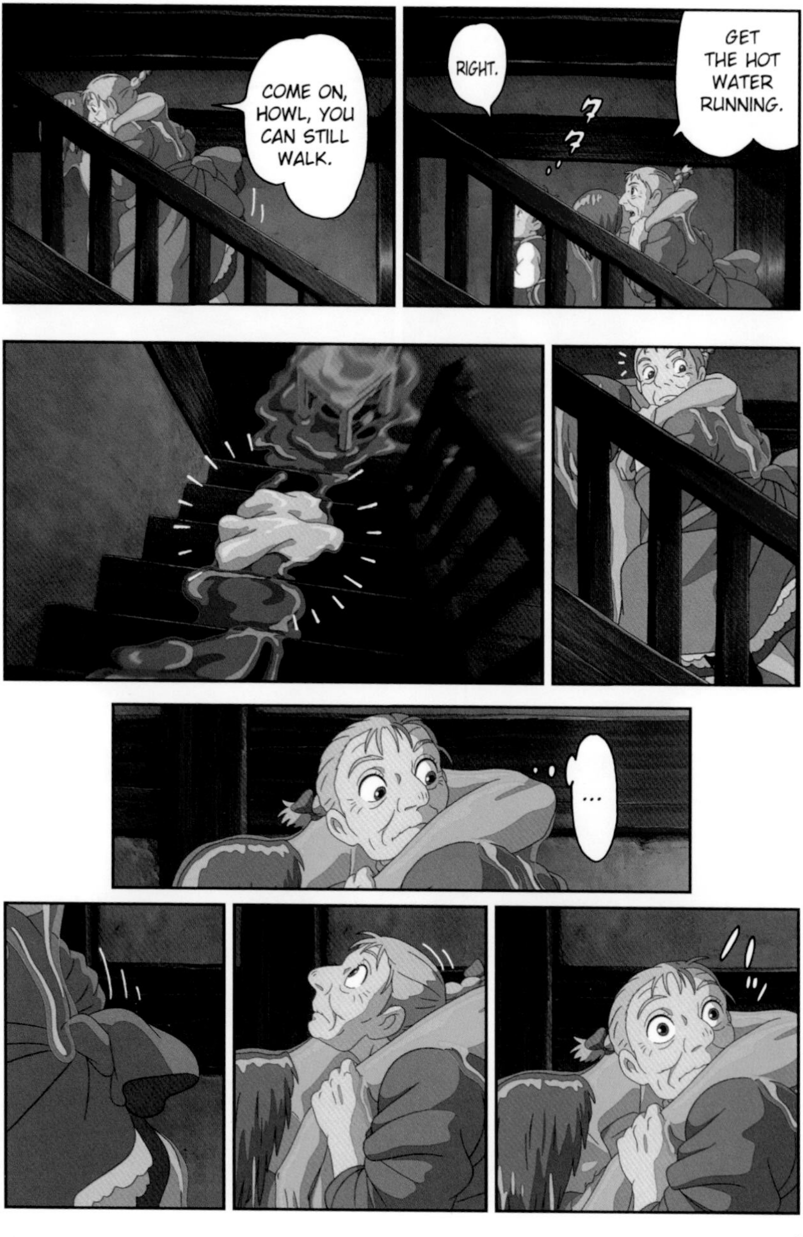
GET THE HOT WATER RUNNING.
RIGHT.
COME ON, HOWL, YOU CAN STILL WALK.
...

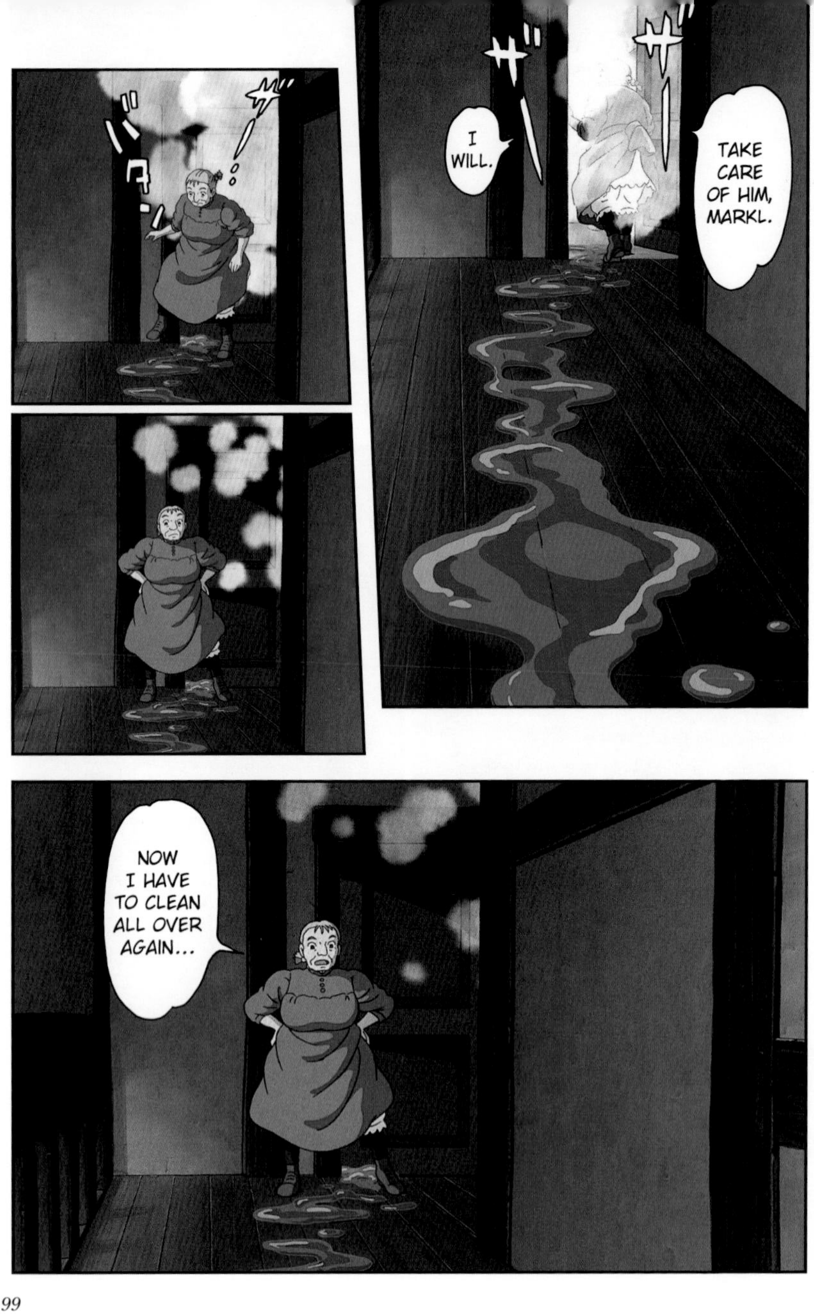
TAKE CARE OF HIM, MARKL.
I WILL.
NOW I HAVE TO CLEAN ALL OVER AGAIN...

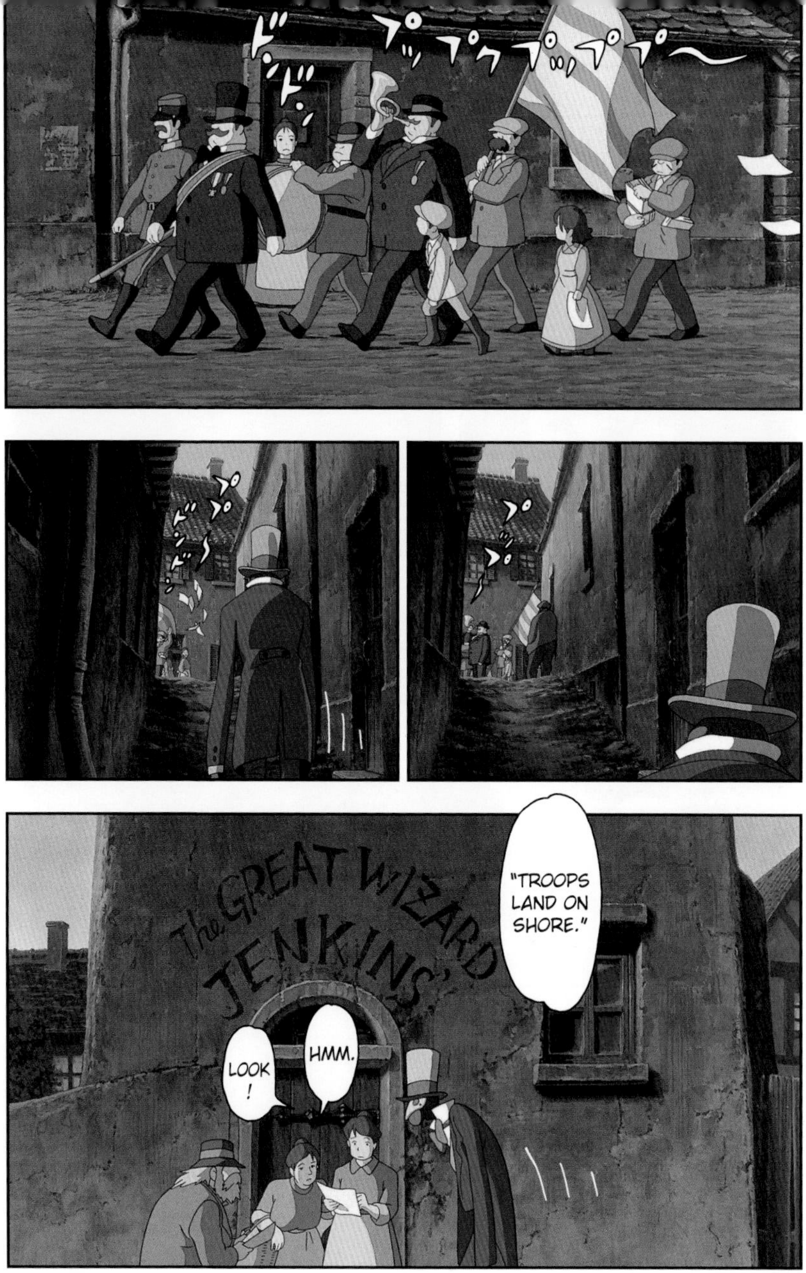
"TROOPS LAND ON SHORE."
The GREAT WIZARD JENKINS'
HMM.
LOOK!

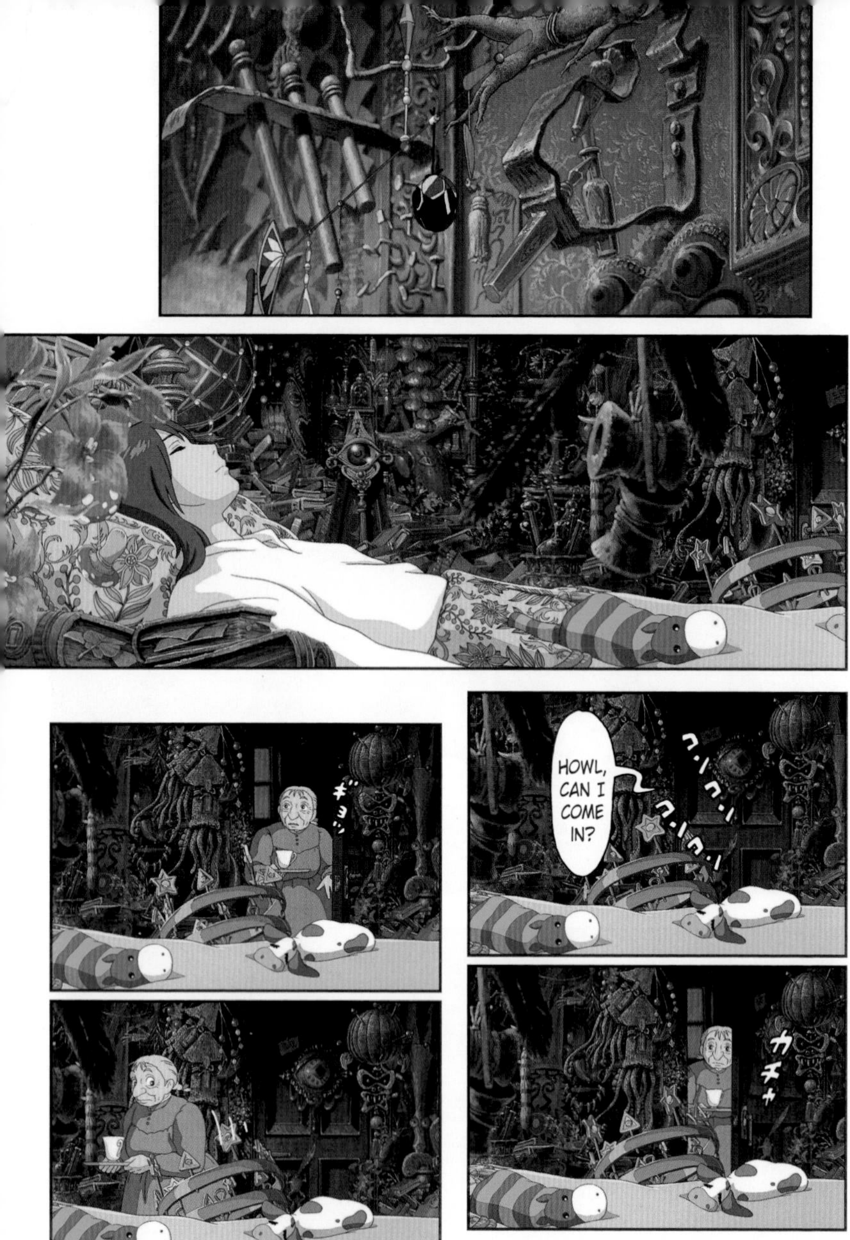
HOWL, CAN I COME IN?
ギョッ
カチャ

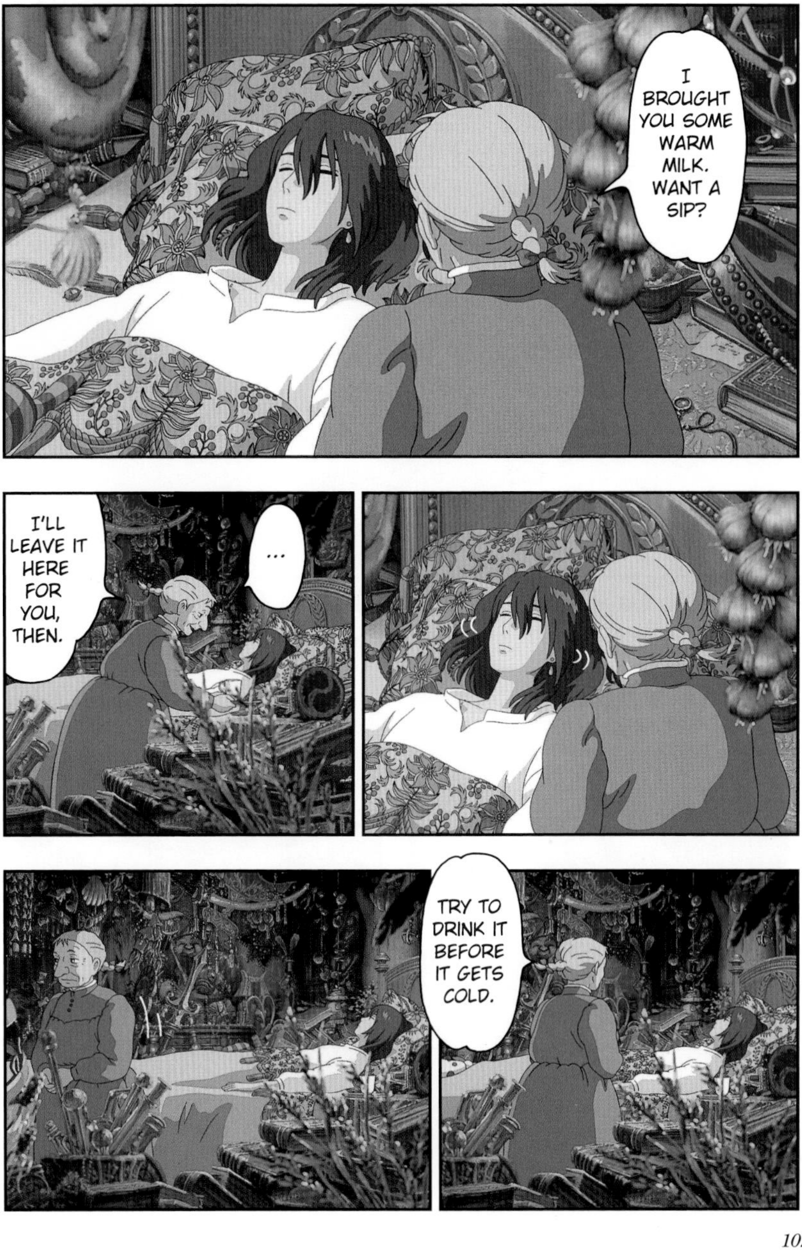
I BROUGHT YOU SOME WARM MILK. WANT A SIP?
...
I'LL LEAVE IT HERE FOR YOU, THEN.
TRY TO DRINK IT BEFORE IT GETS COLD.

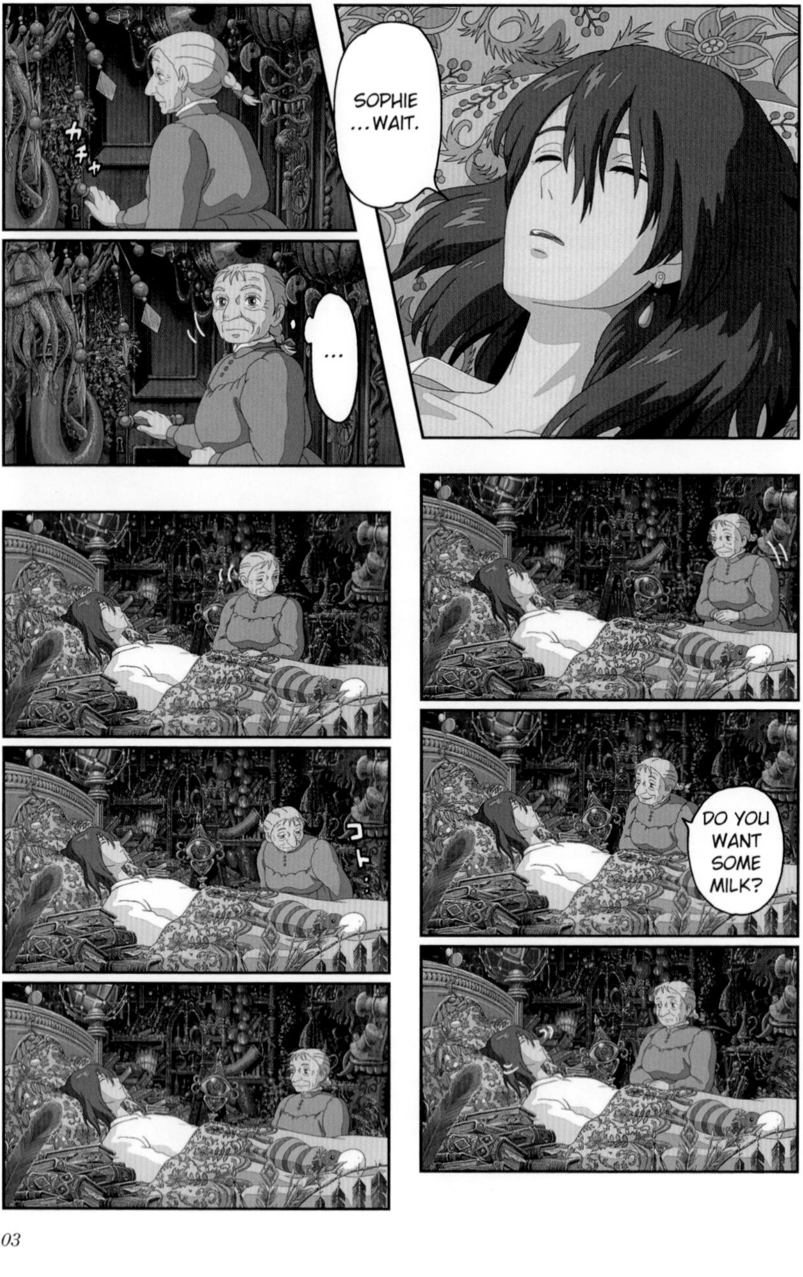
SOPHIE ...WAIT.
カチャ
...
DO YOU WANT SOME MILK?
コト

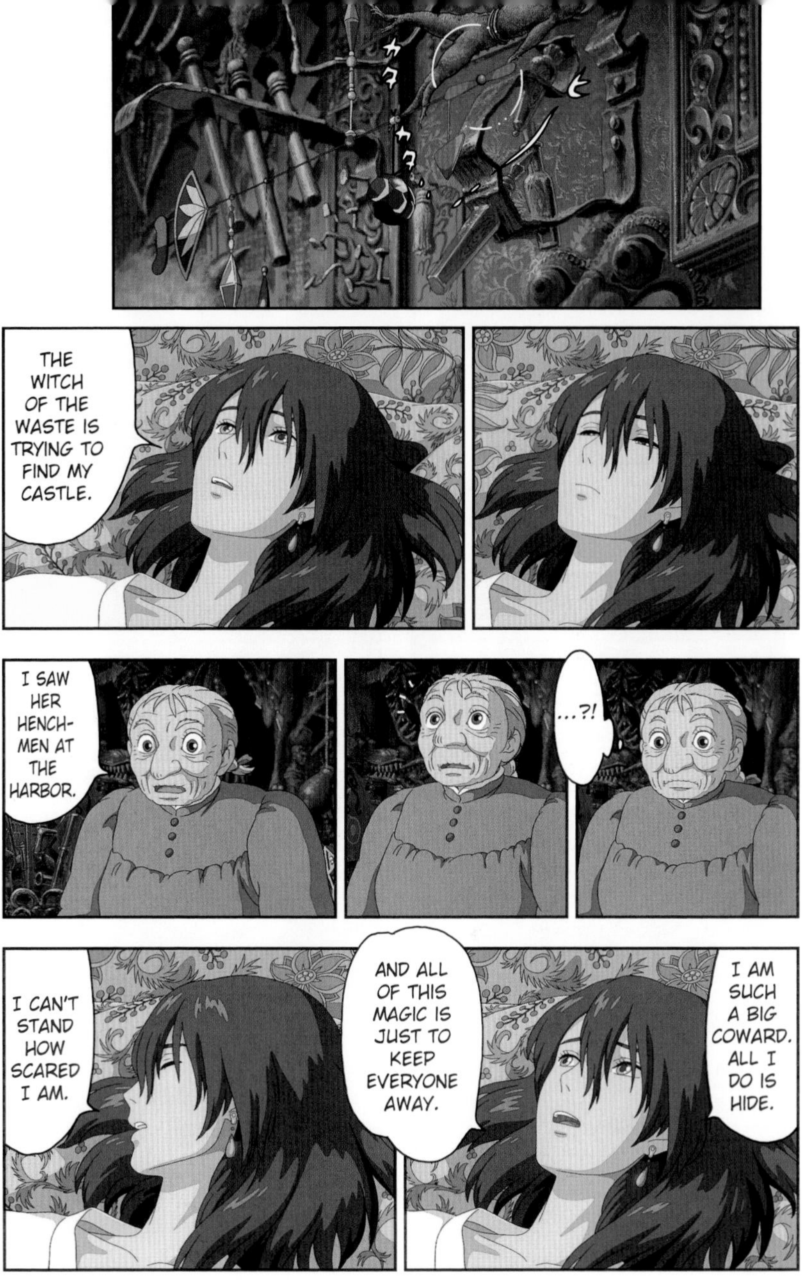
THE WITCH OF THE WASTE IS TRYING TO FIND MY CASTLE.
...?!
I SAW HER HENCHMEN AT THE HARBOR.
I AM SUCH A BIG COWARD. ALL I DO IS HIDE.
AND ALL OF THIS MAGIC IS JUST TO KEEP EVERYONE AWAY.
I CAN'T STAND HOW SCARED I AM.

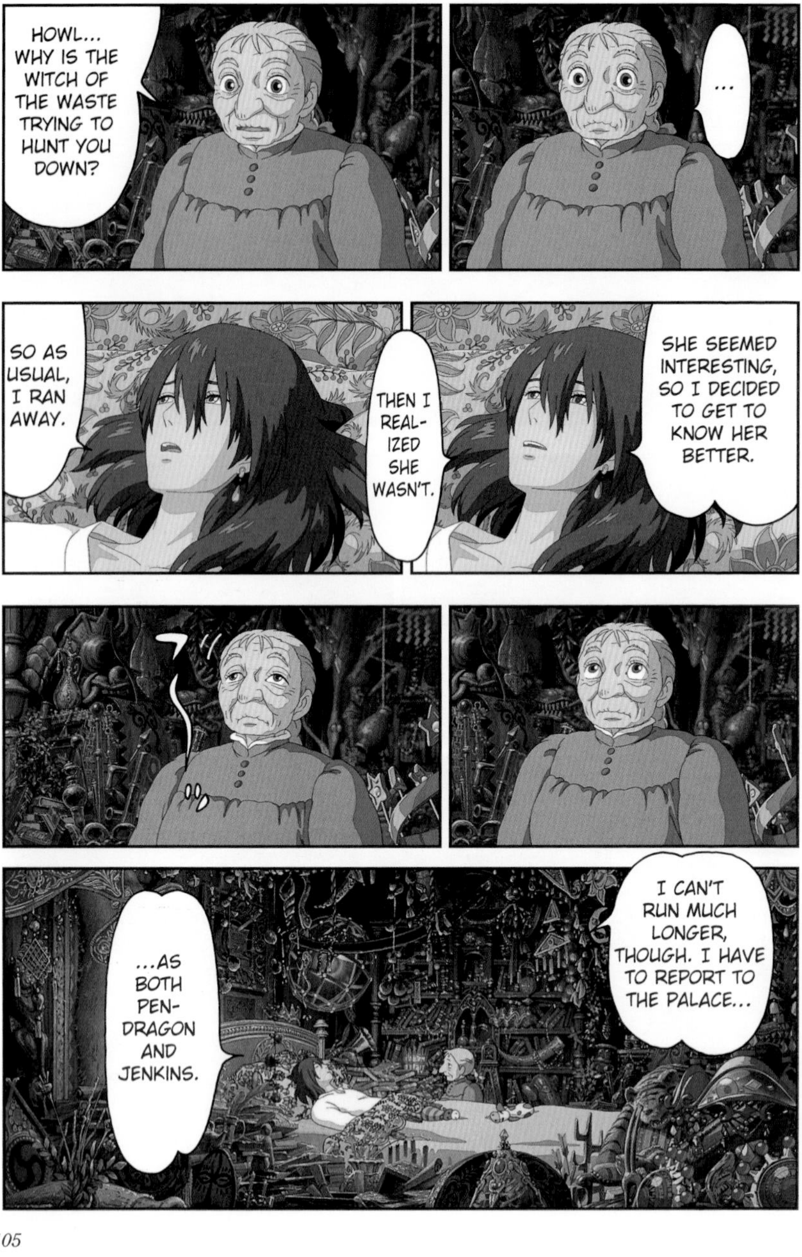
...
HOWL... WHY IS THE WITCH OF THE WASTE TRYING TO HUNT YOU DOWN?
SHE SEEMED INTERESTING, SO I DECIDED TO GET TO KNOW HER BETTER.
THEN I REALIZED SHE WASN'T.
SO AS USUAL, I RAN AWAY.
I CAN'T RUN MUCH LONGER, THOUGH. I HAVE TO REPORT TO THE PALACE...
...AS BOTH PENDRAGON AND JENKINS.

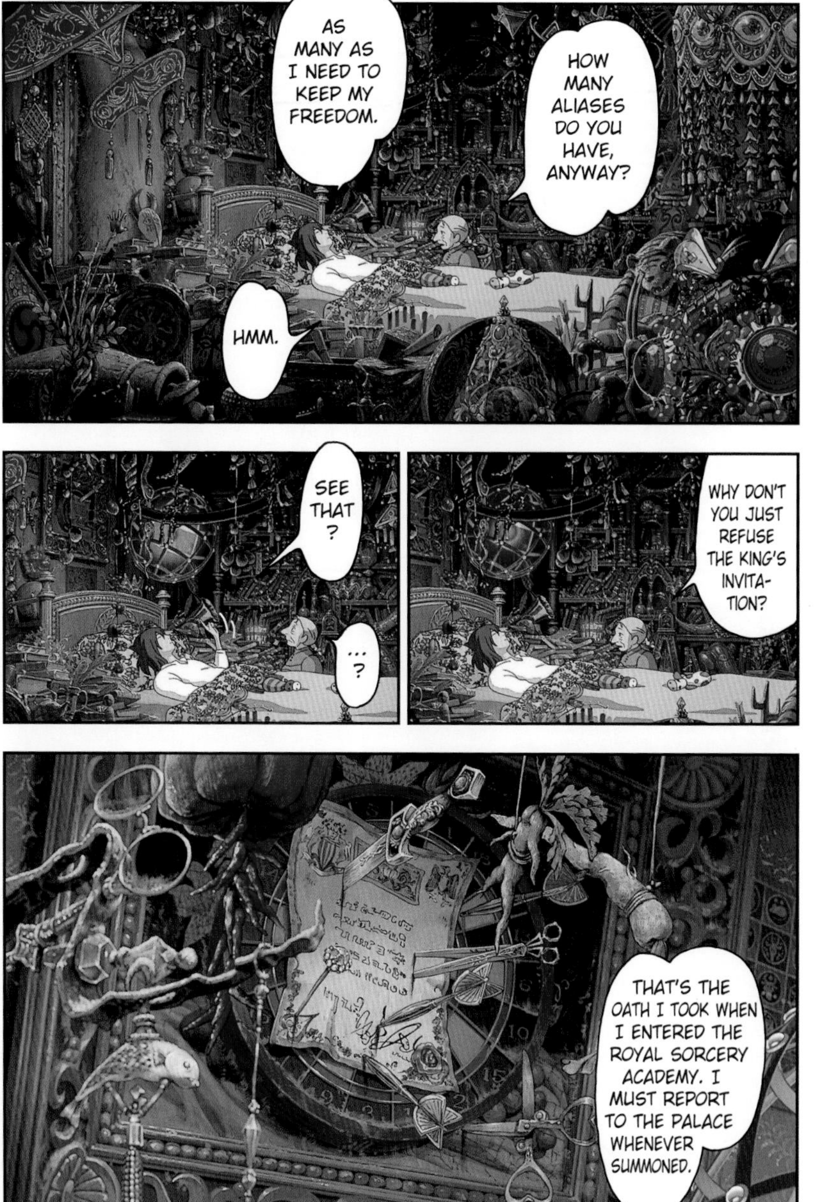
HOW MANY ALIASES DO YOU HAVE, ANYWAY?
AS MANY AS I NEED TO KEEP MY FREEDOM.
HMM.
WHY DON'T YOU JUST REFUSE THE KING'S INVITA-TION?
SEE THAT?
...?
THAT'S THE OATH I TOOK WHEN I ENTERED THE ROYAL SORCERY ACADEMY. I MUST REPORT TO THE PALACE WHENEVER SUMMONED.

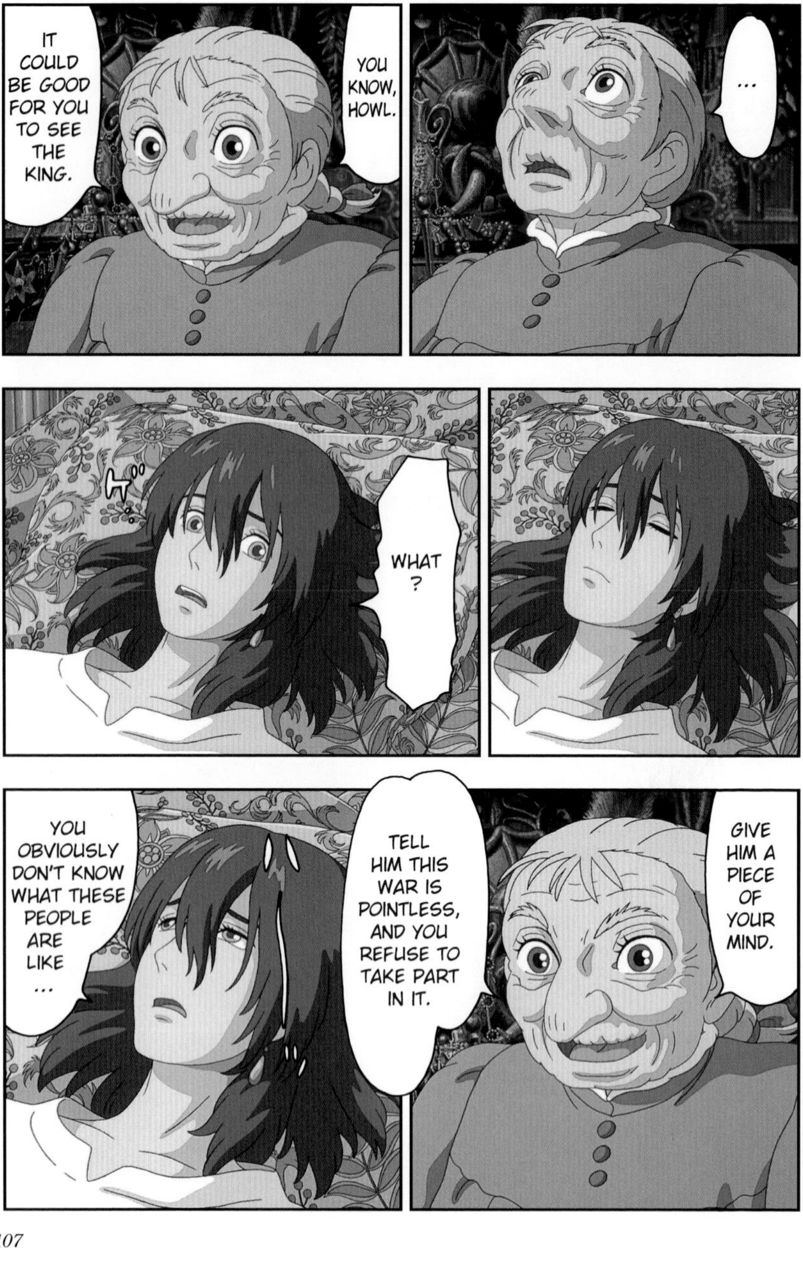
...
YOU KNOW, HOWL.
IT COULD BE GOOD FOR YOU TO SEE THE KING.
WHAT?
GIVE HIM A PIECE OF YOUR MIND.
TELL HIM THIS WAR IS POINTLESS, AND YOU REFUSE TO TAKE PART IN IT.
YOU OBVIOUSLY DON'T KNOW WHAT THESE PEOPLE ARE LIKE ...

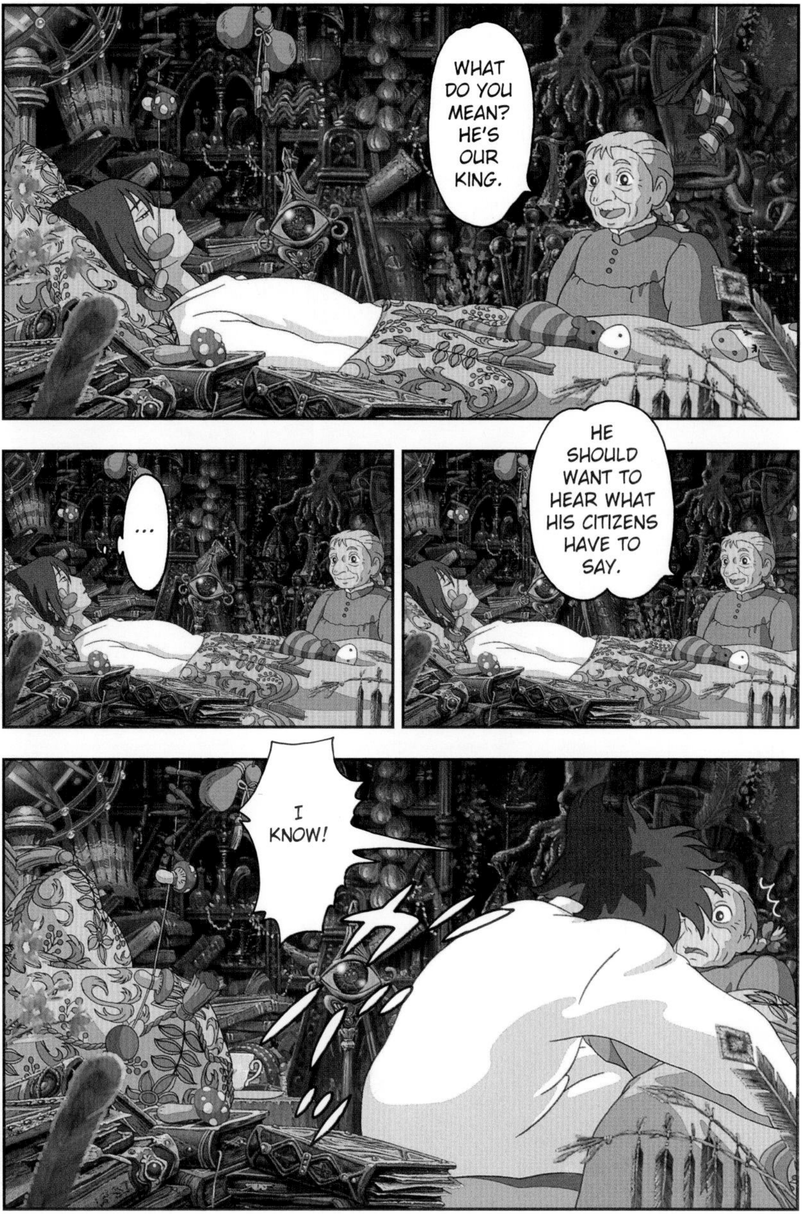
WHAT DO YOU MEAN? HE'S OUR KING.
HE SHOULD WANT TO HEAR WHAT HIS CITIZENS HAVE TO SAY.
...
I KNOW!

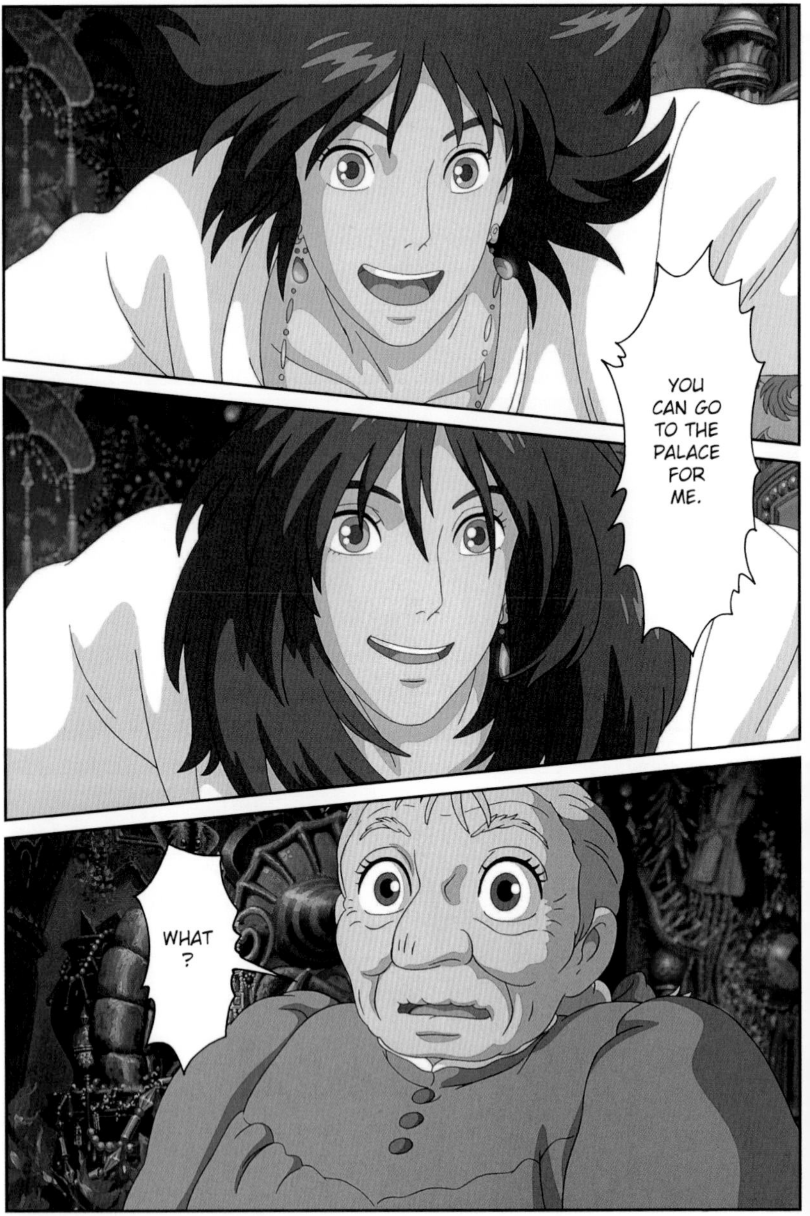
YOU CAN GO TO THE PALACE FOR ME.
WHAT?

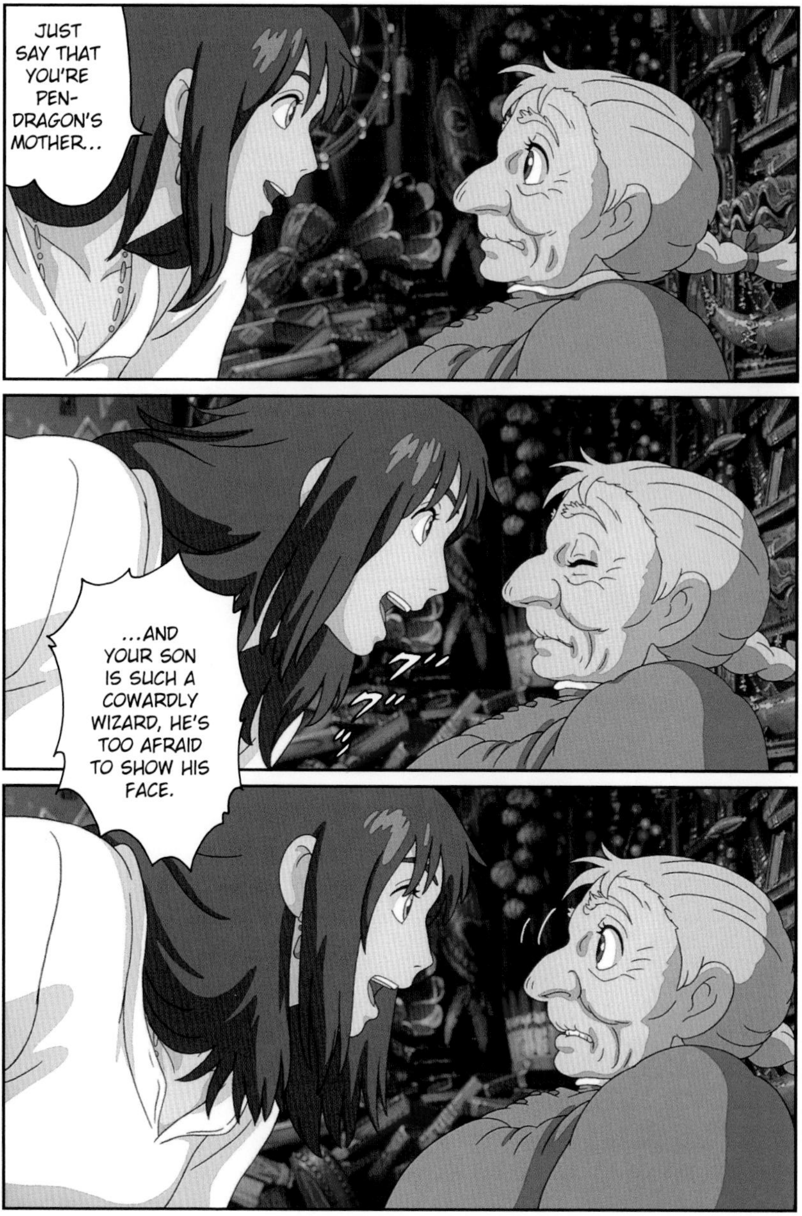
JUST SAY THAT YOU'RE PEN-DRAGON'S MOTHER...
...AND YOUR SON IS SUCH A COWARDLY WIZARD, HE'S TOO AFRAID TO SHOW HIS FACE.

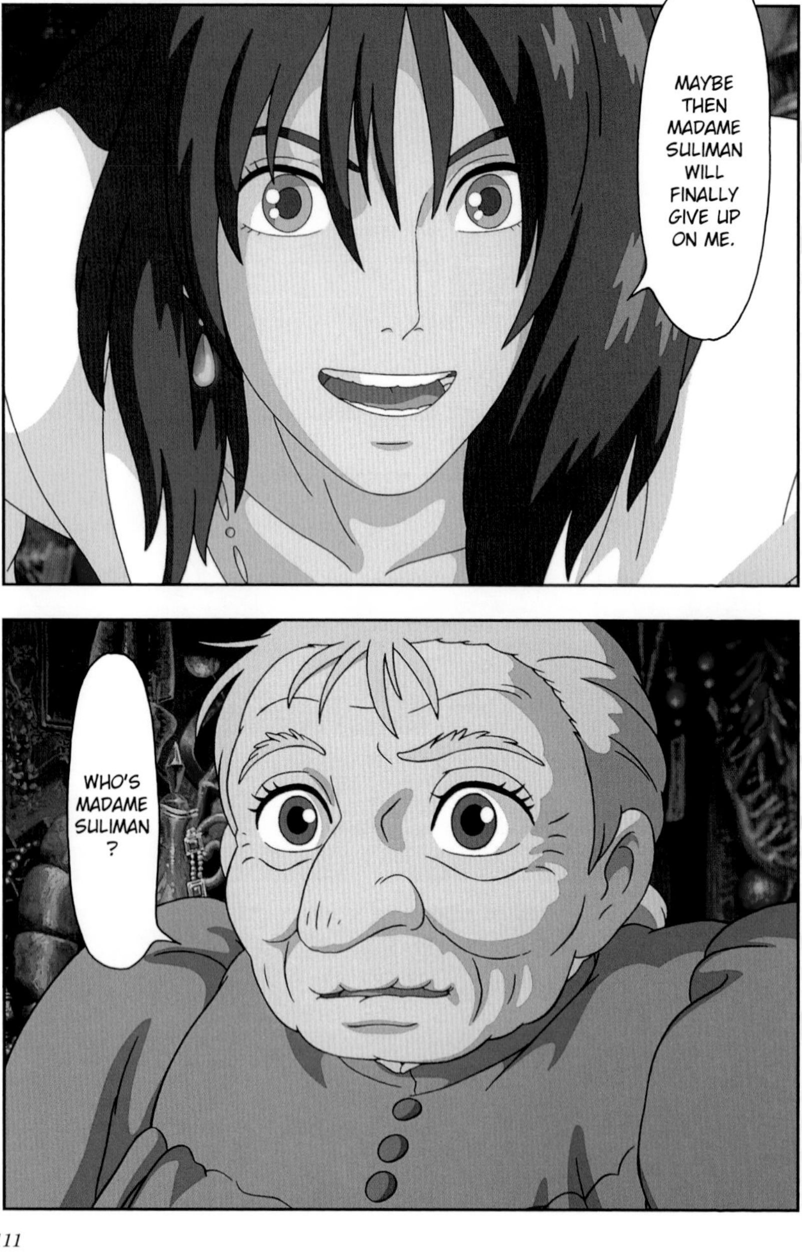
MAYBE THEN MADAME SULIMAN WILL FINALLY GIVE UP ON ME.
WHO'S MADAME SULIMAN?

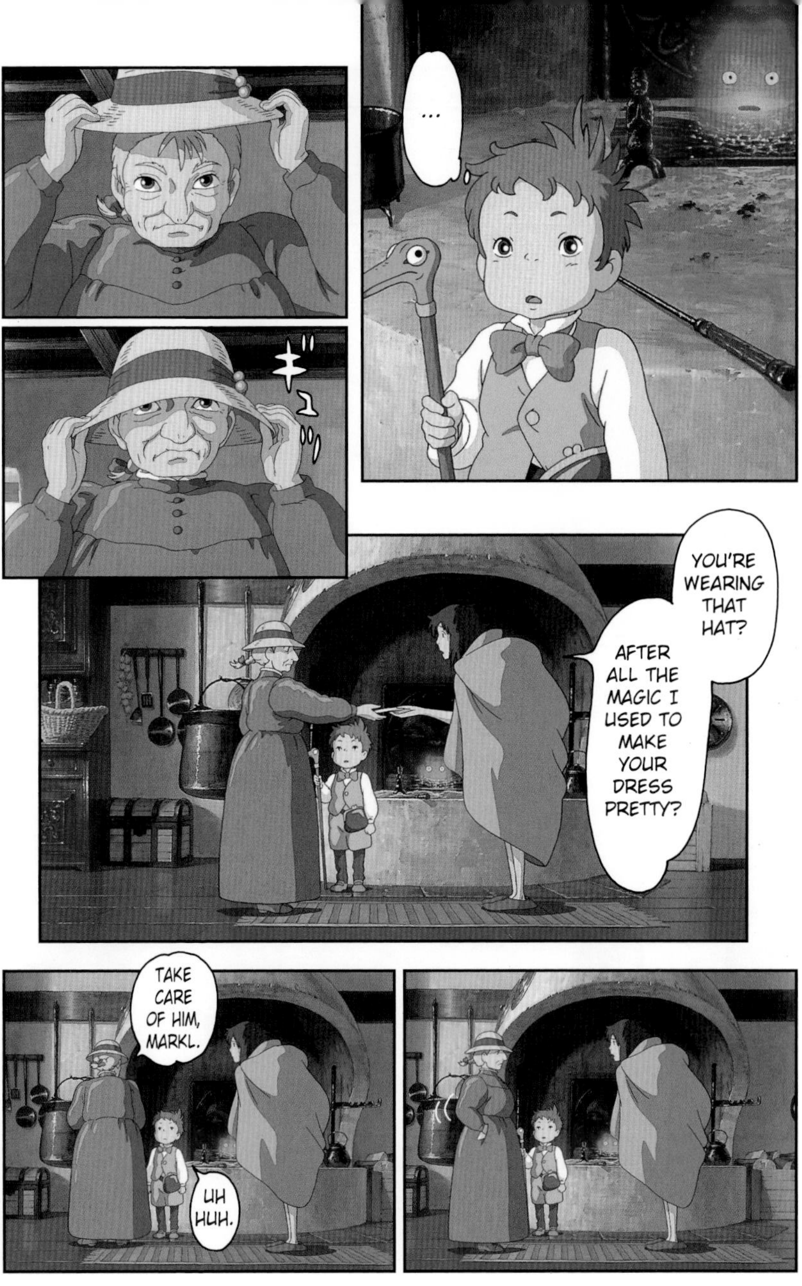
...
ギュッ
YOU'RE WEARING THAT HAT?
AFTER ALL THE MAGIC I USED TO MAKE YOUR DRESS PRETTY?
TAKE CARE OF HIM, MARKL.
UH HUH.

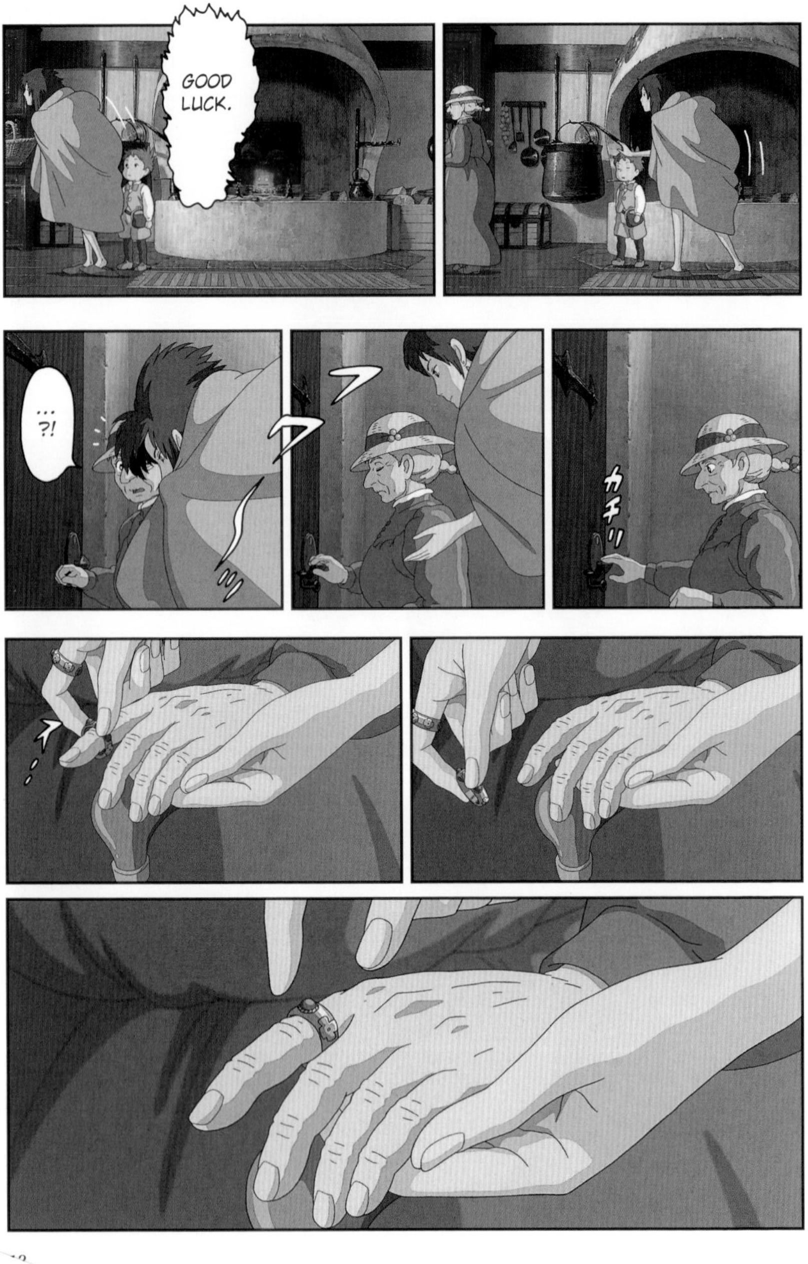
GOOD LUCK.
カチリ
...?!

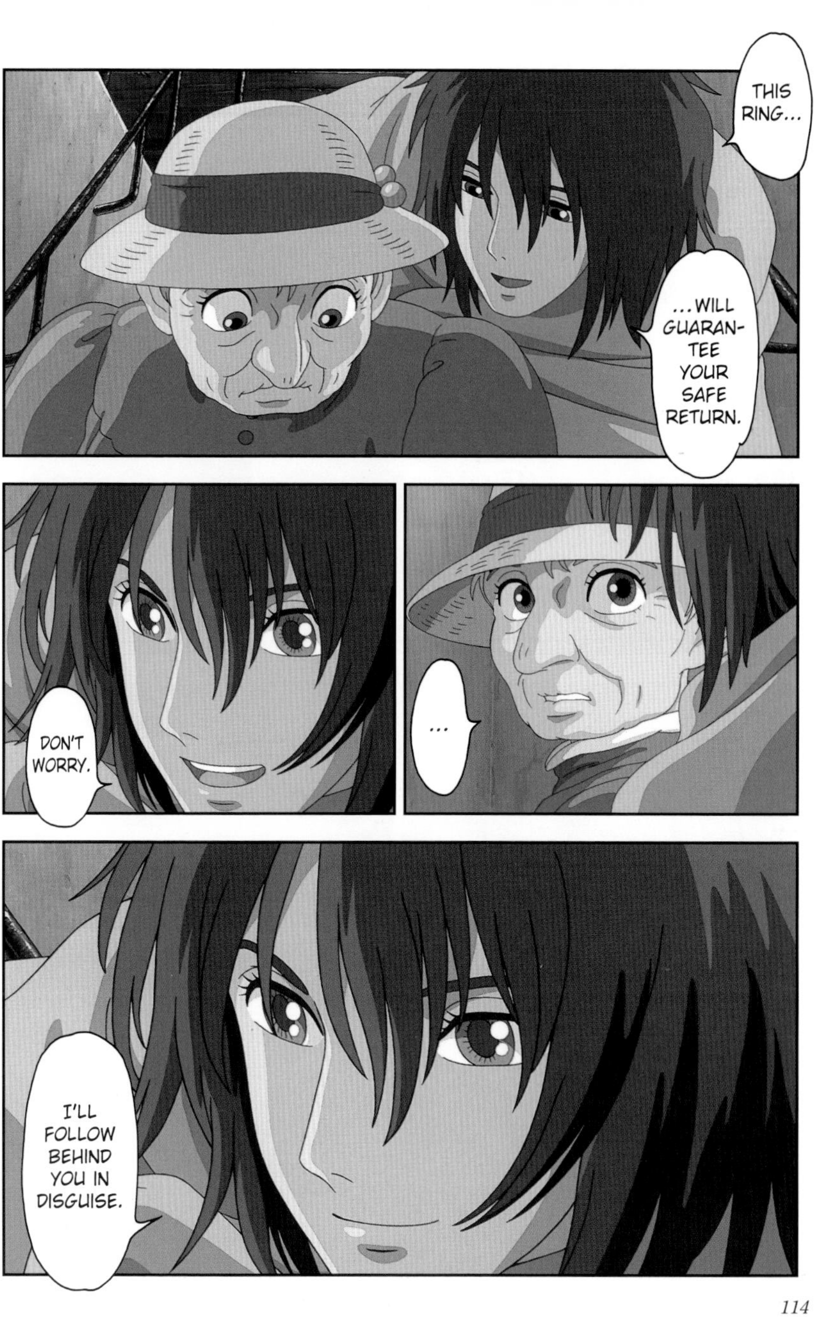
THIS RING...
...WILL GUARANTEE YOUR SAFE RETURN.
...
DON'T WORRY.
I'LL FOLLOW BEHIND YOU IN DISGUISE.

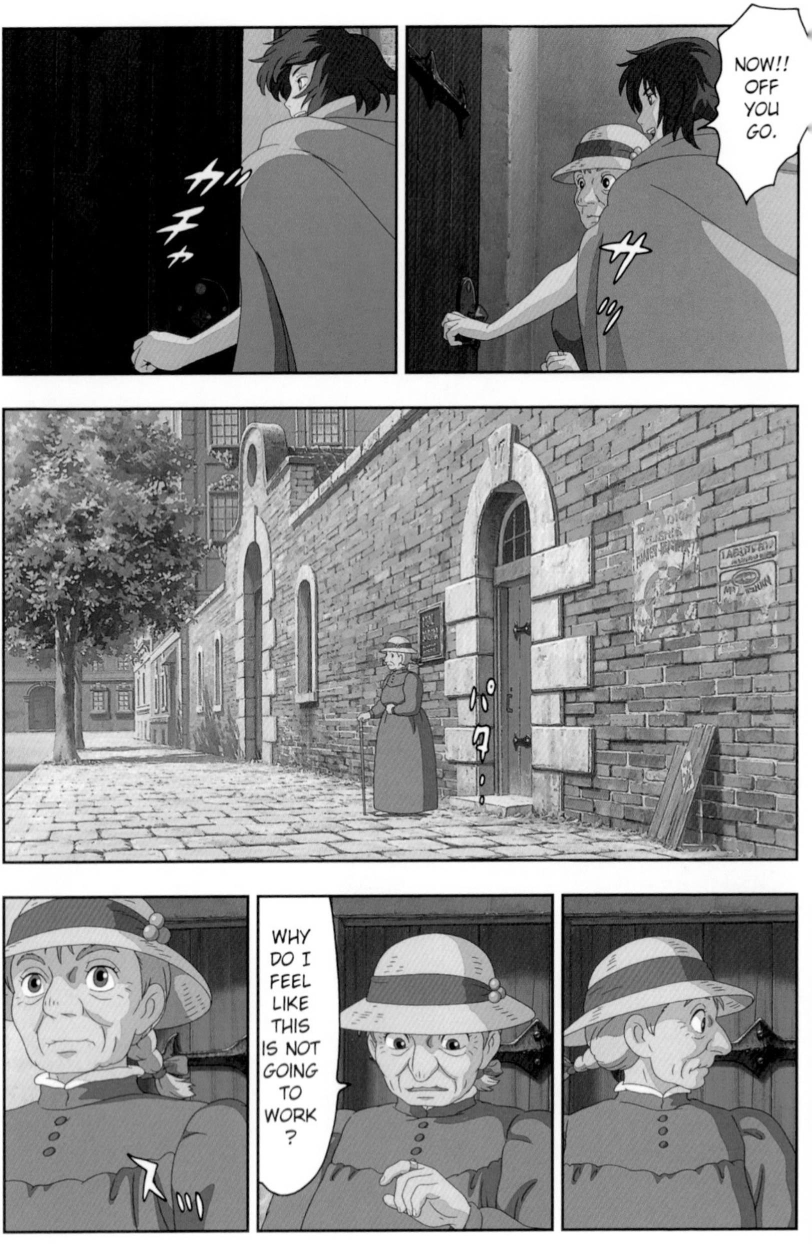
NOW!! OFF YOU GO.
サッ
ガチャ
パタ
WHY DO I FEEL LIKE THIS IS NOT GOING TO WORK?
スッ

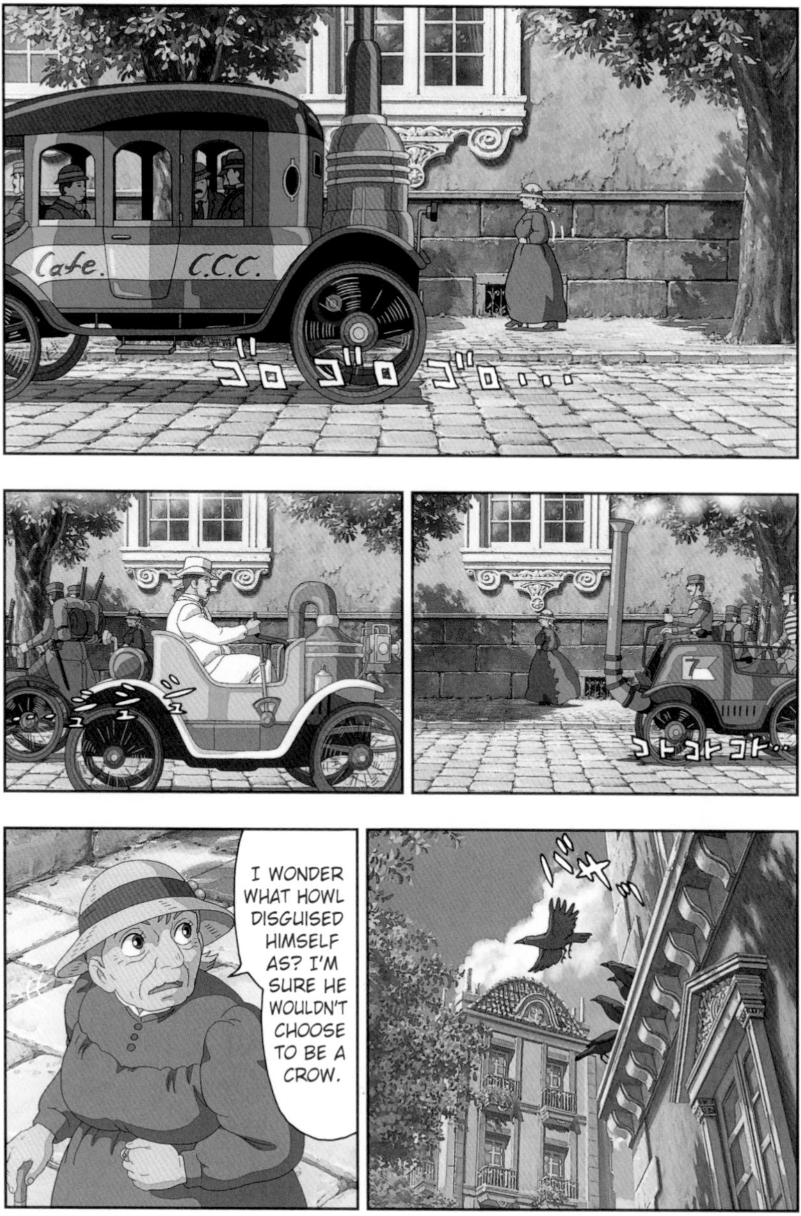
ゴロゴロゴロ…
コトコトコト‥
I WONDER WHAT HOWL DISGUISED HIMSELF AS? I'M SURE HE WOULDN'T CHOOSE TO BE A CROW.

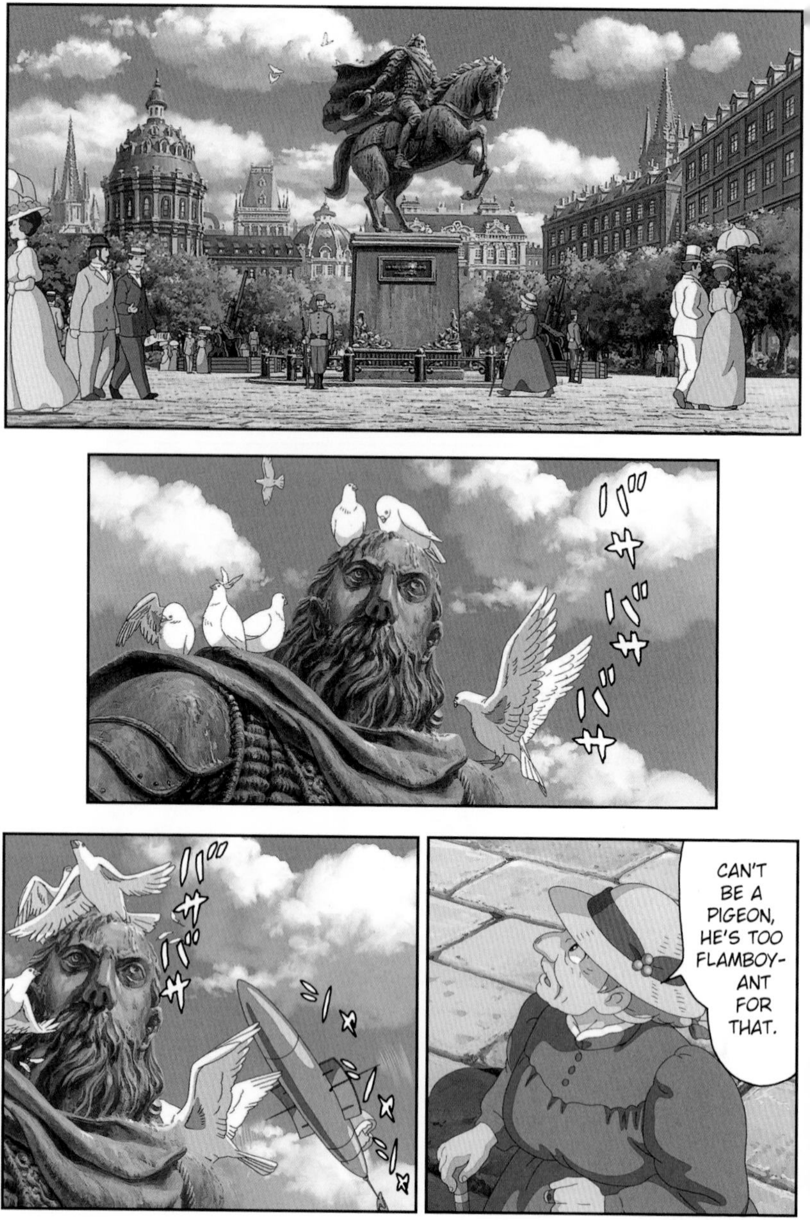
バサ
バサ
バサ
CAN'T BE A PIGEON, HE'S TOO FLAMBOY-ANT FOR THAT.
バサ
バサ

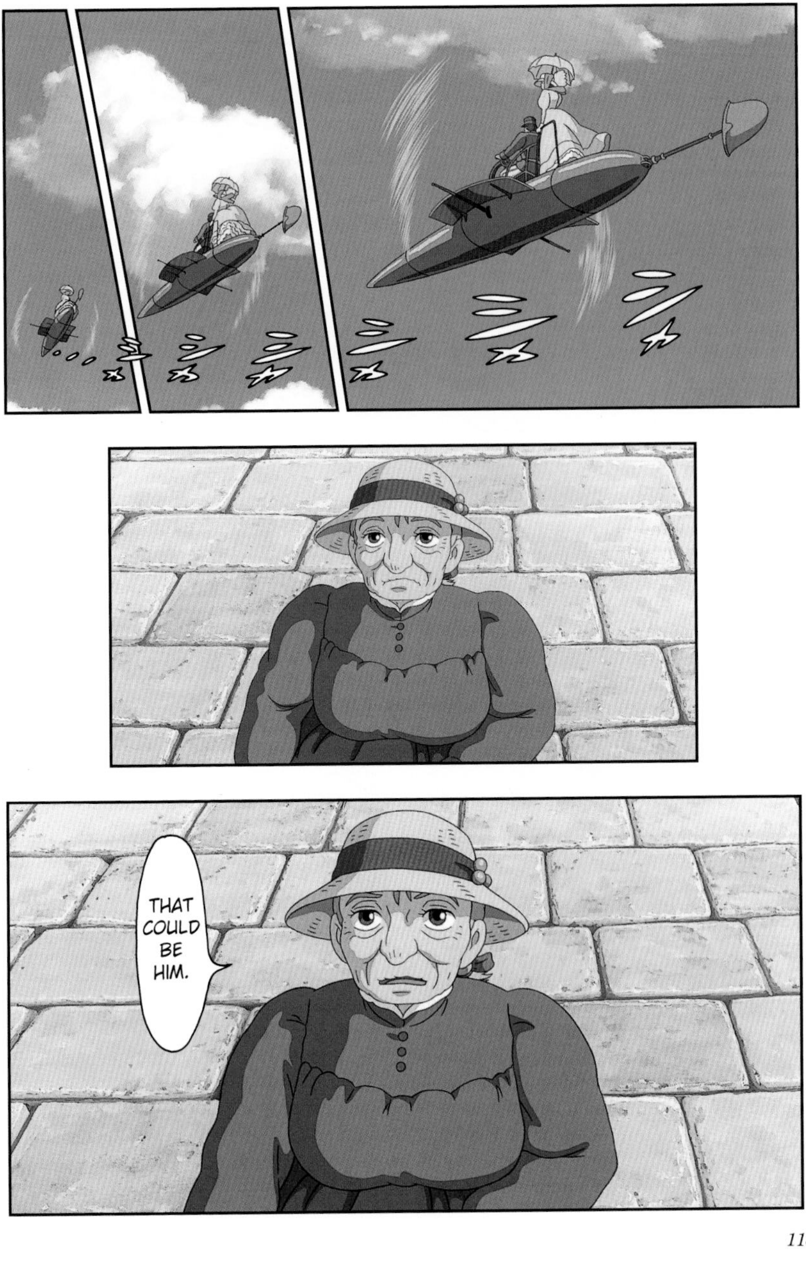
THAT COULD BE HIM.

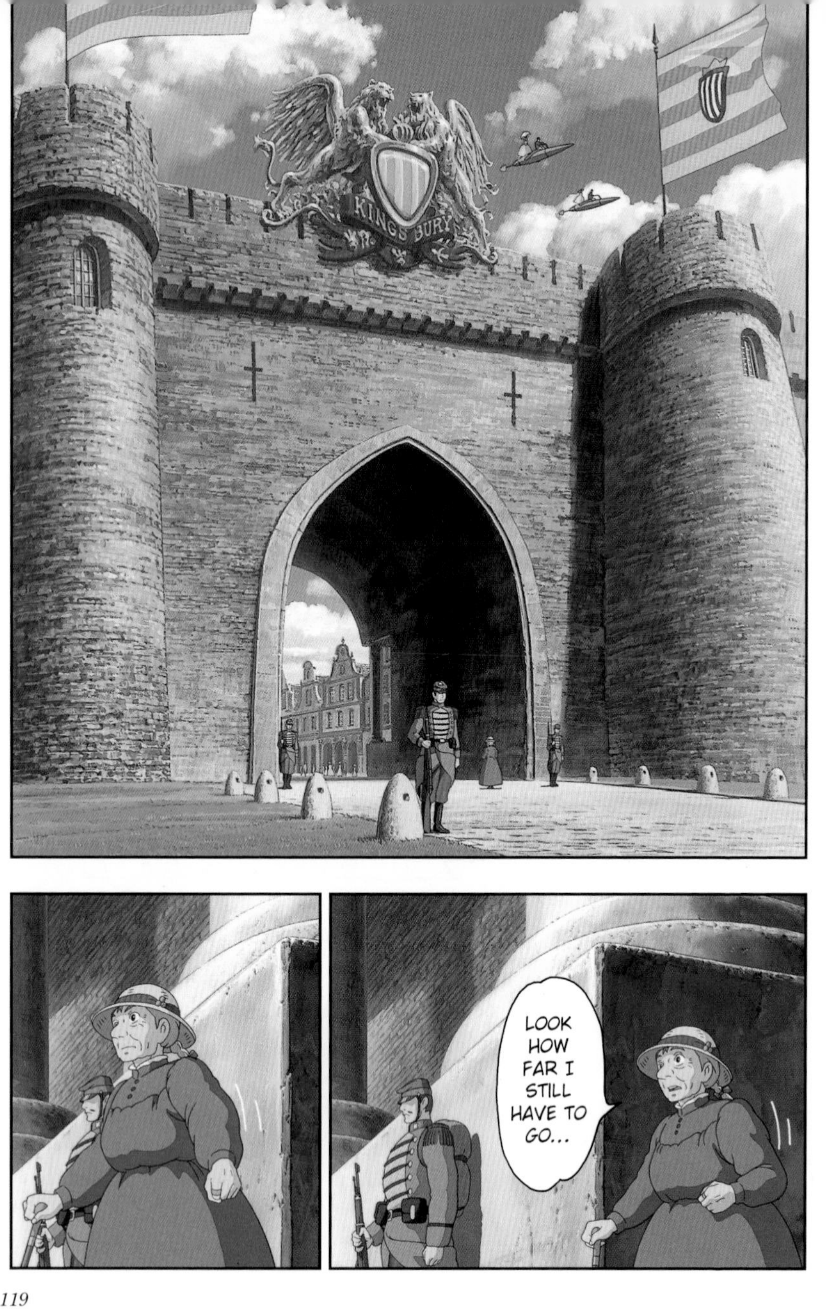
KINGS BURY
LOOK HOW FAR I STILL HAVE TO GO...

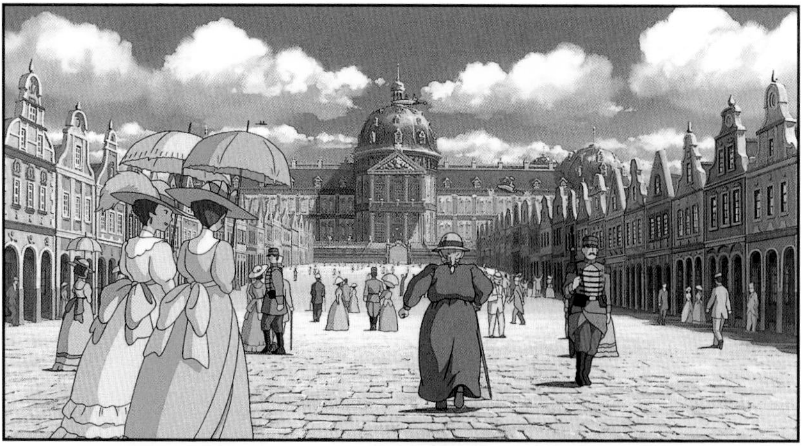

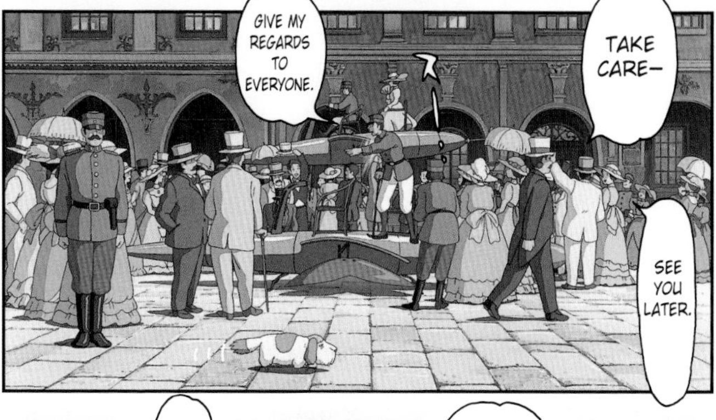
TAKE CARE—
GIVE MY REGARDS TO EVERYONE.
SEE YOU LATER.

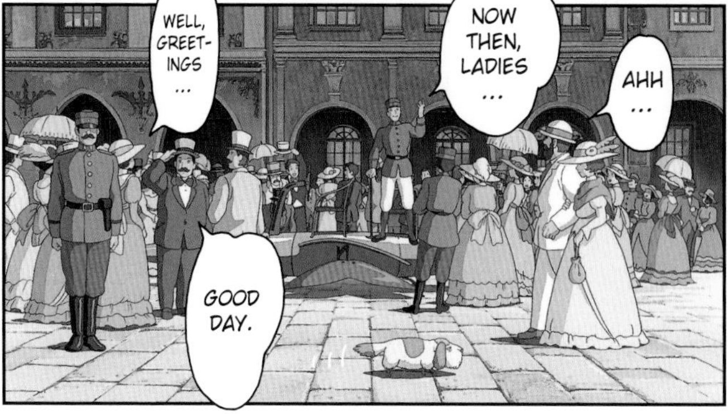
AHH ...
NOW THEN, LADIES ...
WELL, GREET-INGS ...
GOOD DAY.

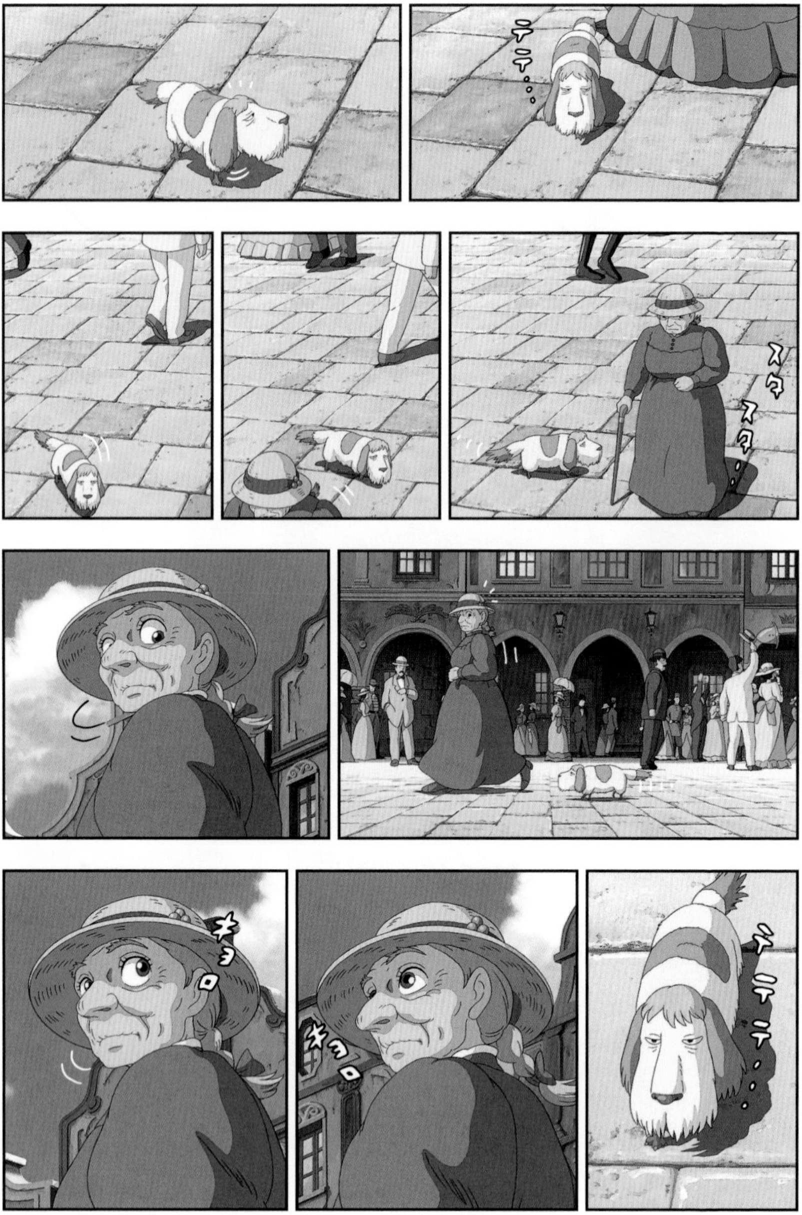

テテ・・・
スタ スタ・・・
テテテ・・・
キョロ
キョロ

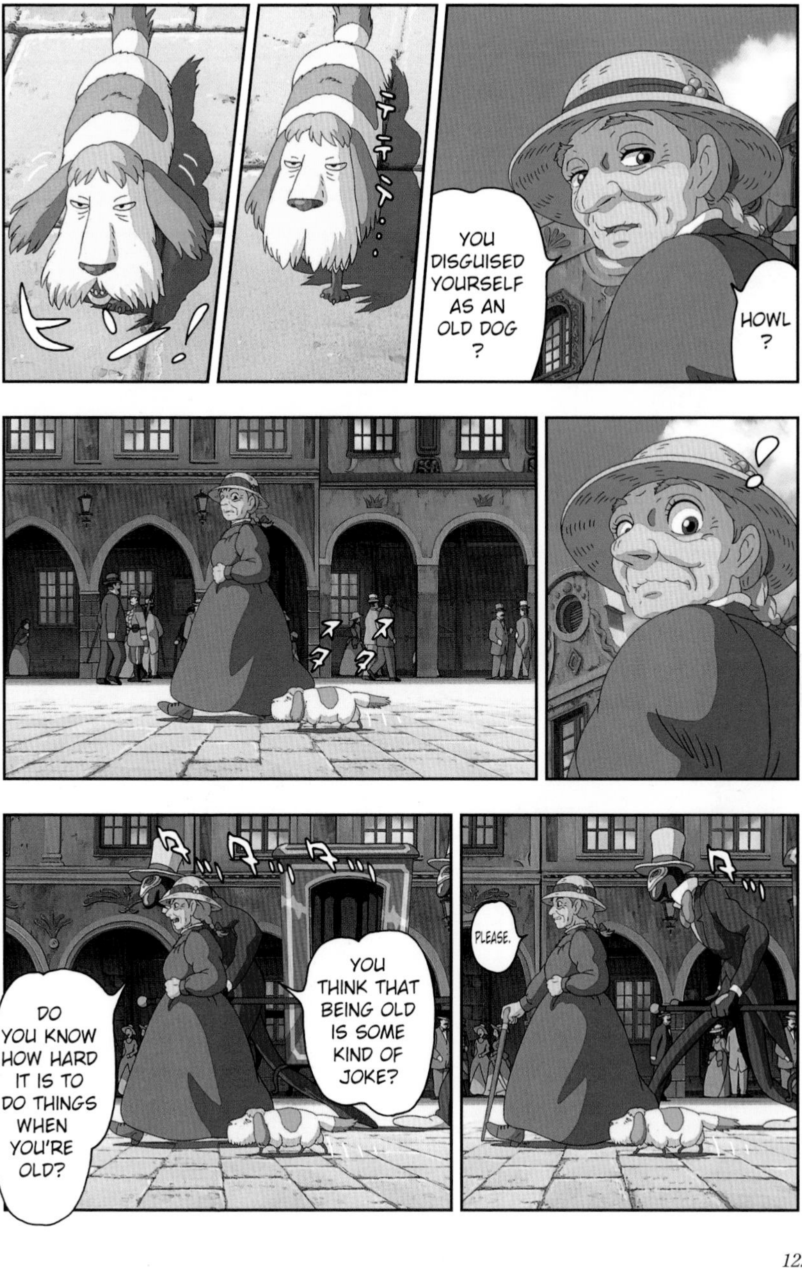
HOWL?
YOU DISGUISED YOURSELF AS AN OLD DOG?
PLEASE.
YOU THINK THAT BEING OLD IS SOME KIND OF JOKE?
DO YOU KNOW HOW HARD IT IS TO DO THINGS WHEN YOU'RE OLD?

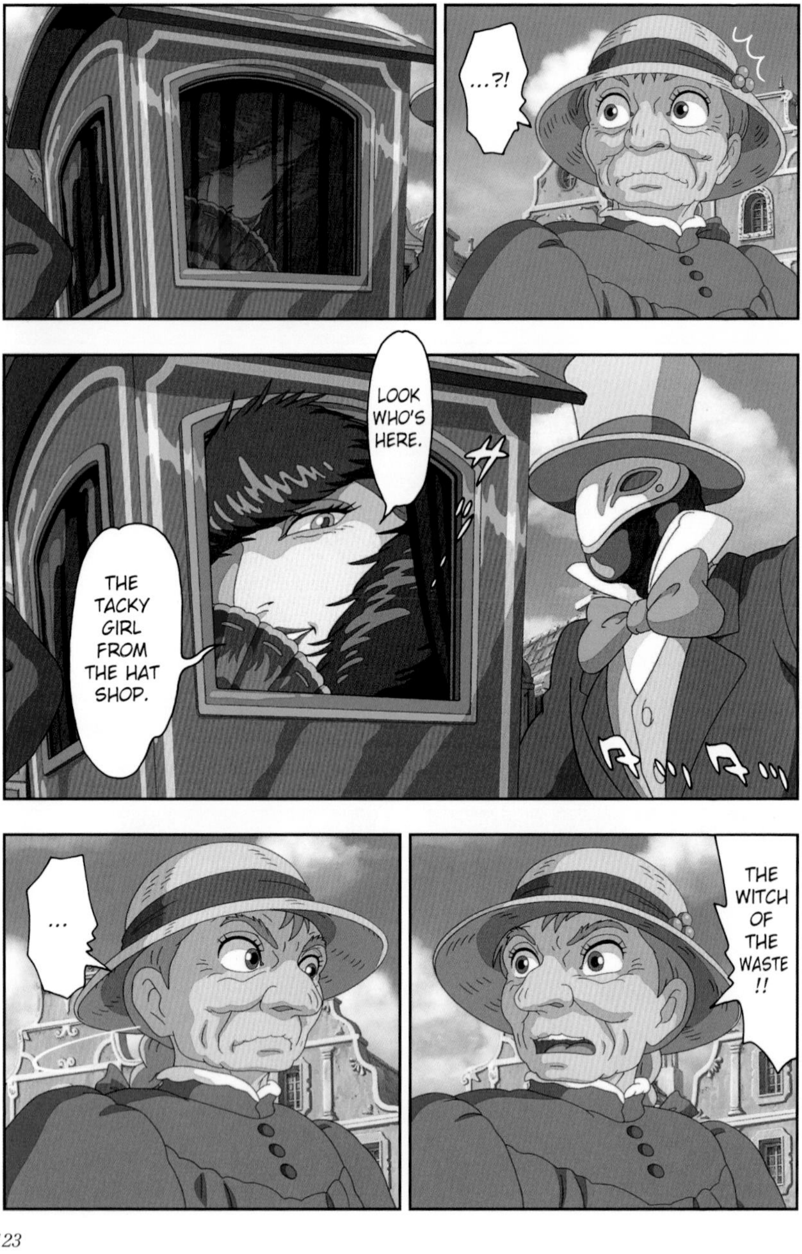
...?!
LOOK WHO'S HERE.
THE TACKY GIRL FROM THE HAT SHOP.
THE WITCH OF THE WASTE!!
...

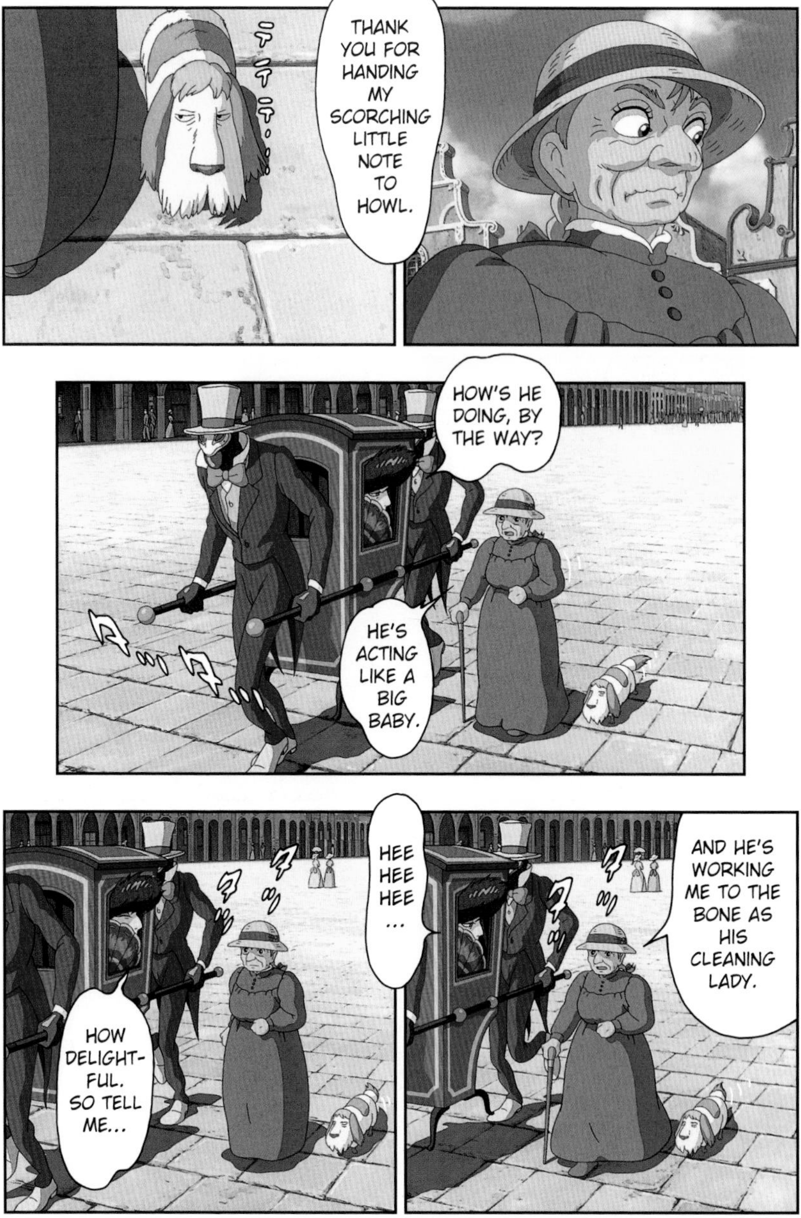
THANK YOU FOR HANDING MY SCORCHING LITTLE NOTE TO HOWL.
HOW'S HE DOING, BY THE WAY?
HE'S ACTING LIKE A BIG BABY.
AND HE'S WORKING ME TO THE BONE AS HIS CLEANING LADY.
HEE HEE HEE ...
HOW DELIGHT-FUL. SO TELL ME...

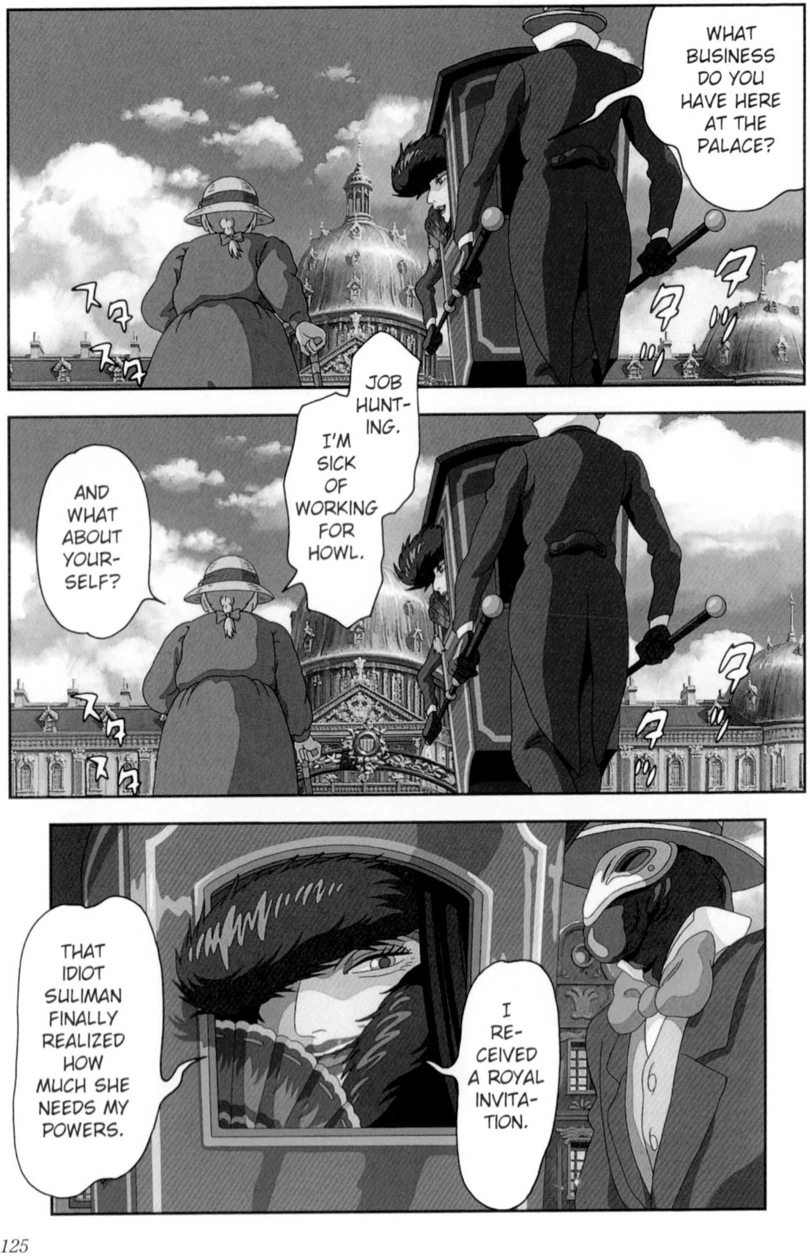
WHAT BUSINESS DO YOU HAVE HERE AT THE PALACE?
JOB HUNTING. I'M SICK OF WORKING FOR HOWL.
AND WHAT ABOUT YOURSELF?
I RECEIVED A ROYAL INVITATION.
THAT IDIOT SULIMAN FINALLY REALIZED HOW MUCH SHE NEEDS MY POWERS.

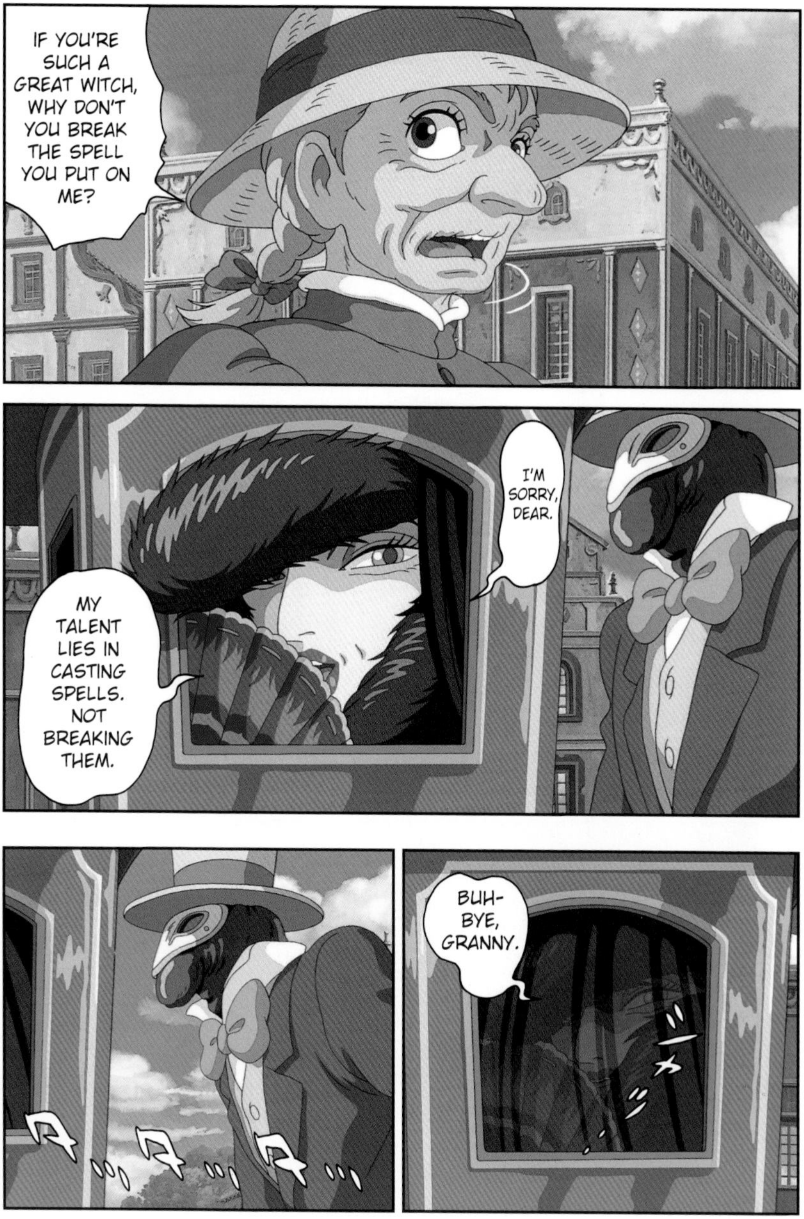
IF YOU'RE SUCH A GREAT WITCH, WHY DON'T YOU BREAK THE SPELL YOU PUT ON ME?
I'M SORRY, DEAR.
MY TALENT LIES IN CASTING SPELLS. NOT BREAKING THEM.
BUH-BYE, GRANNY.

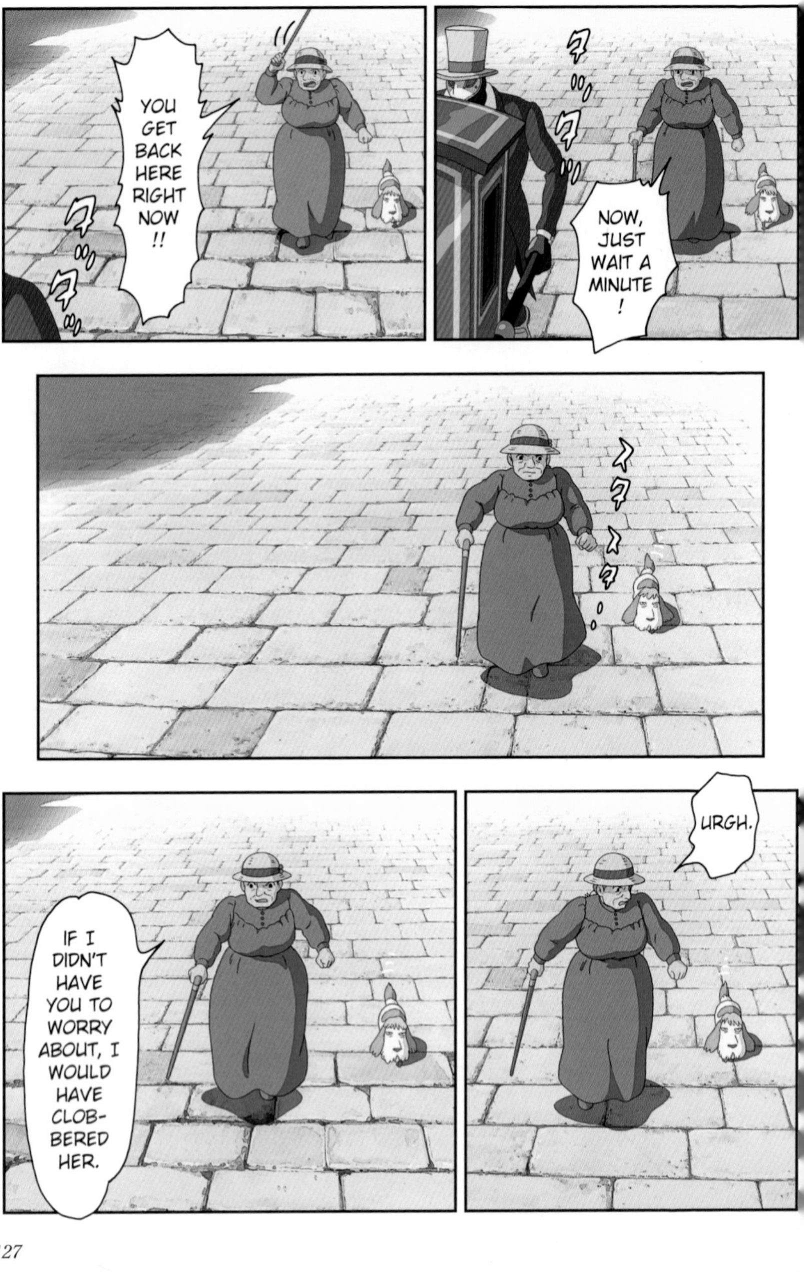
NOW, JUST WAIT A MINUTE!
YOU GET BACK HERE RIGHT NOW!!
URGH.
IF I DIDN'T HAVE YOU TO WORRY ABOUT, I WOULD HAVE CLOBBERED HER.

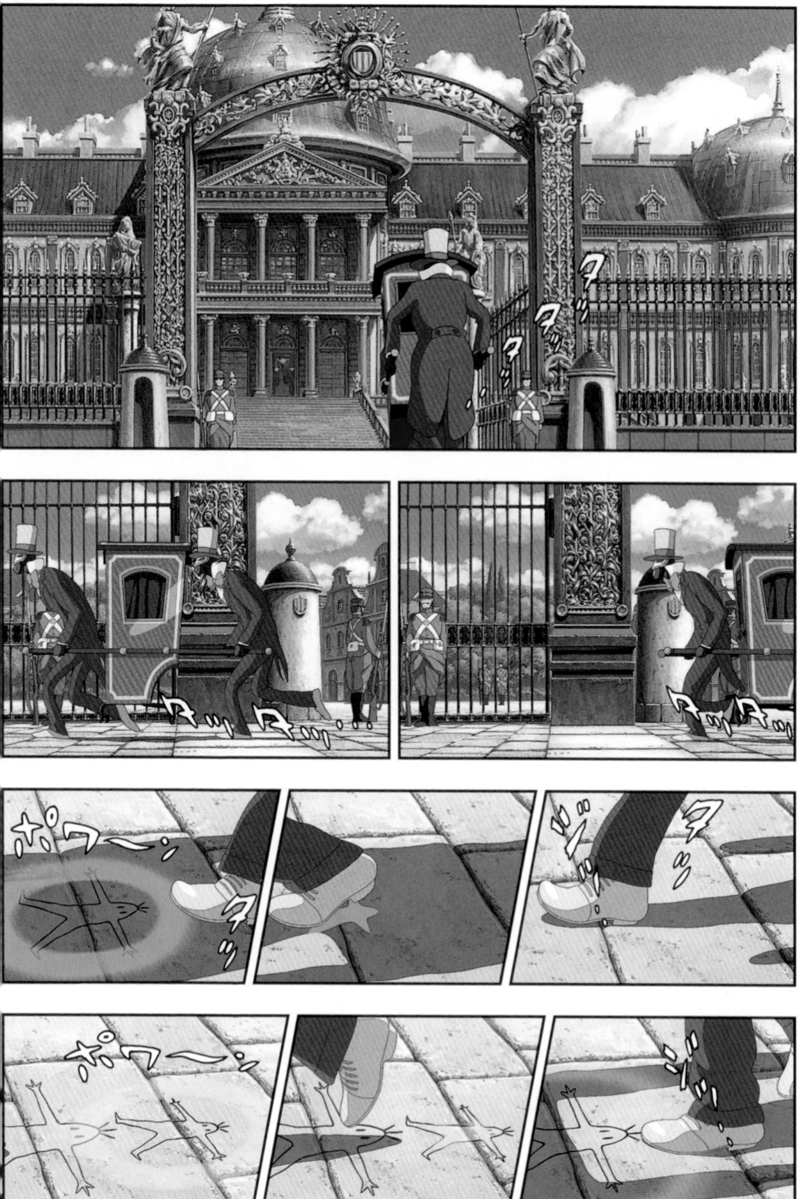
タッ
タッ
タッ
タッ
タッ
タッ
タッ
タッ
ポワ〜
タッ
ポワ〜

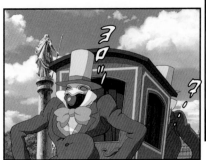

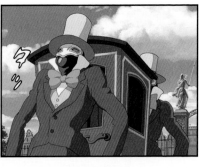

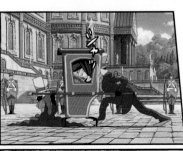

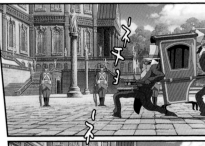

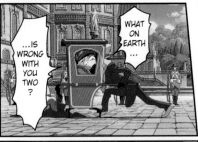

WHAT
ON
EARTH
...

...IS
WRONG
WITH
YOU
TWO
?

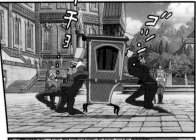

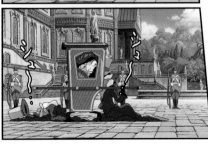

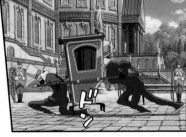

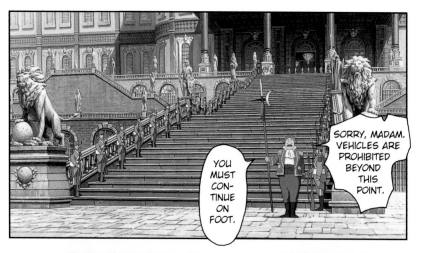

SORRY, MADAM. VEHICLES ARE PROHIBITED BEYOND THIS POINT.

YOU MUST CONTINUE ON FOOT.

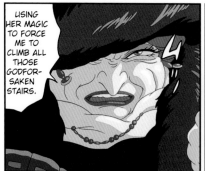

USING HER MAGIC TO FORCE ME TO CLIMB ALL THOSE GODFORSAKEN STAIRS.

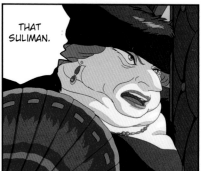

THAT SULIMAN.

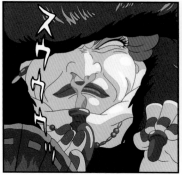

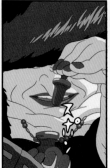

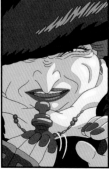

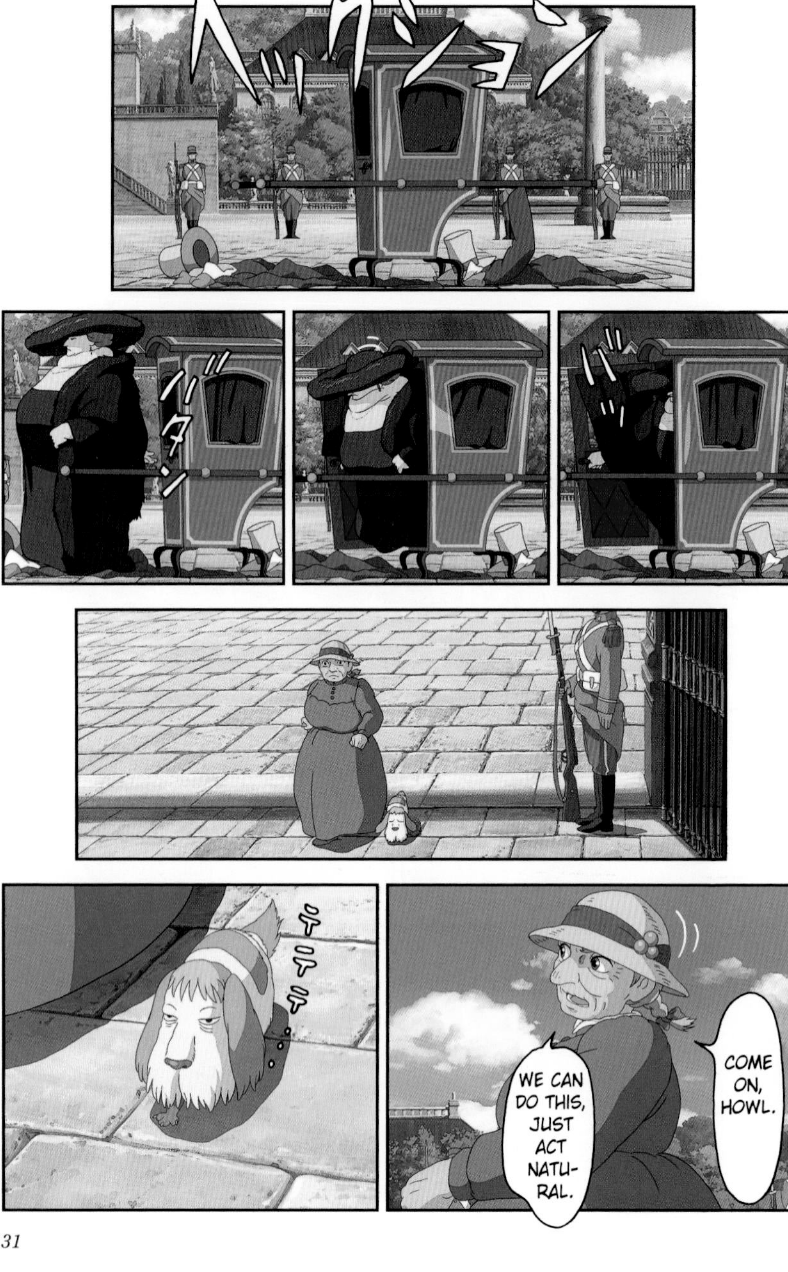
ヘックション
バ
バタン
COME ON, HOWL.
WE CAN DO THIS, JUST ACT NATURAL.
テテテテ

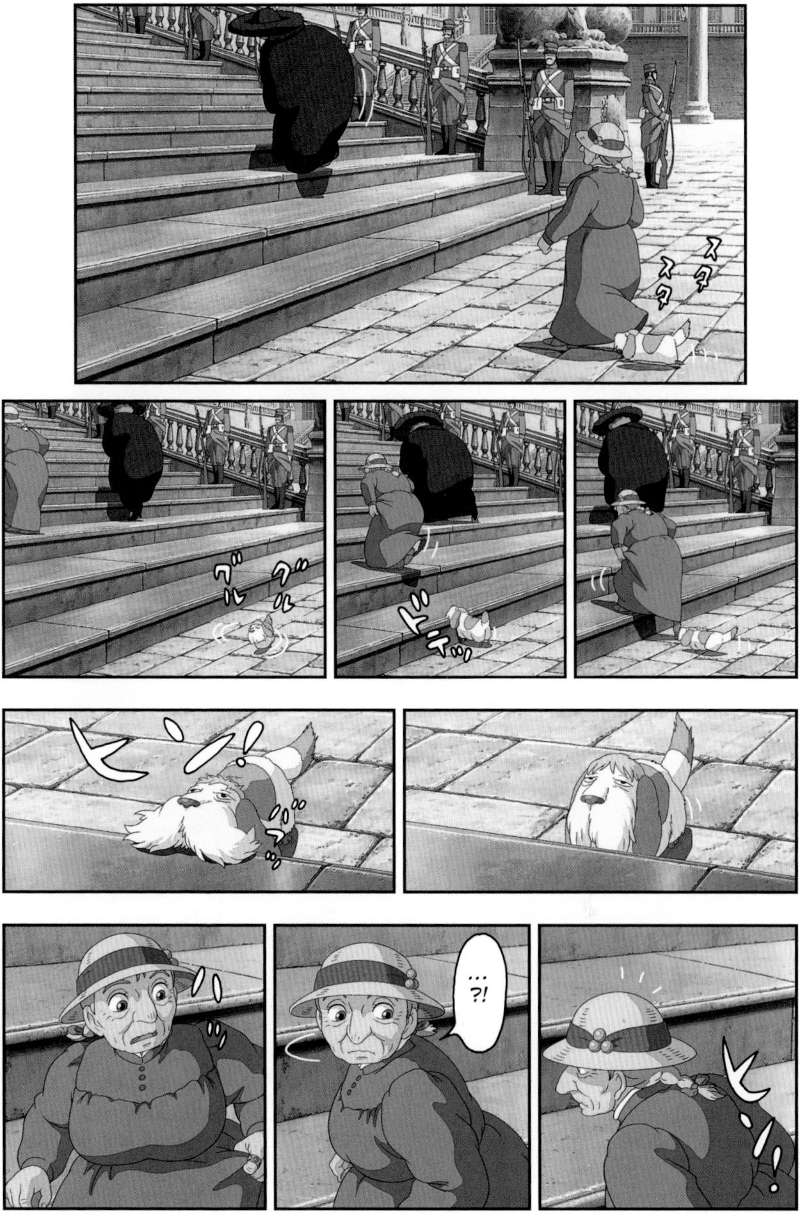
スタスタ
ドテッ
グルグル
ヒン!
ヒン!
...?!

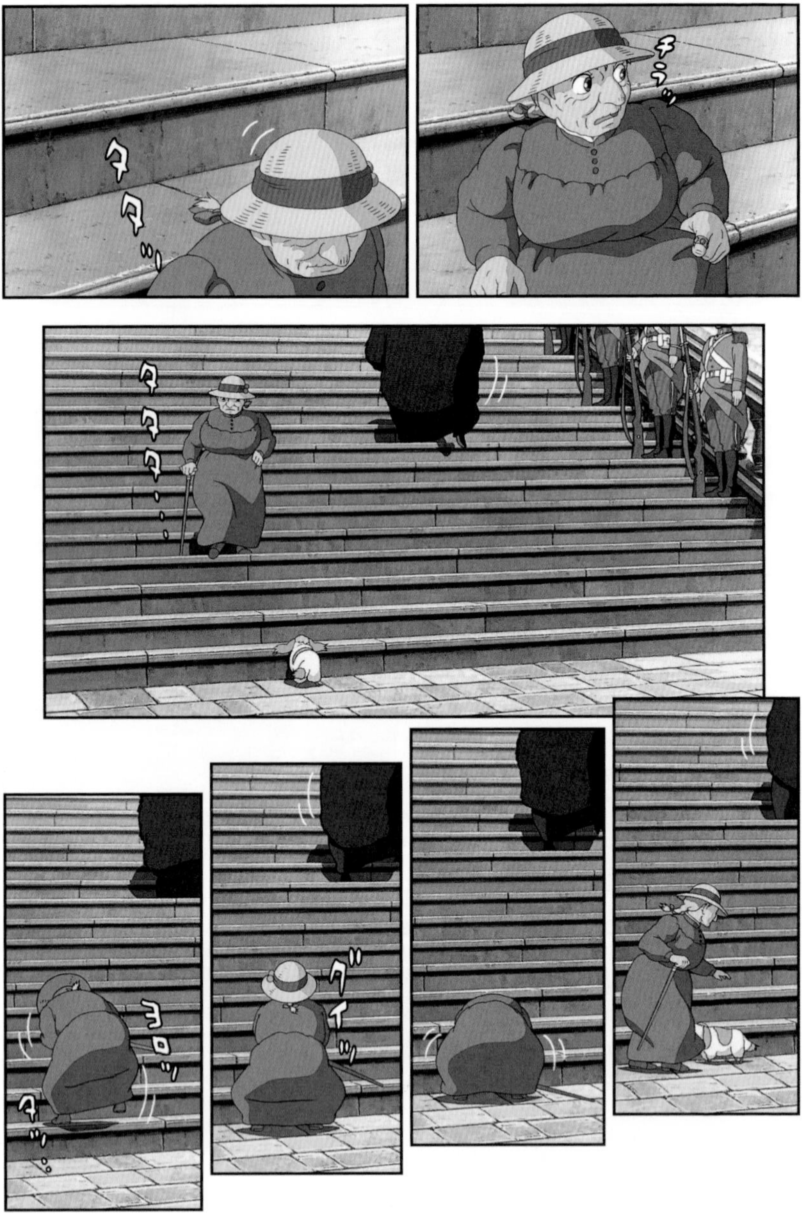
チラッ
タタッ
タタタ…
グイッ
ヨロッ
タッ…

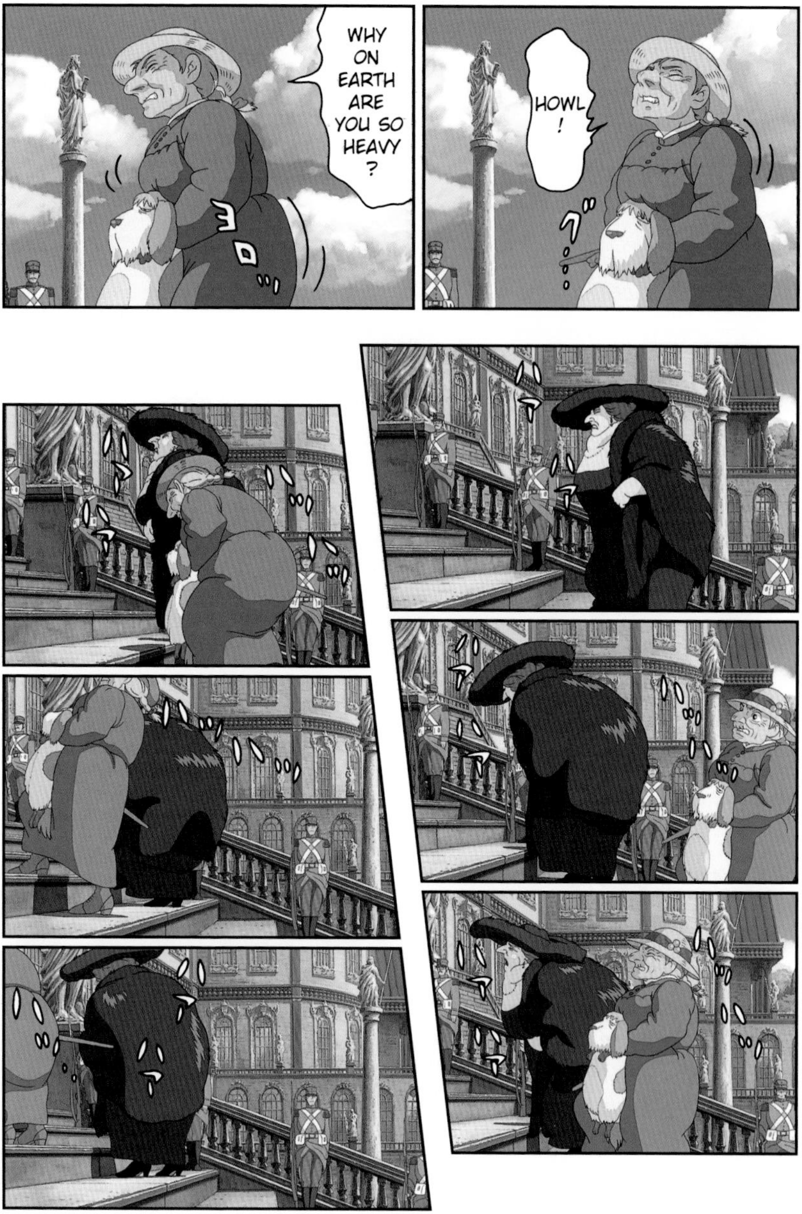
HOWL!
WHY ON EARTH ARE YOU SO HEAVY?

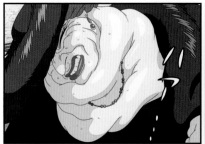
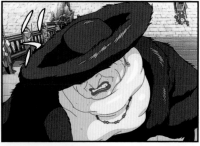

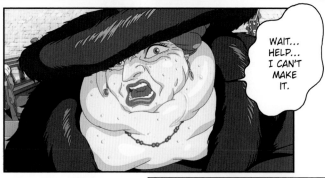

WAIT...
HELP...
I CAN'T
MAKE
IT.

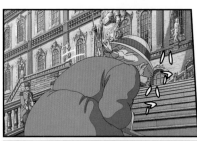

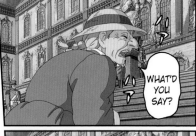

WHAT'D
YOU
SAY?

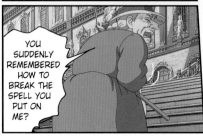

YOU
SUDDENLY
REMEMBERED
HOW TO
BREAK THE
SPELL YOU
PUT ON
ME?

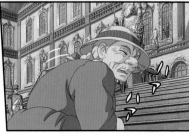

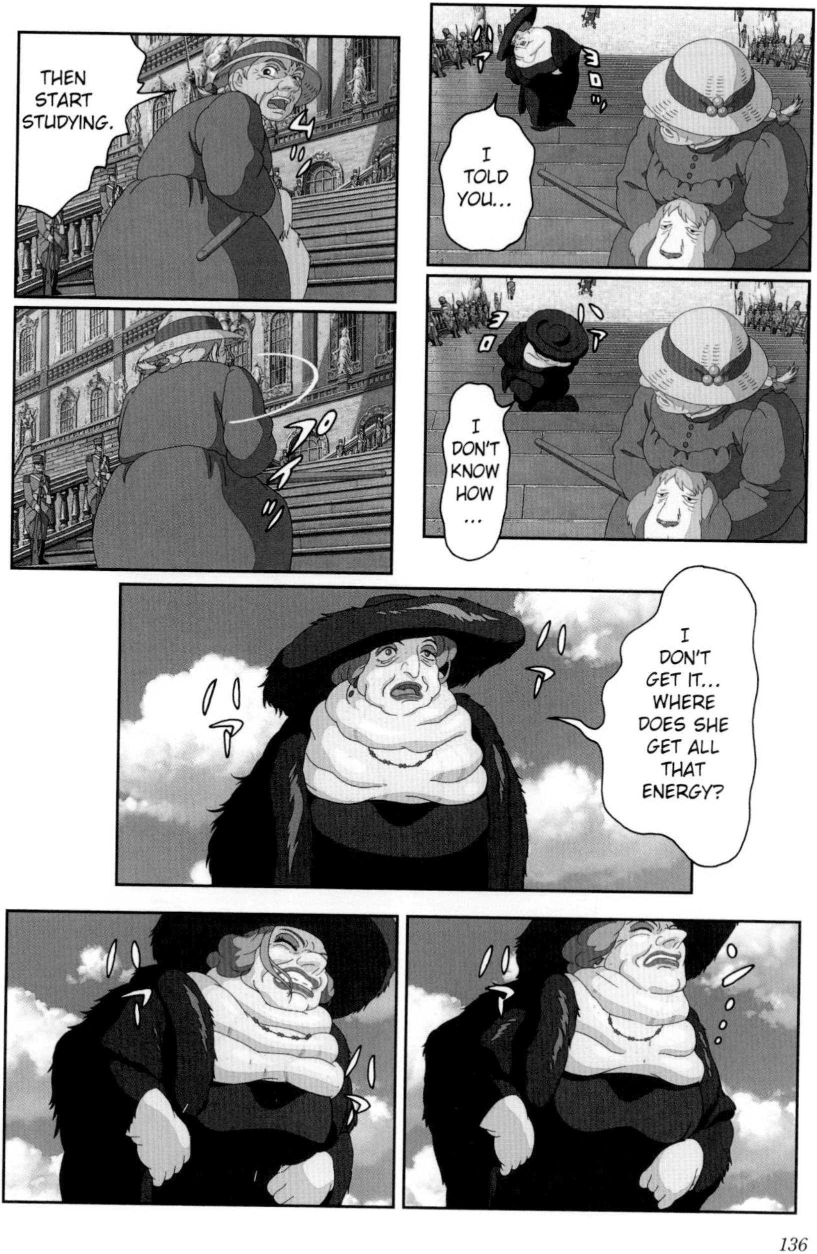
I TOLD YOU...
THEN START STUDYING.
I DON'T KNOW HOW ...
I DON'T GET IT... WHERE DOES SHE GET ALL THAT ENERGY?

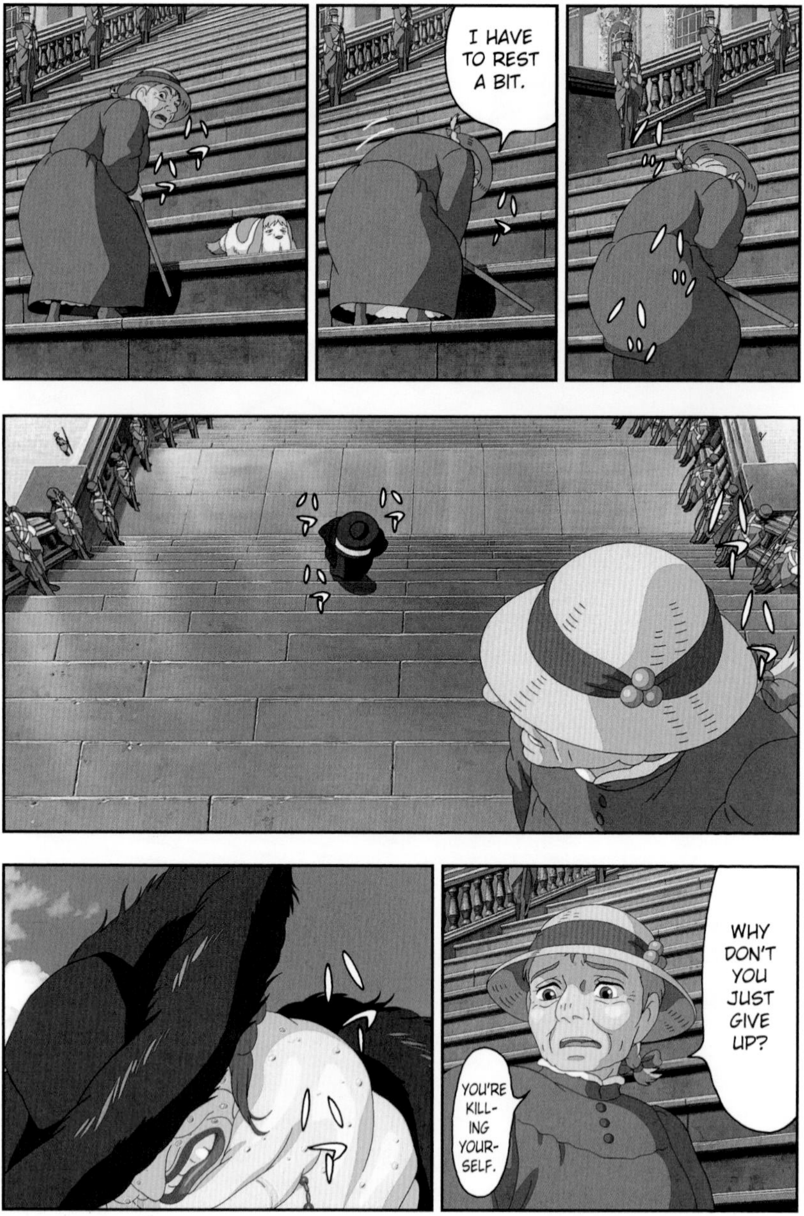
I HAVE TO REST A BIT.
WHY DON'T YOU JUST GIVE UP?
YOU'RE KILL-ING YOUR-SELF.

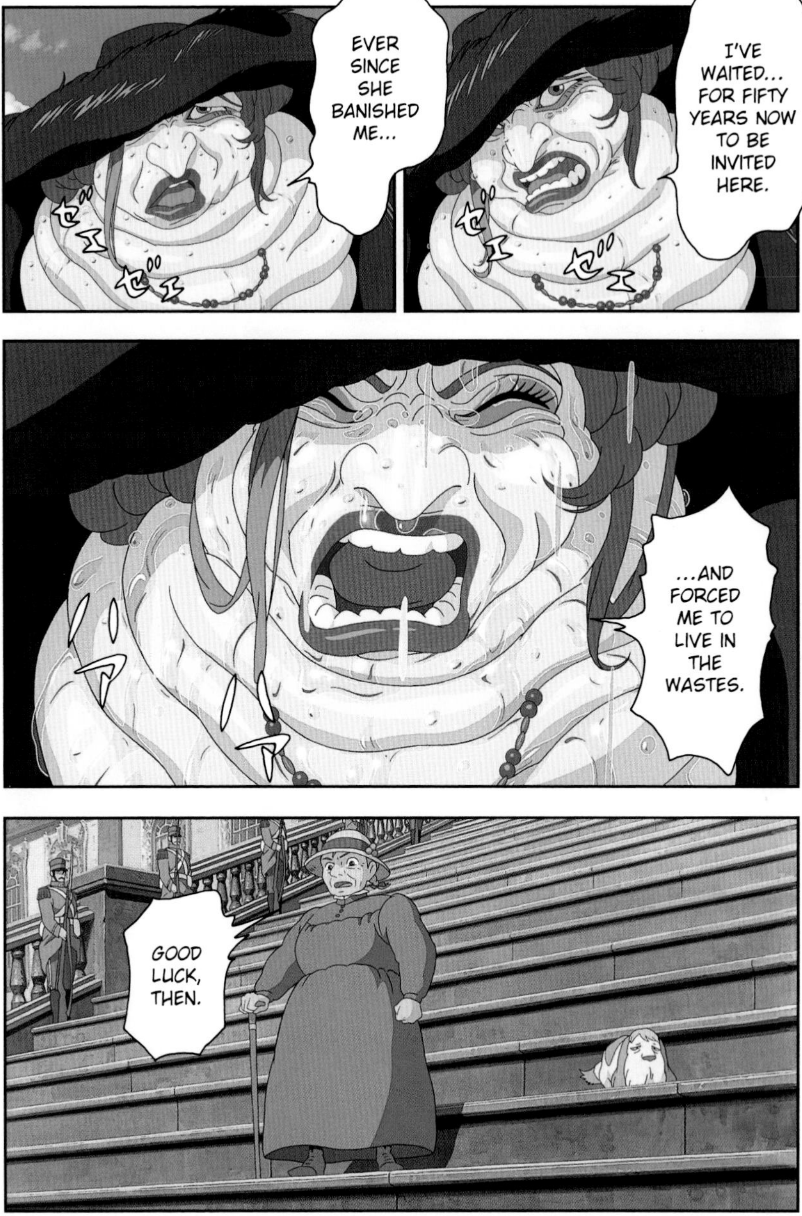
I'VE WAITED... FOR FIFTY YEARS NOW TO BE INVITED HERE.
EVER SINCE SHE BANISHED ME...
...AND FORCED ME TO LIVE IN THE WASTES.
GOOD LUCK, THEN.

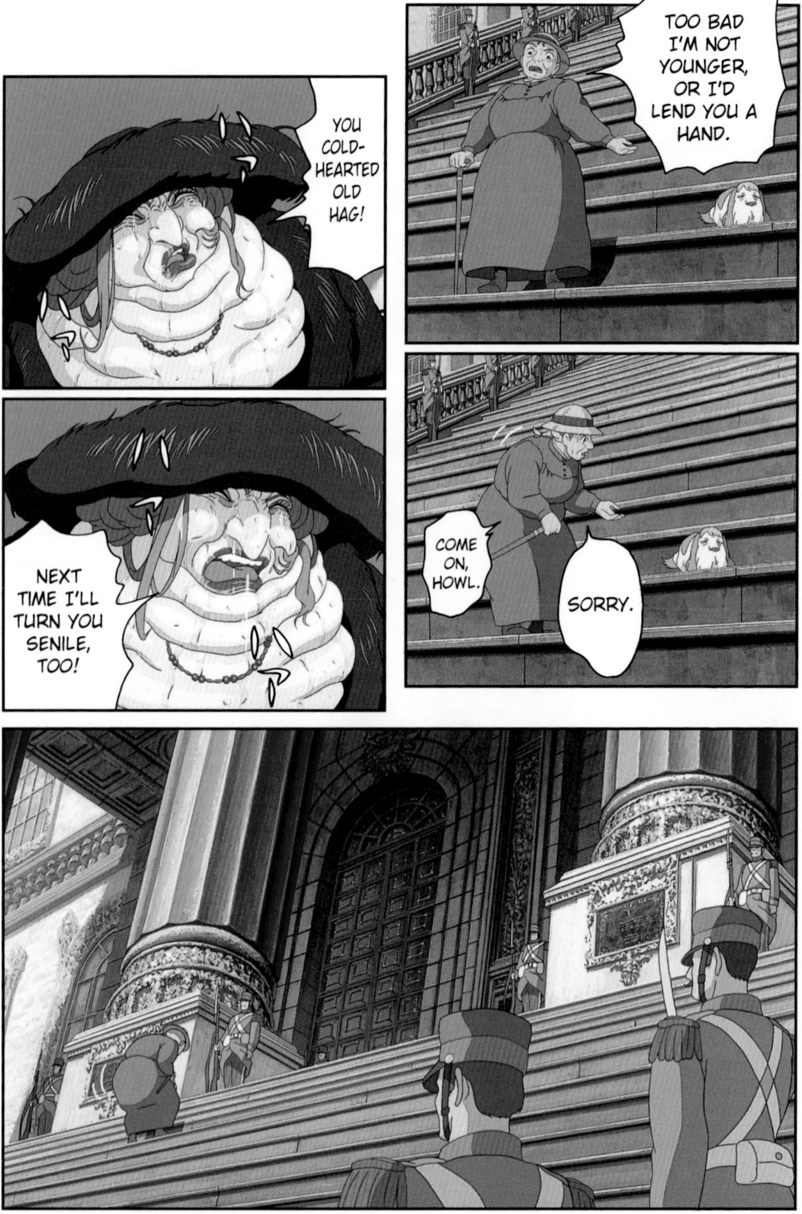
TOO BAD I'M NOT YOUNGER, OR I'D LEND YOU A HAND.
YOU COLD-HEARTED OLD HAG!
SORRY.
COME ON, HOWL.
NEXT TIME I'LL TURN YOU SENILE, TOO!

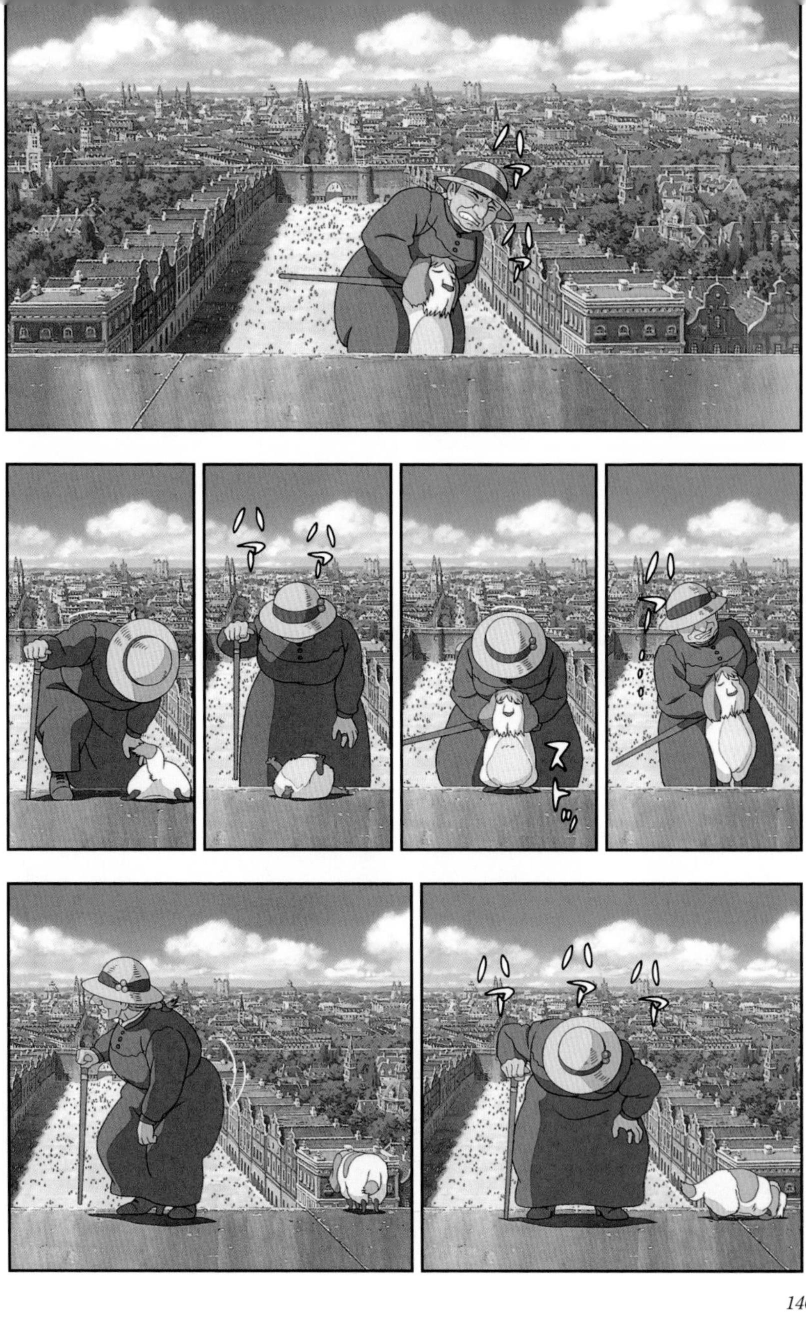
ハァ
ハァ
ハァ
ストッ
ハァ
ハァ
ハァ
ハァ
ハァ

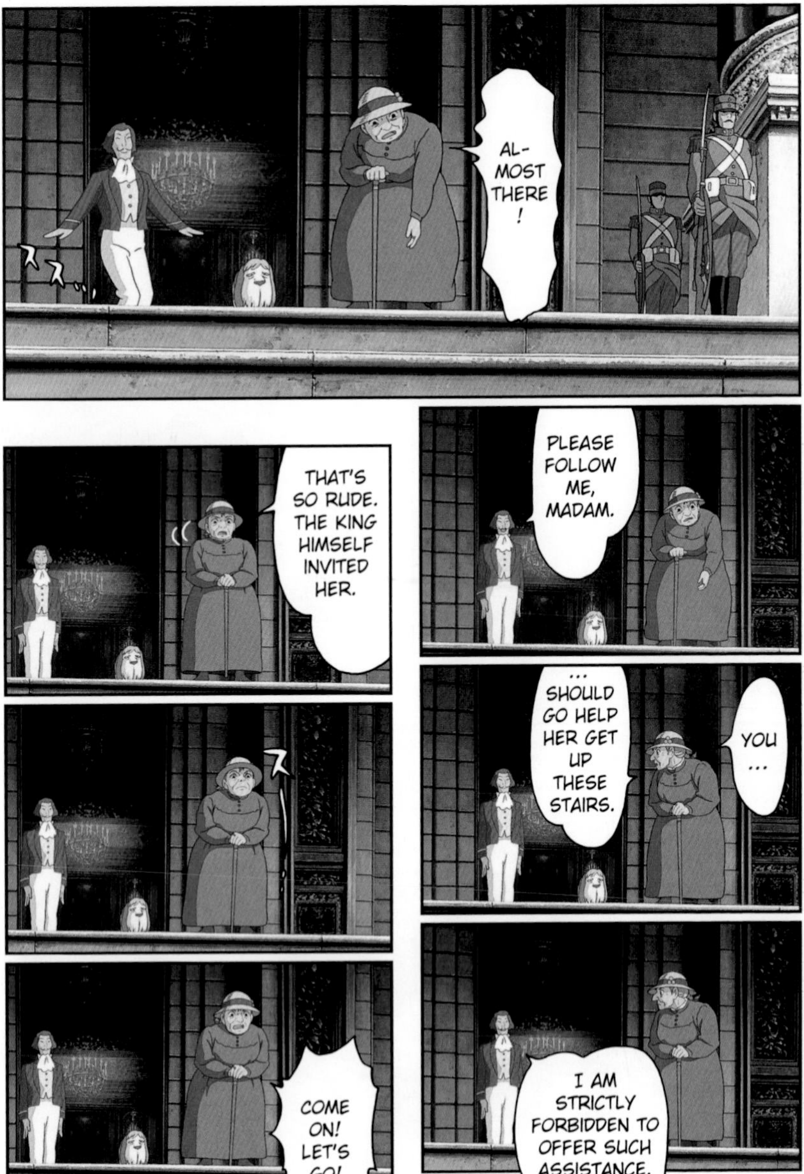
スス‥
AL-MOST THERE!
PLEASE FOLLOW ME, MADAM.
YOU ...
... SHOULD GO HELP HER GET UP THESE STAIRS.
I AM STRICTLY FORBIDDEN TO OFFER SUCH ASSISTANCE.
THAT'S SO RUDE. THE KING HIMSELF INVITED HER.
ス
COME ON! LET'S GO!

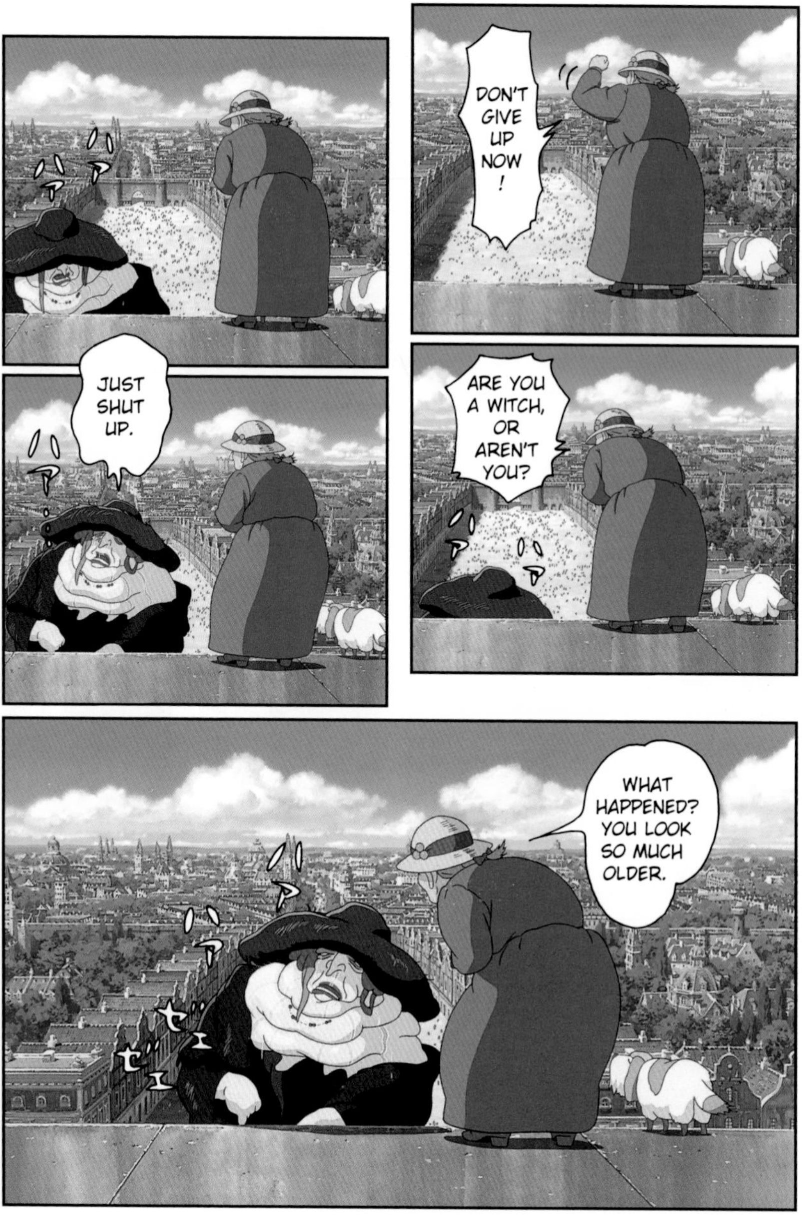
DON'T GIVE UP NOW!
ARE YOU A WITCH, OR AREN'T YOU?
JUST SHUT UP.
WHAT HAPPENED? YOU LOOK SO MUCH OLDER.

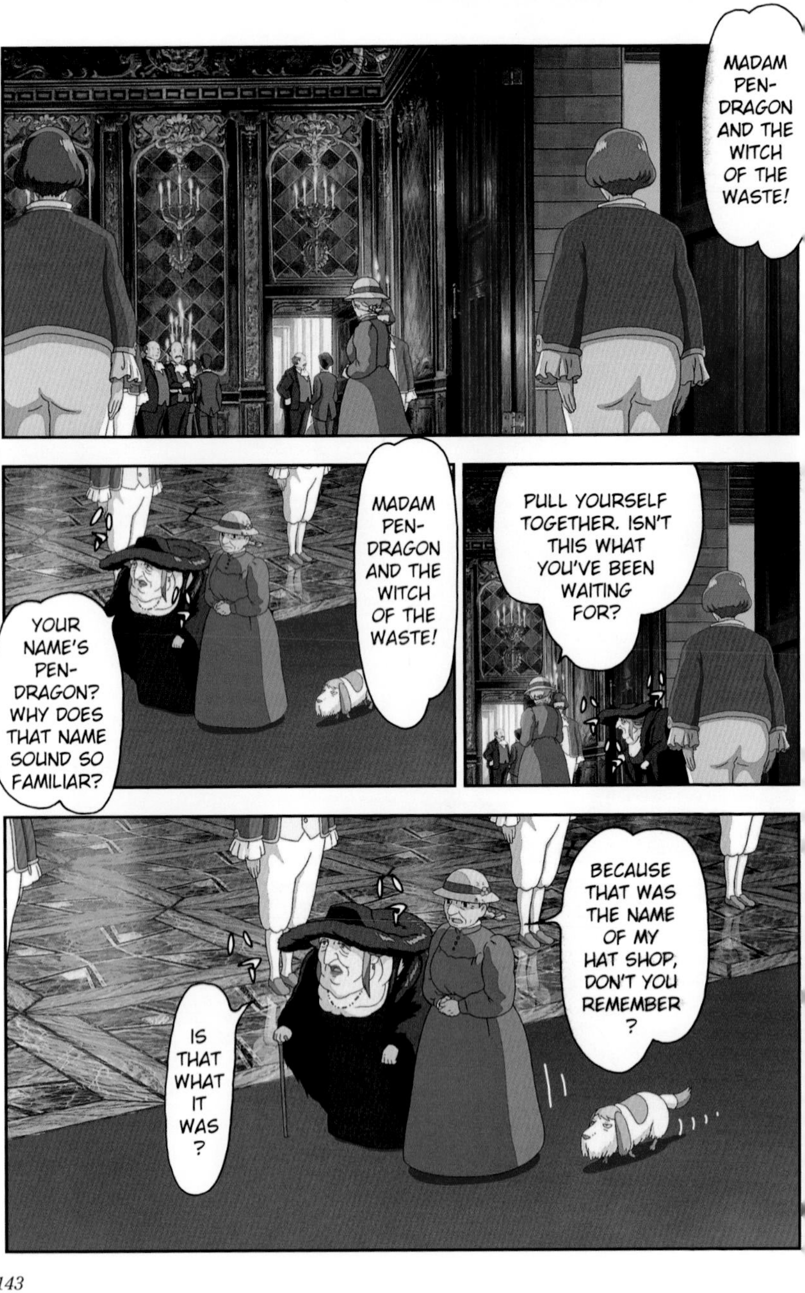
MADAM PEN-DRAGON AND THE WITCH OF THE WASTE!
PULL YOURSELF TOGETHER. ISN'T THIS WHAT YOU'VE BEEN WAITING FOR?
MADAM PEN-DRAGON AND THE WITCH OF THE WASTE!
YOUR NAME'S PEN-DRAGON? WHY DOES THAT NAME SOUND SO FAMILIAR?
BECAUSE THAT WAS THE NAME OF MY HAT SHOP, DON'T YOU REMEMBER?
IS THAT WHAT IT WAS?

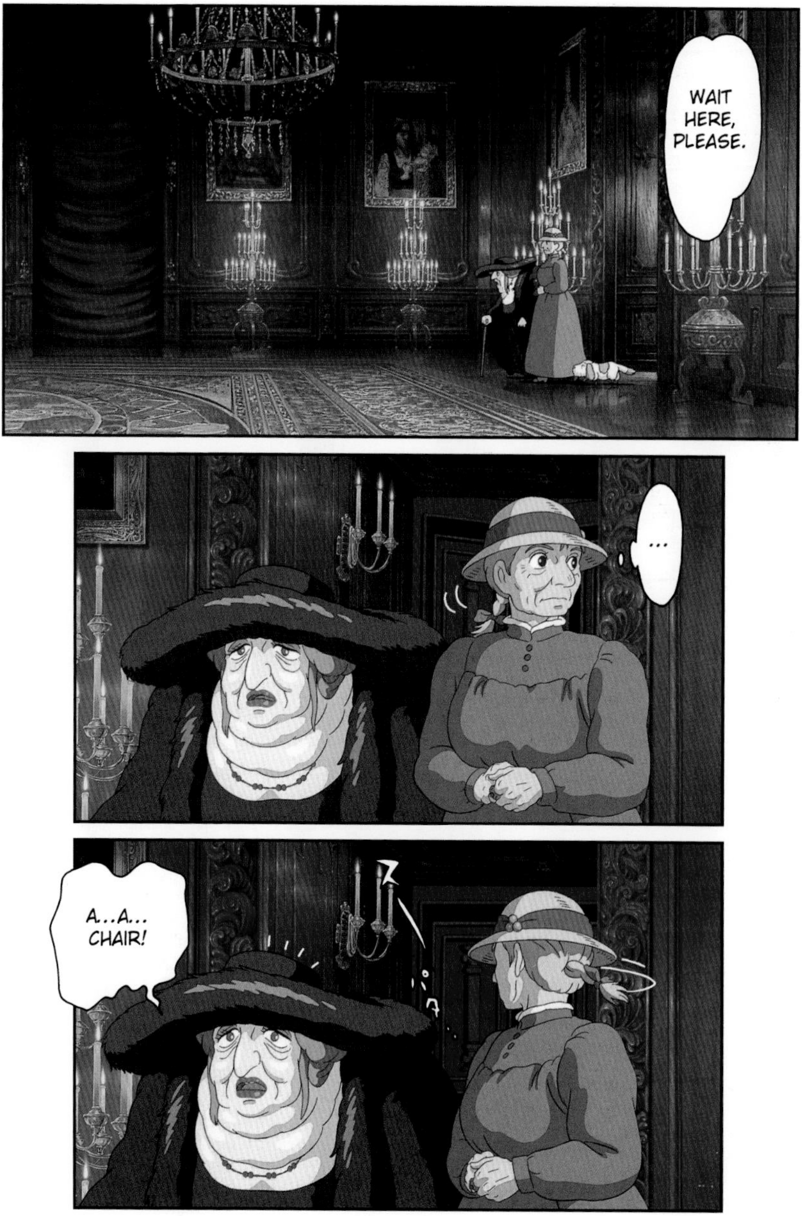
WAIT HERE, PLEASE.
...
A...A... CHAIR!

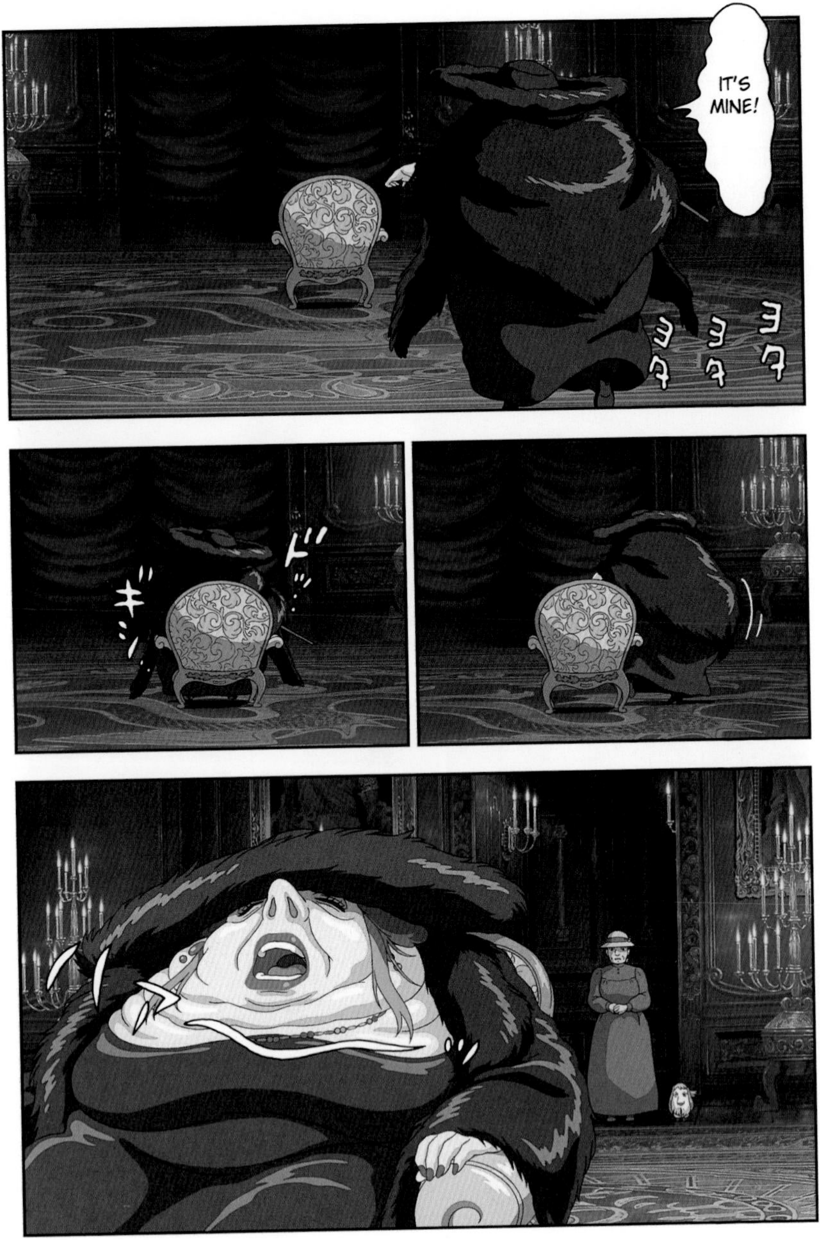
IT'S MINE!
ヨタ
ヨタ
ヨタ
ド
ギ

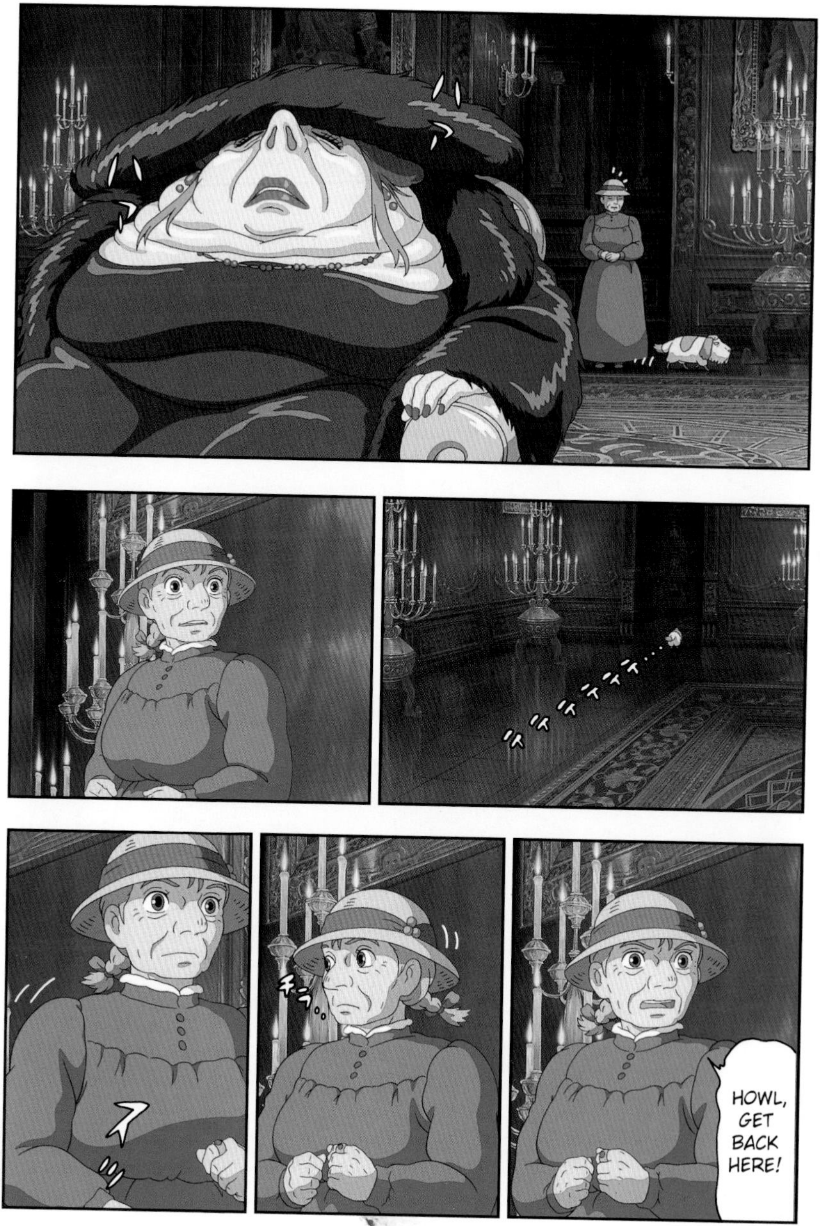
HOWL, GET BACK HERE!

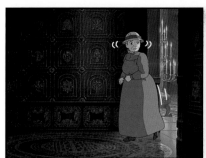

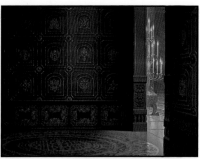

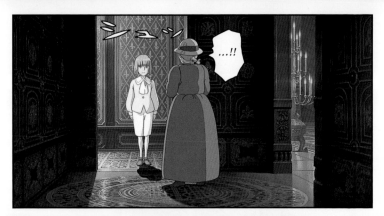

...!!

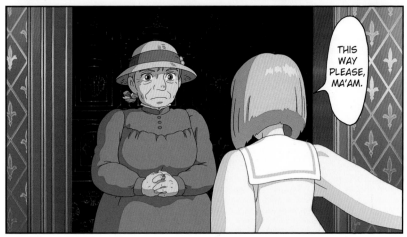

THIS WAY PLEASE, MA'AM.

147

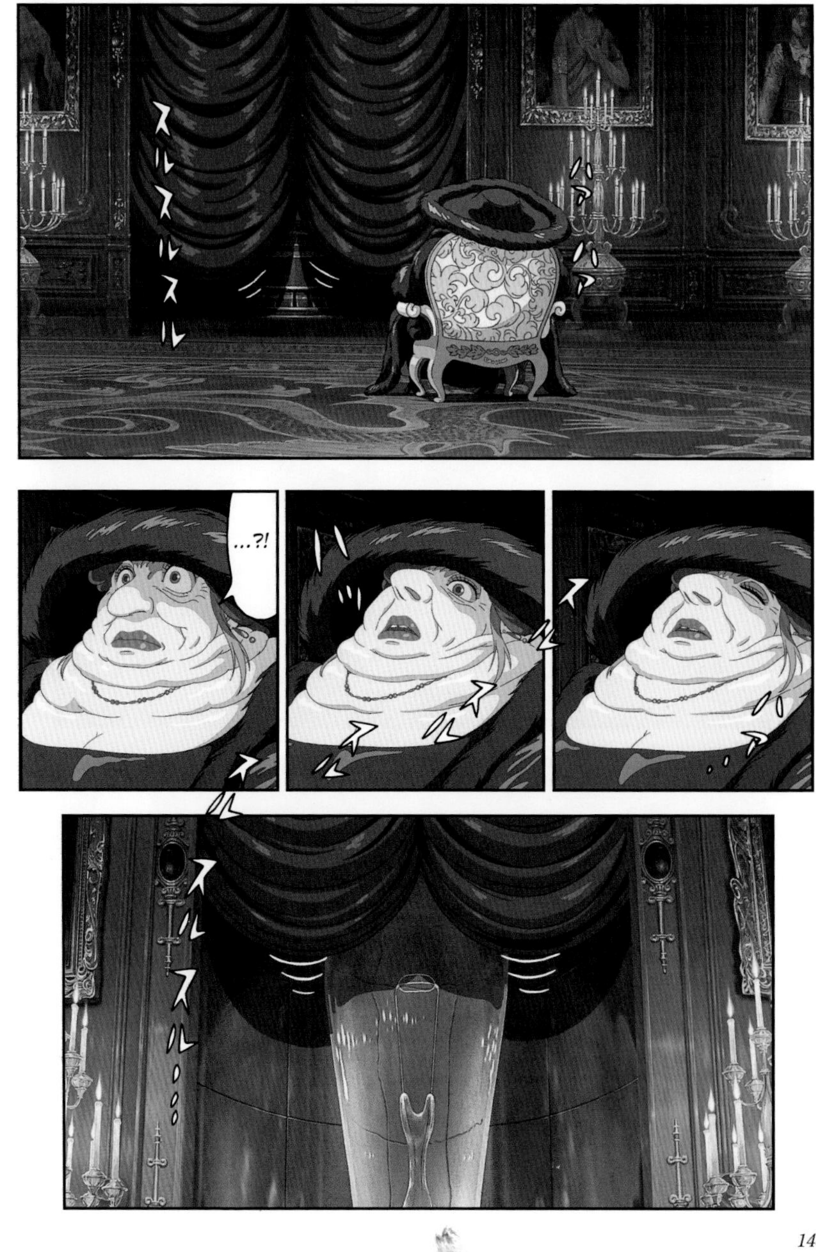
ハァハァ
スルスルスル
スル
ハァ…
スル
スル
…?!
スル
スルスル…

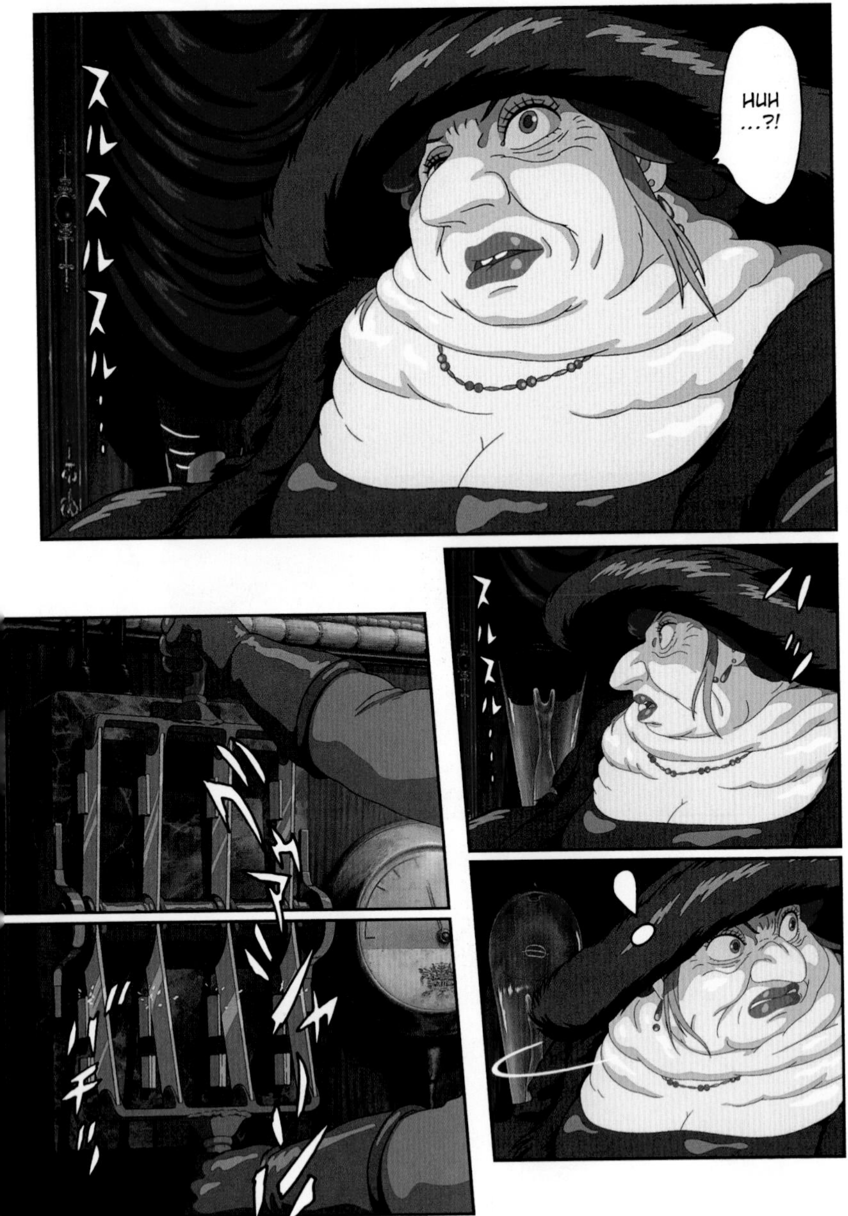
スルスルスル・・・
HUH ...?!
スルスル…

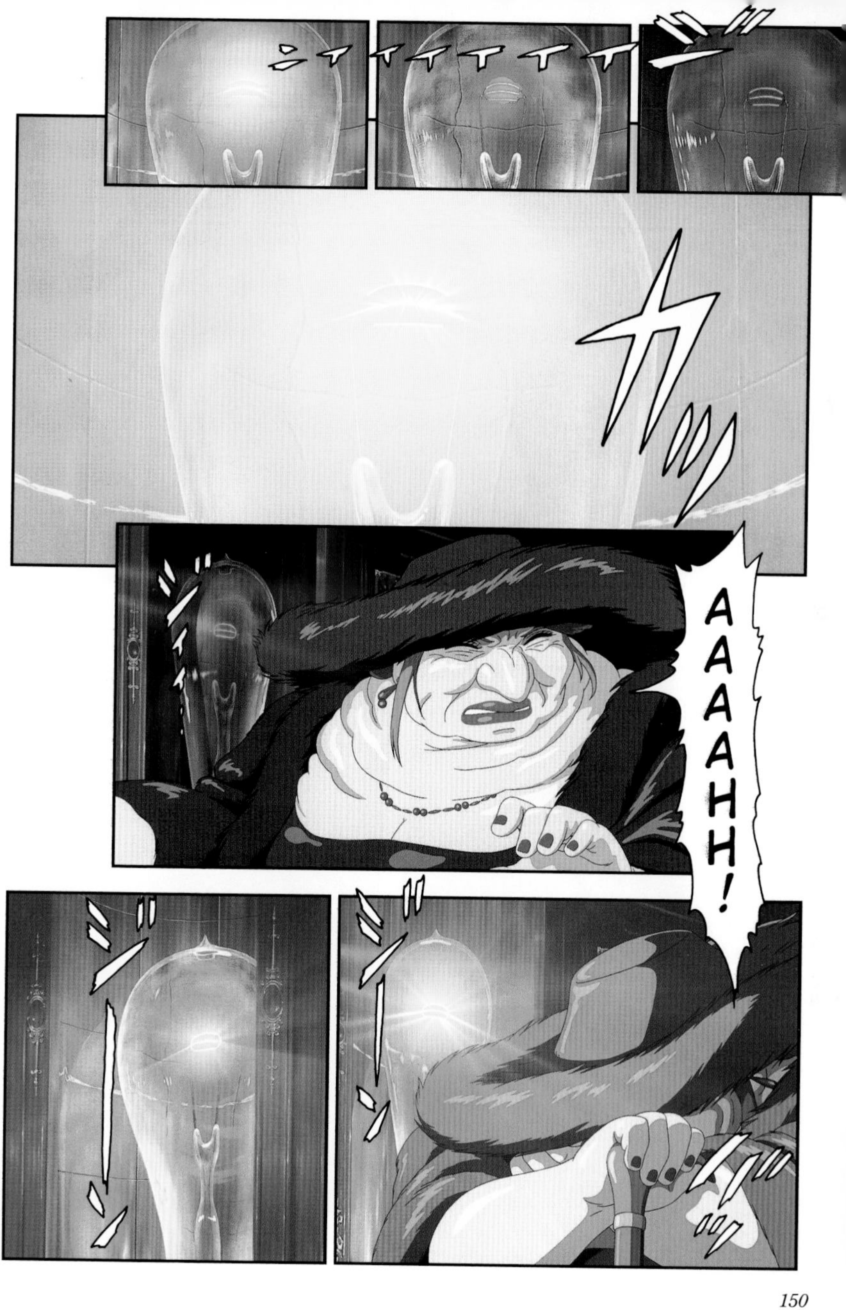
カッ
AAAAAHH!

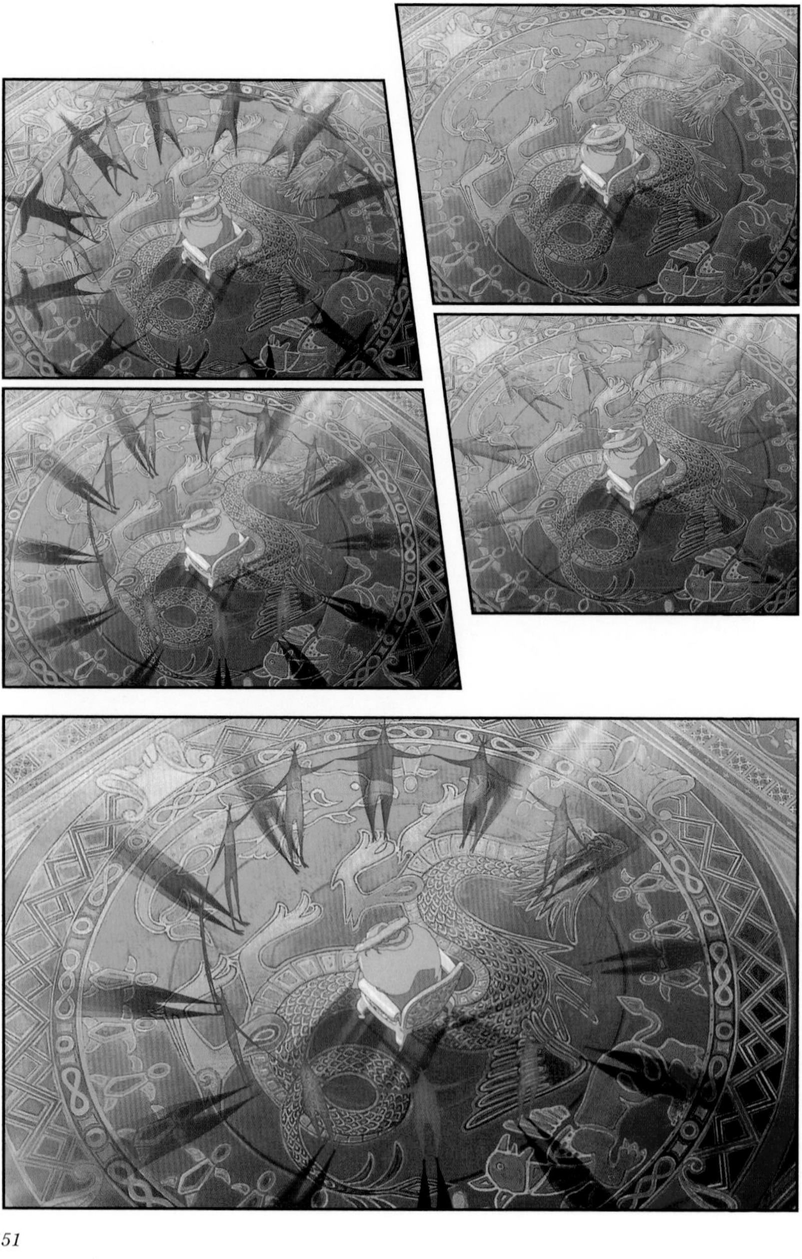

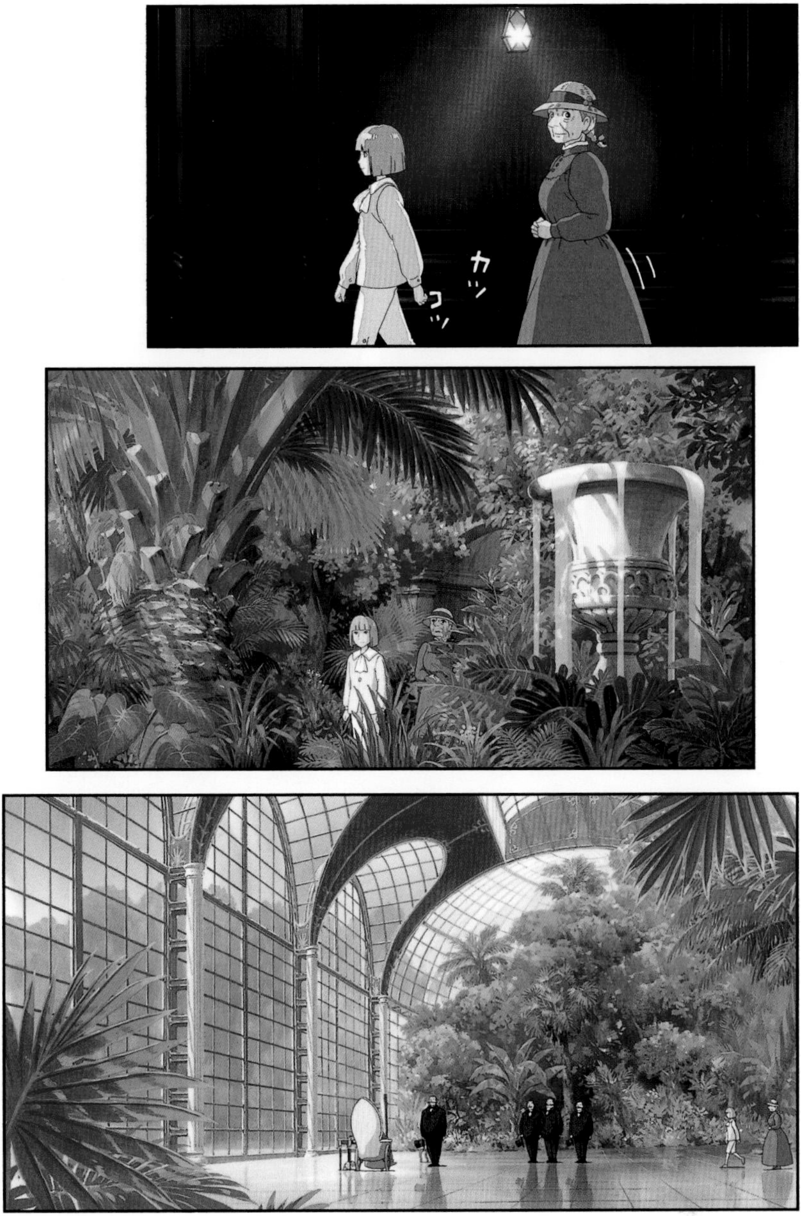
カッ
コッ

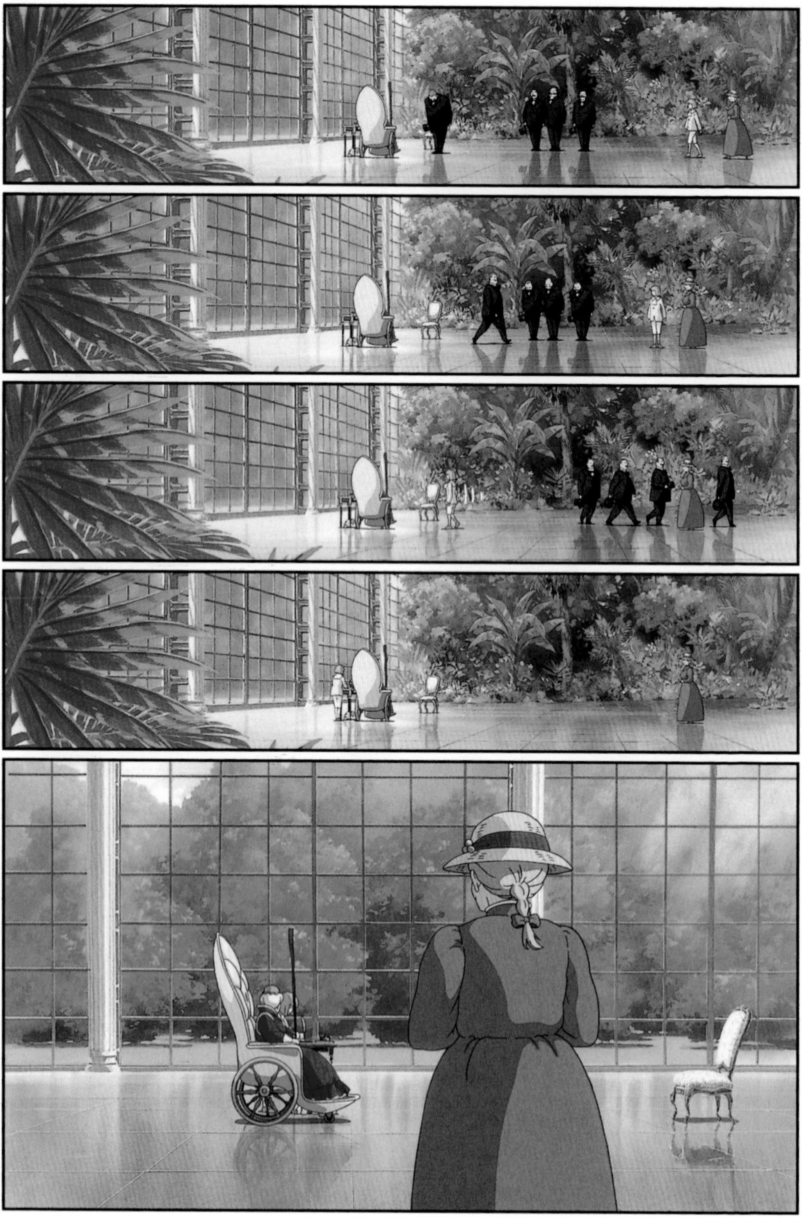

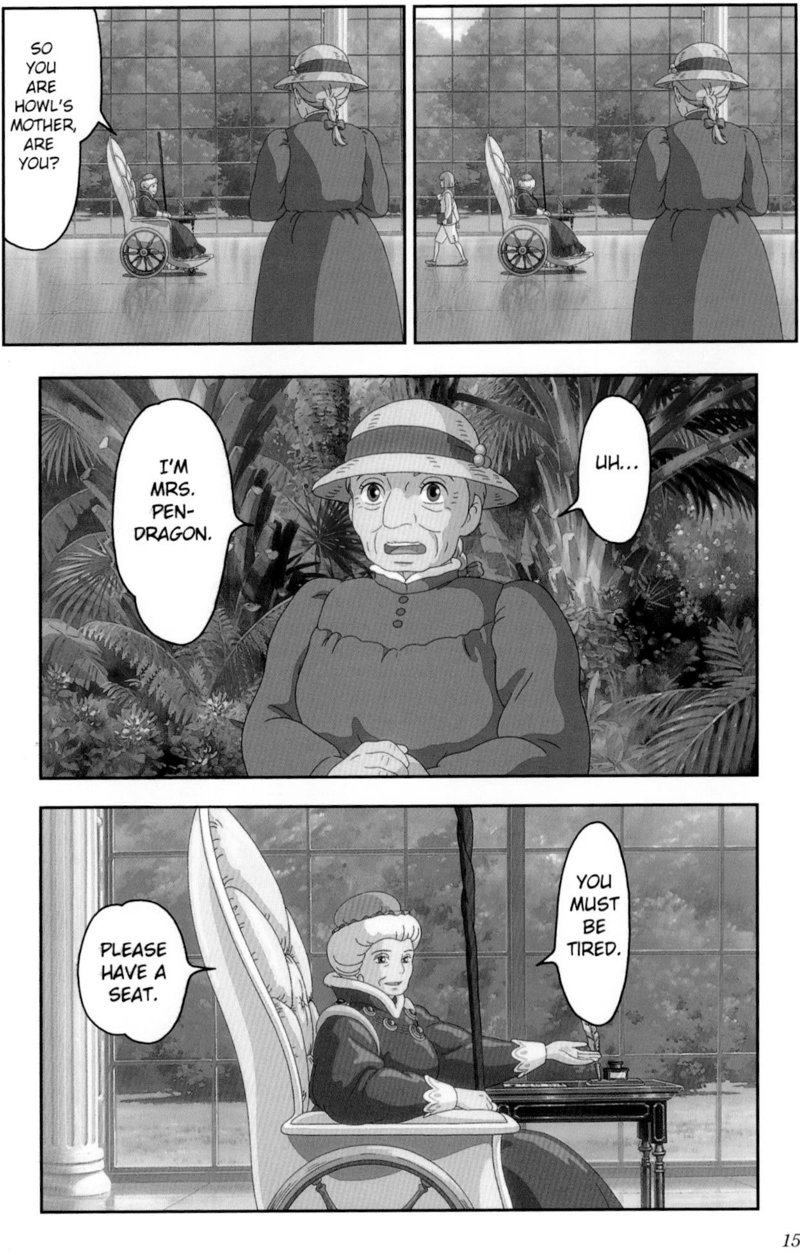
SO YOU ARE HOWL'S MOTHER, ARE YOU?
UH...
I'M MRS. PEN-DRAGON.
YOU MUST BE TIRED.
PLEASE HAVE A SEAT.

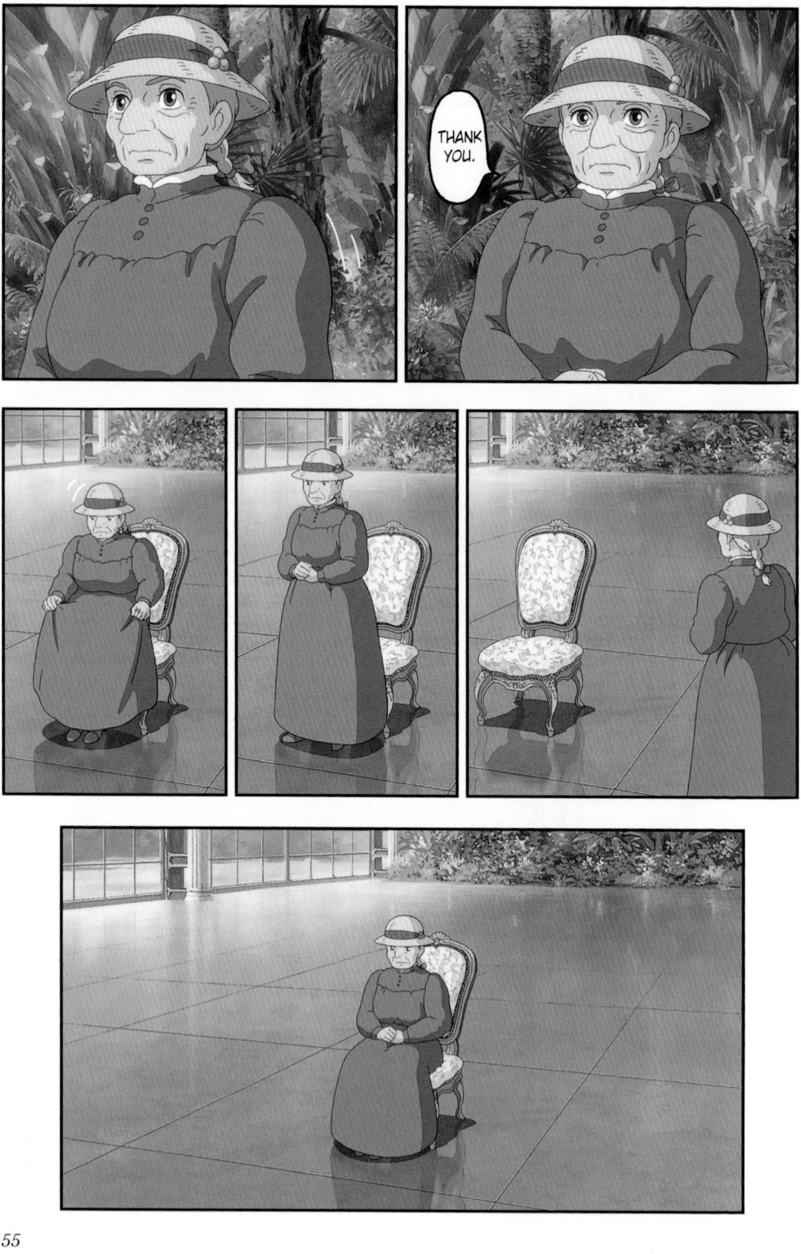
THANK YOU.

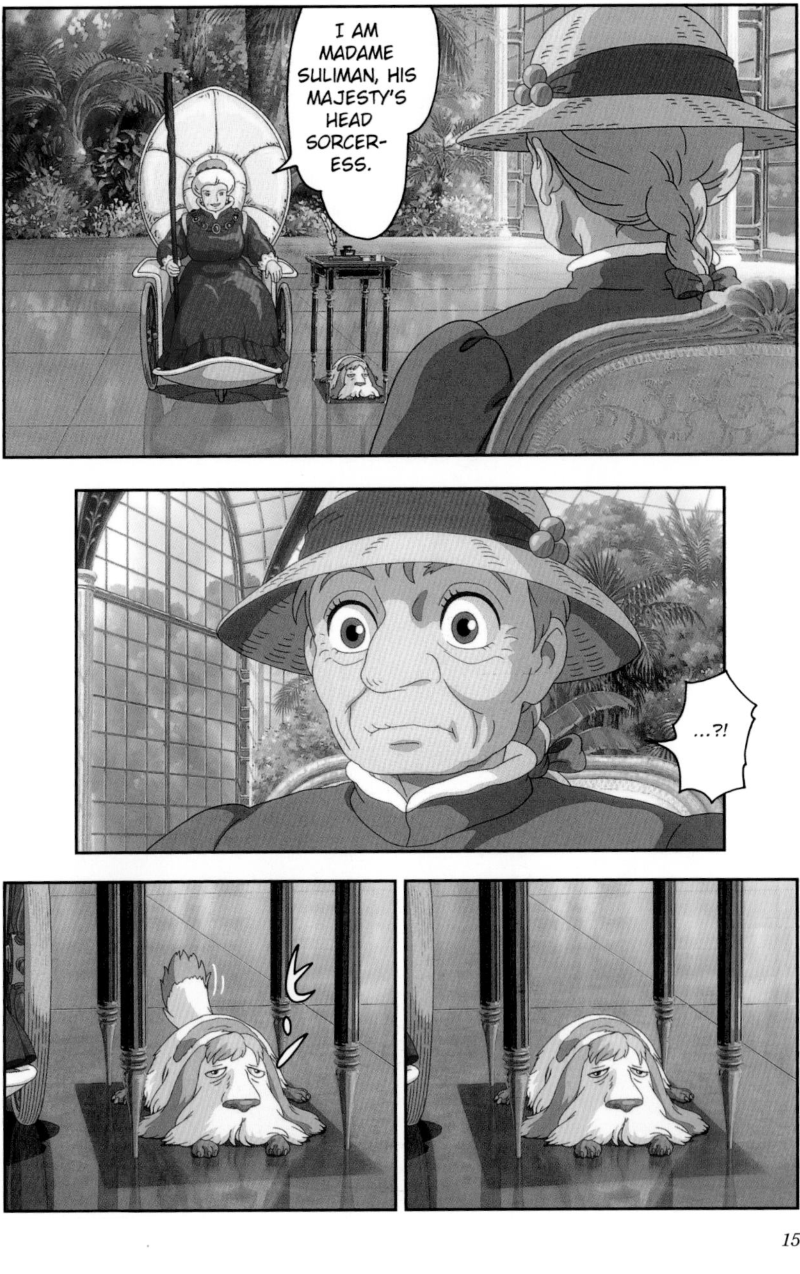
I AM MADAME SULIMAN, HIS MAJESTY'S HEAD SORCER-ESS.
...?!

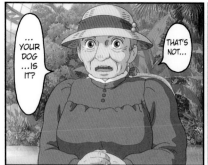

...YOUR DOG ...IS IT?

THAT'S NOT...

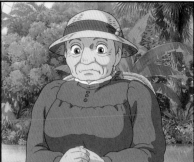

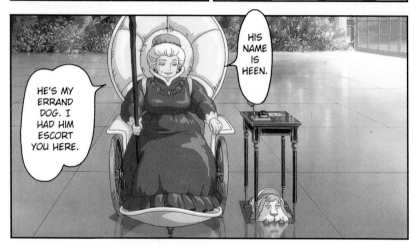

HIS NAME IS HEEN.

HE'S MY ERRAND DOG. I HAD HIM ESCORT YOU HERE.

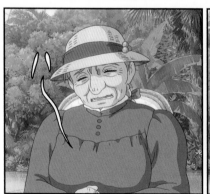

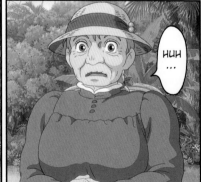

HUH ...

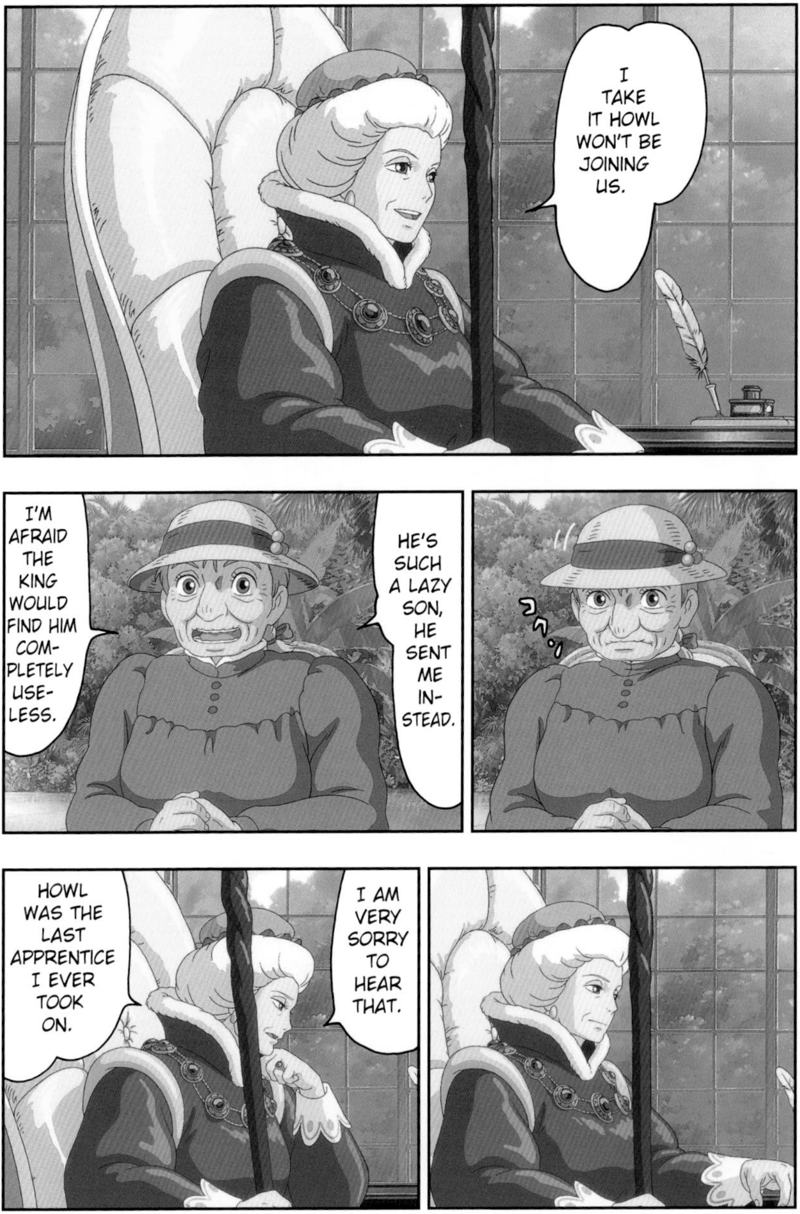
I TAKE IT HOWL WON'T BE JOINING US.
HE'S SUCH A LAZY SON, HE SENT ME IN-STEAD.
I'M AFRAID THE KING WOULD FIND HIM COM-PLETELY USE-LESS.
I AM VERY SORRY TO HEAR THAT.
HOWL WAS THE LAST APPRENTICE I EVER TOOK ON.

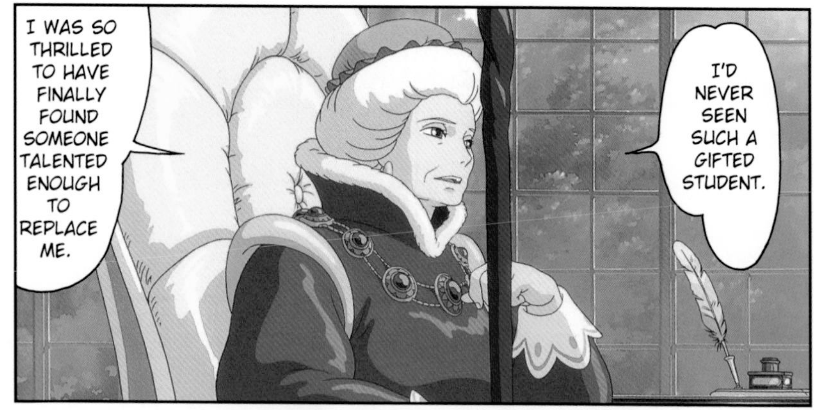
I'D NEVER SEEN SUCH A GIFTED STUDENT.
I WAS SO THRILLED TO HAVE FINALLY FOUND SOMEONE TALENTED ENOUGH TO REPLACE ME.

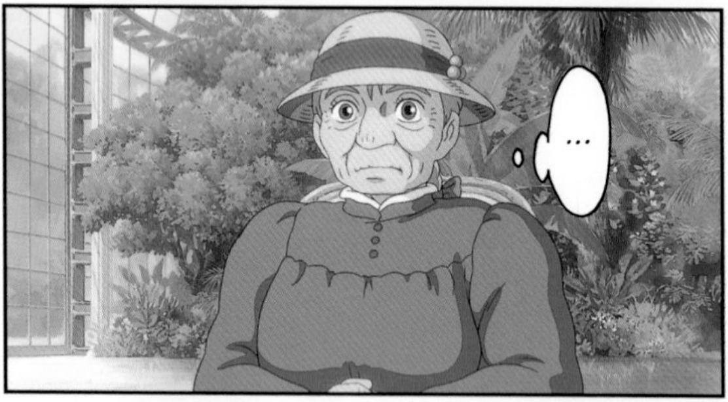
...

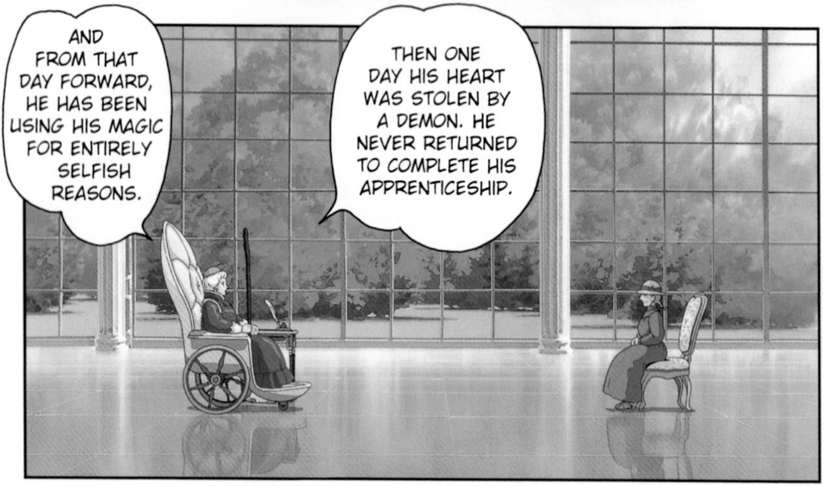
THEN ONE DAY HIS HEART WAS STOLEN BY A DEMON. HE NEVER RETURNED TO COMPLETE HIS APPRENTICESHIP.
AND FROM THAT DAY FORWARD, HE HAS BEEN USING HIS MAGIC FOR ENTIRELY SELFISH REASONS.

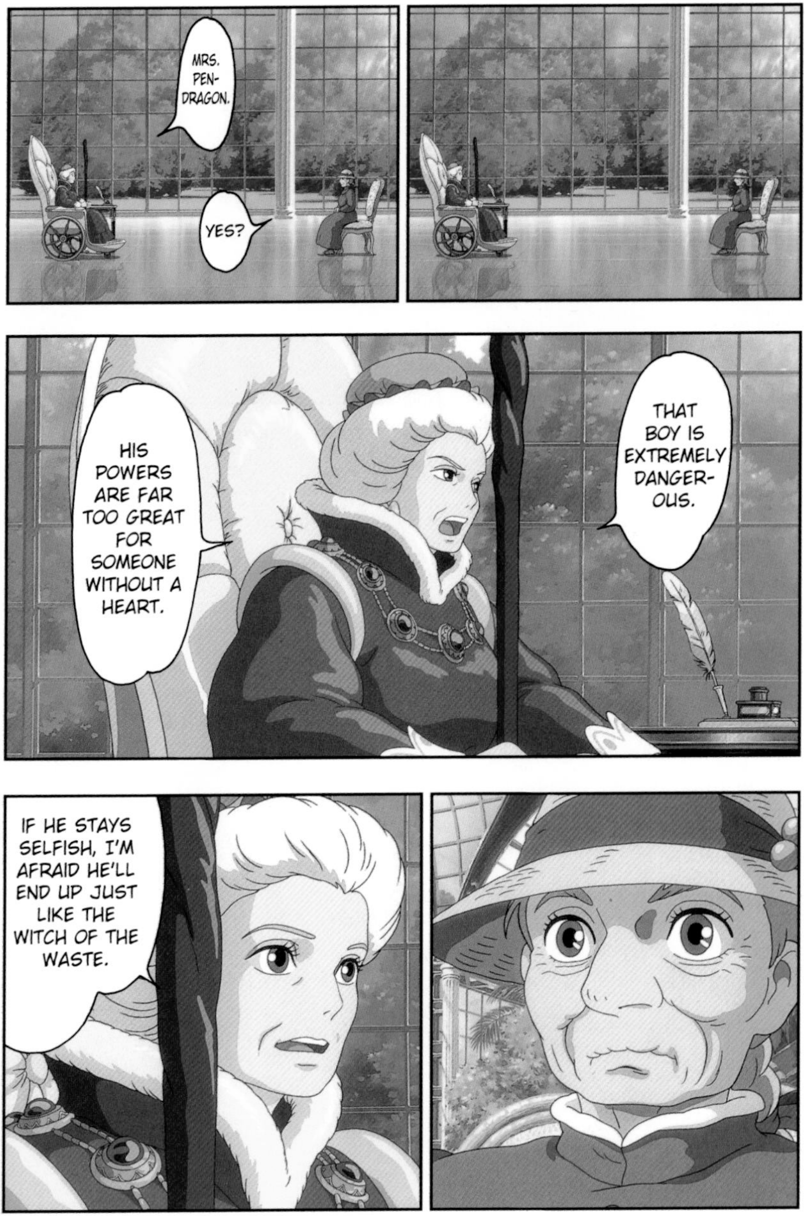
MRS. PEN-DRAGON.
YES?
THAT BOY IS EXTREMELY DANGER-OUS.
HIS POWERS ARE FAR TOO GREAT FOR SOMEONE WITHOUT A HEART.
IF HE STAYS SELFISH, I'M AFRAID HE'LL END UP JUST LIKE THE WITCH OF THE WASTE.

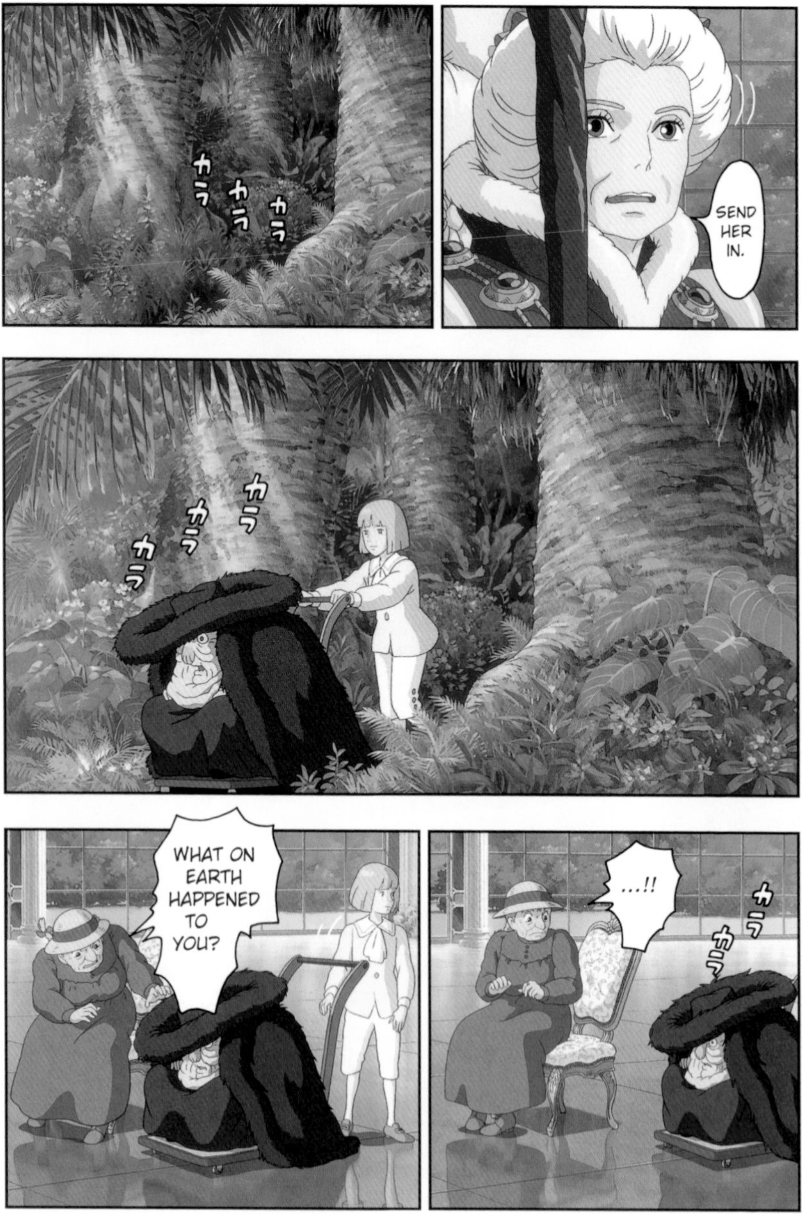
SEND HER IN.
カラ
カラ
カラ
カラ
カラ
カラ
...!!
カラ
カラ
WHAT ON EARTH HAPPENED TO YOU?

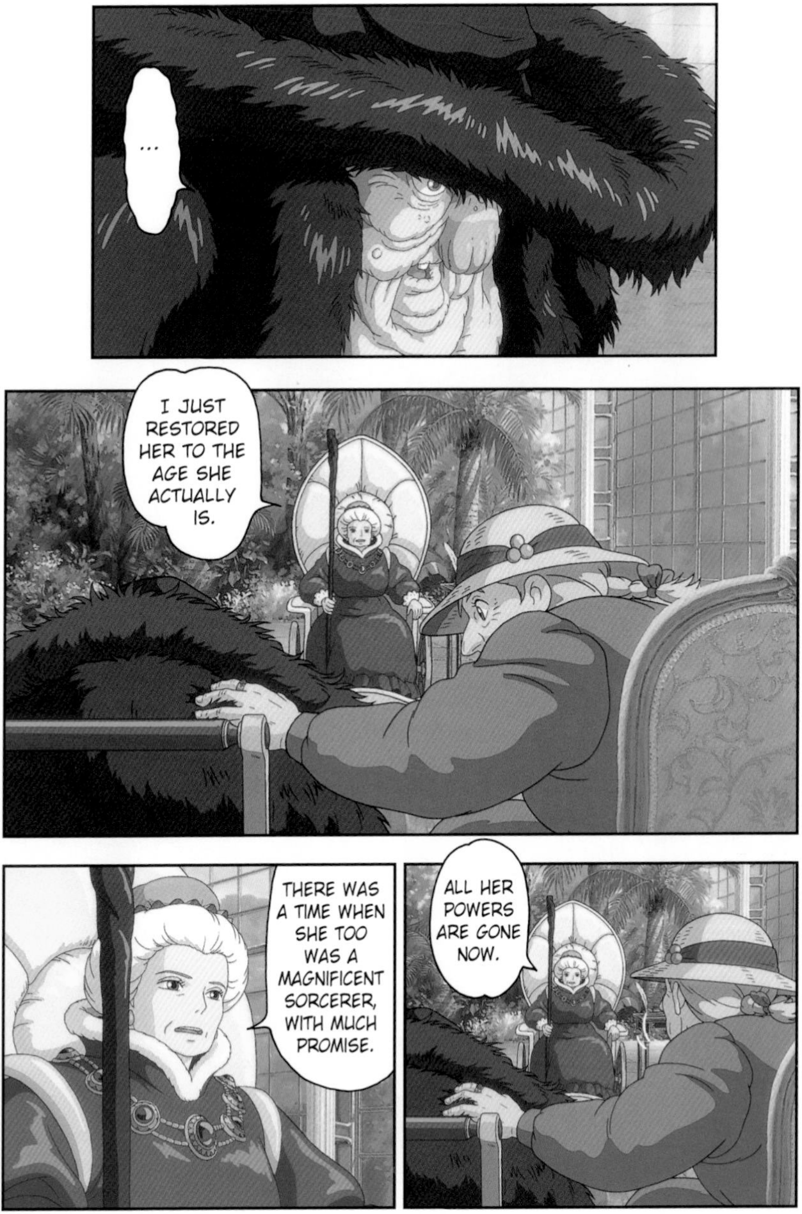
...
I JUST RESTORED HER TO THE AGE SHE ACTUALLY IS.
ALL HER POWERS ARE GONE NOW.
THERE WAS A TIME WHEN SHE TOO WAS A MAGNIFICENT SORCERER, WITH MUCH PROMISE.

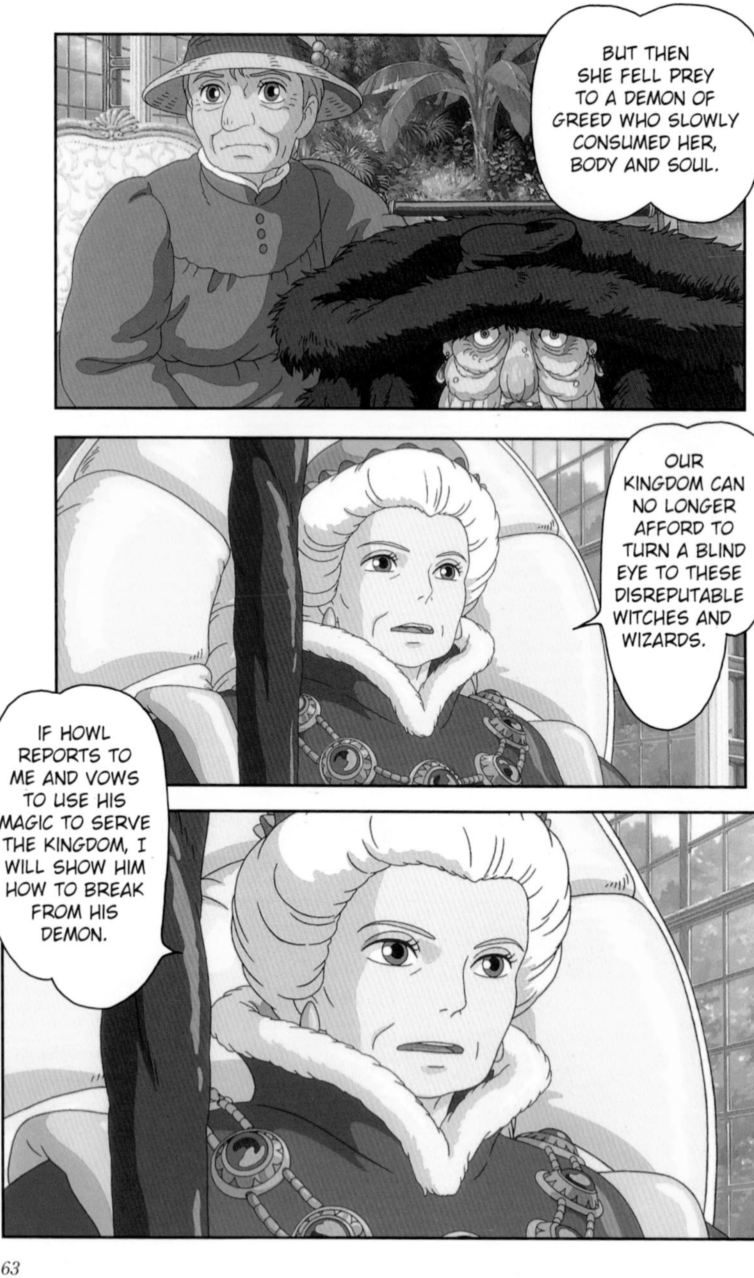
BUT THEN SHE FELL PREY TO A DEMON OF GREED WHO SLOWLY CONSUMED HER, BODY AND SOUL.
OUR KINGDOM CAN NO LONGER AFFORD TO TURN A BLIND EYE TO THESE DISREPUTABLE WITCHES AND WIZARDS.
IF HOWL REPORTS TO ME AND VOWS TO USE HIS MAGIC TO SERVE THE KINGDOM, I WILL SHOW HIM HOW TO BREAK FROM HIS DEMON.

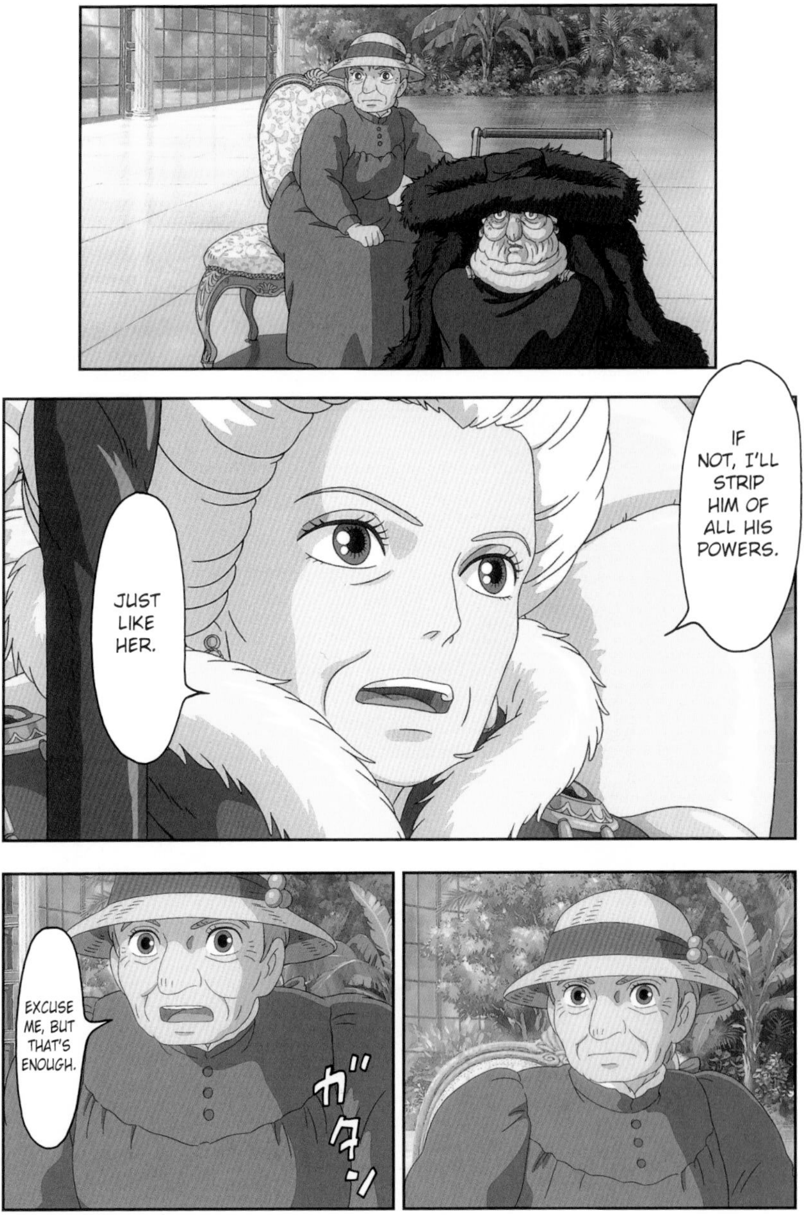
IF NOT, I'LL STRIP HIM OF ALL HIS POWERS.
JUST LIKE HER.
EXCUSE ME, BUT THAT'S ENOUGH.
ガタン

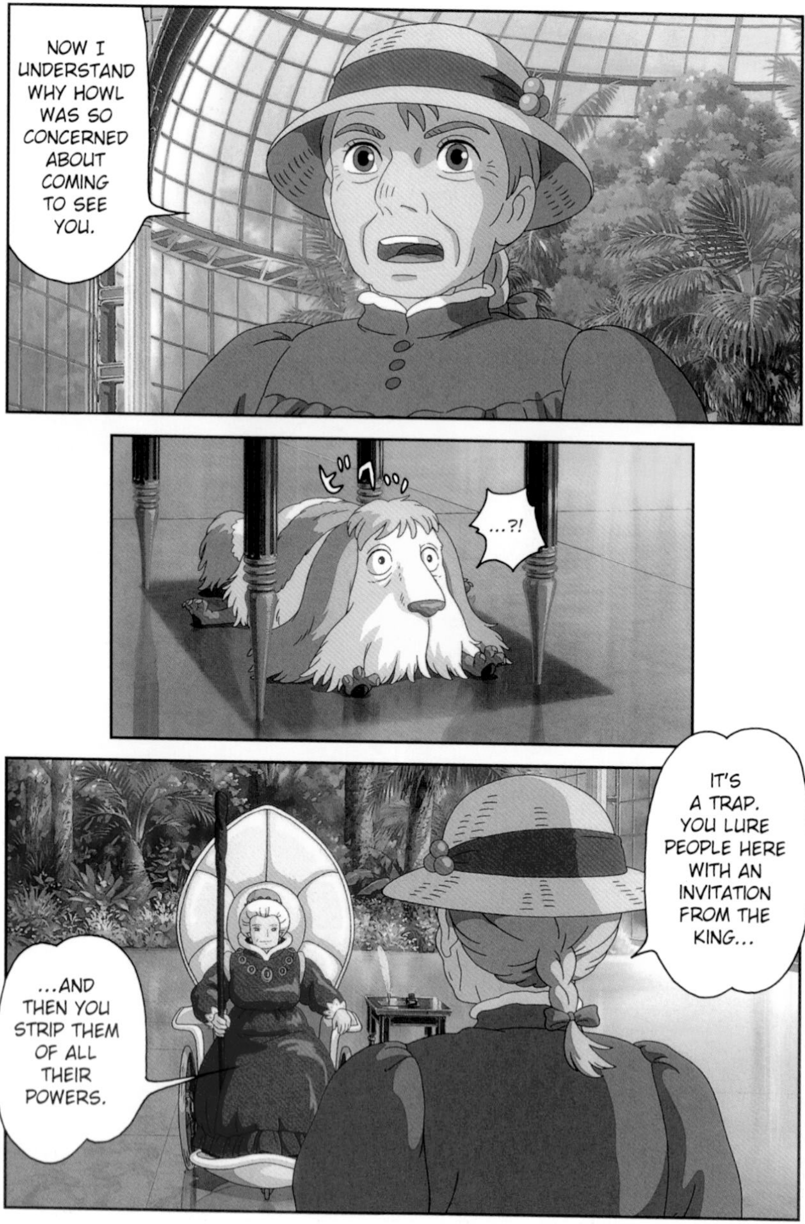
NOW I UNDERSTAND WHY HOWL WAS SO CONCERNED ABOUT COMING TO SEE YOU.
...?!
IT'S A TRAP. YOU LURE PEOPLE HERE WITH AN INVITATION FROM THE KING...
...AND THEN YOU STRIP THEM OF ALL THEIR POWERS.

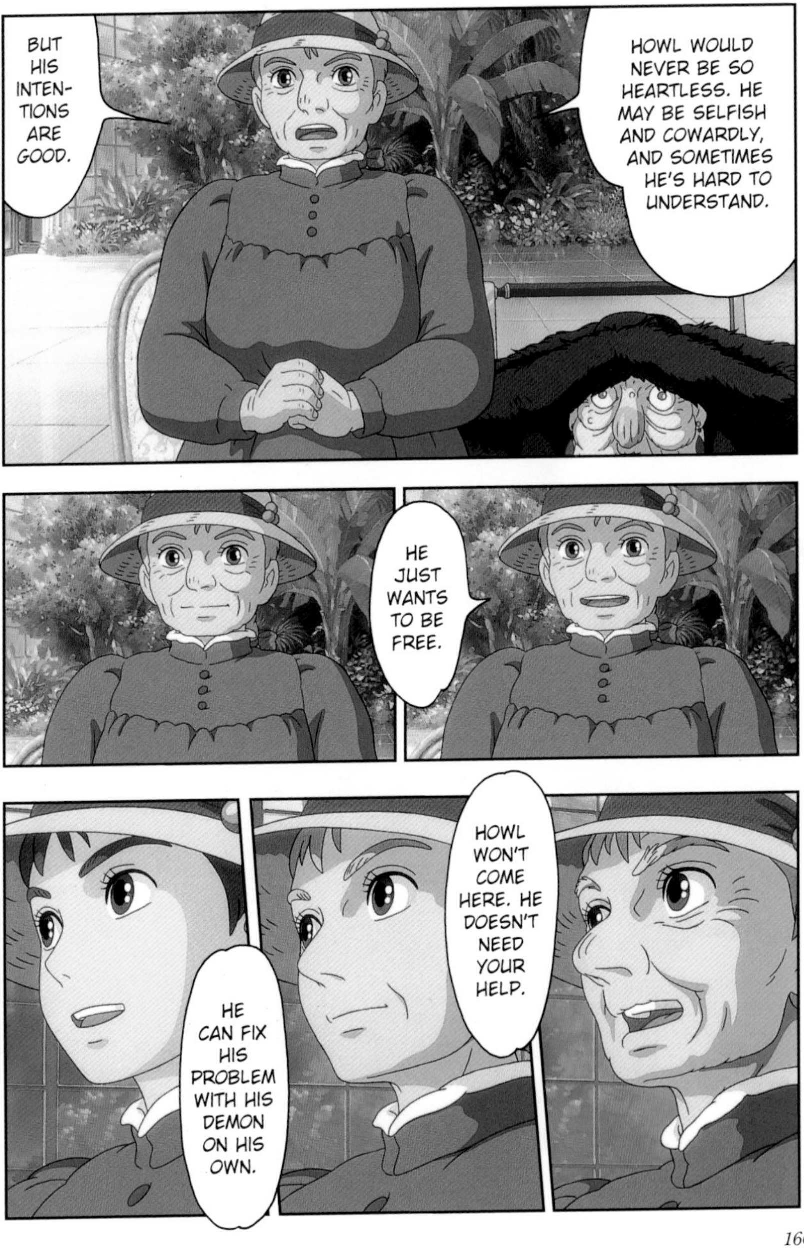
HOWL WOULD NEVER BE SO HEARTLESS. HE MAY BE SELFISH AND COWARDLY, AND SOMETIMES HE'S HARD TO UNDERSTAND.
BUT HIS INTEN-TIONS ARE GOOD.
HE JUST WANTS TO BE FREE.
HOWL WON'T COME HERE. HE DOESN'T NEED YOUR HELP.
HE CAN FIX HIS PROBLEM WITH HIS DEMON ON HIS OWN.

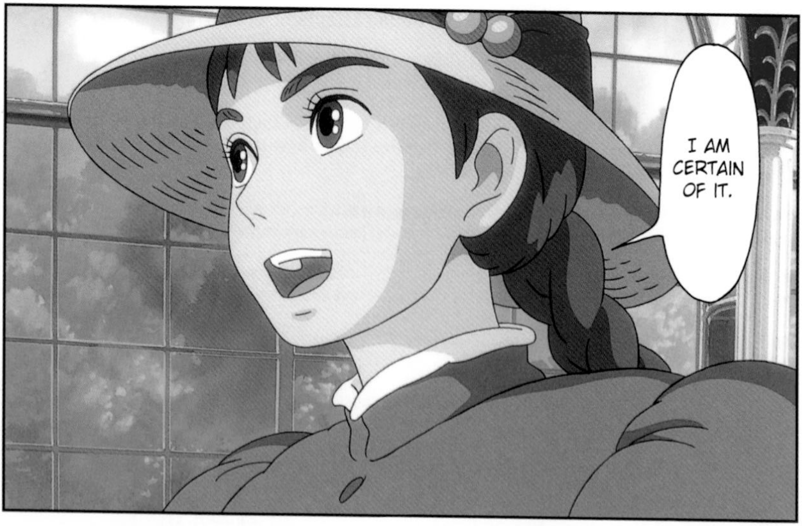
I AM CERTAIN OF IT.

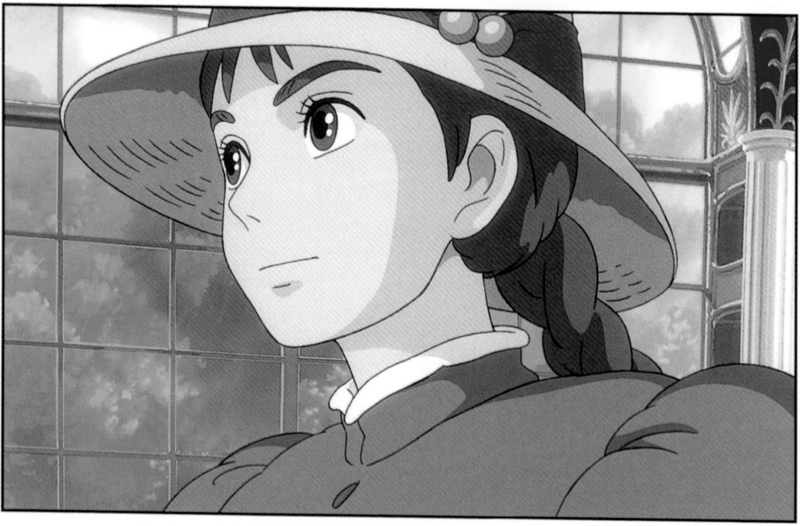

TO BE CONTINUED...

Your Guide to HOWL'S MOVING CASTLE Sound Effects!

To increase your enjoyment of the distinctive Japanese visual style of HOWL'S MOVING CASTLE we've included a listing of and guide to the sound effects used in this comic adaptation of the movie. In the comic, these sound effects are written in the Japanese phonetic characters called katakana.

In the sound effects glossary for HOWL'S MOVING CASTLE, sound effects are listed by page and panel number, for example, 6.1 means page 6, panel 1 – if there is more than one sound effect in a panel, the sound effects are listed in order (so, 12.1.1 means page 12, panel 1, first sound effect). Remember that all numbers are given in the original Japanese reading order: right-to-left.

After the page and panel numbers, you'll see the literally translated sound spelled out by the katakana, followed by how this sound effect might have been spelled out, or what it stands for, in English – it is interesting to see the different ways Japanese people describe the sounds of things!

You'll sometimes see a long dash at the end of a sound effects listing. This is just a way of showing that the sound is the kind that lasts for a while; similarly, sounds that fade-out are indicated by three dots. When a sound effect goes through more than one panel, a hyphen and number indicate the panels affected.

Now you are ready to use the HOWL'S MOVING CASTLE Sound Effects Guide!

25.7 FX: DADADA [tmp tmp tmp]
25.8 FX: DA [tmp]

26.7 FX: KACHA [chak]

27.2 FX: MOWAA [wowom]
3 FX: DOYOHN [gwump]

28.4 FX: GU [grab]
28.5 FX: DOSU DOSU DOSU [fump fump fump]

29.1 FX: GATA GATA [klak klak]
29.2 FX: BAN [thud]

30.1.1 FX: GASHON GASHON [klang klang]
30.1.2 FX: GISHI GISHI [whirr whirr]
30.2 FX: GASHON GASHON [klang klang]

31.1-3 FX: BYUUUUU… [whoooooo……]

32.1 FX: BAN [thump]
32.3 FX: DOTA DOTA DOTA [fump fump fump]

33.1 FX: TE HE HE… [heh heh heh…]
33.2 FX: GOOHH… [rrrrah…]
32.3.1 FX: GOOH— [rrrah—]
32.3.2 FX: BUOHH— [vroom—]
32.3.3 FX: PIII— [tweet—]
32.3.4 FX: BUSHUU— [fwooosh—]
32.4.1 FX: GASHA GASHA GASHA GASHA [klang klang klang klang]
32.4.2 FX: GUHE GUHE [burrp burrp]

34.1 FX: TA [tmp]
34.2 FX: BATAN [thud]
34.6 FX: GU [tugg]
34.7.1 FX: BAAN [whoomp]
34.7.2 FX: GOOH… [rrrrah…]

15.1 FX: DOSU DOSU… [tump tump…]
15.2.1 FX: BAN [thud]
15.2.2 FX: GATA GATA [klak klak]
15.3 FX: DOSU DOSU [tump tump]
15.6 FX: NU [fip]
15.7 FX: GASHI [tunk]

16.2 FX: SU [fip]
16.8 FX: SU [fsh]

17.1 FX: ZAZAA [swissh]
17.2 FX: ZAZAA [swoosh]
17.4 FX: ZAA [swisssh]

19.4 FX: POWAAN [ploosh]
19.6 FX: SU [fsh]
19.9 FX: GOTON GOTON [thunk thunk]

20.3 FX: FUU… [whooo…]

21.4 FX: SU [fsh]

22.2 FX: SU [fsh]
22.3 FX: KATSU KOTSU [tak tok]
22.4 FX: KATSU [tak]
22.7 FX: KURI [krik]
FX: KACHI [klik]

23.3.1 FX: GACHA [chak]
23.3.2 FX: BYUUU… [fweee…]
23.4 FX: BUWA [fwoosh]
23.5 FX: GI [kreek]
23.6 FX: BATAN [thud]

24.2 FX: KURI [krik]
24.9 FX: TATA [tmp tmp]
24.10 FX: DA [tmp]

25.3 FX: NIYARI [grin]
25.5 FX: CHIRA [glance]

5.3 FX: SU [fsh]
5.4 FX: JIJIJI… [sizzz…]

6.1 FX: JIJI… [sizz…]
6.2 FX: JUUU… [sizzz…]
6.3 FX: JUUU [sizzz…]
6.4 FX: JUUU… [sizzz…]

7.1 FX: JUUU… [sizzz…]

8.1 FX: SU [fsh]
8.3 FX: KATSU KATSU [tak tak]
8.5 FX: MOGU MOGU [mnch mnch]
FX: KATSU KATSU [tak tak]

9.2 FX: KOTSU KOTSU [tok tok]

10.2 FX: GYU… [mmph…]
10.3 FX: GUU… [mmmph…]
10.4 FX: GUGU [mmph mmph]
10.5 FX: MUGU… [ungh…]

11.1 FX: GABA [woosh]
11.2.1 FX: DAN [slam]
11.2.2 FX: GARA GARA [klak klak]
11.5 FX: MUSHA MUSHA [mnch mnch]

12.2 FX: ZAZA— [fsssh—]
12.3 FX: ZA ZA [fsh fsh]
12.4 FX: ZA [fsh]
12.6 FX: ZA [fsh]
12.7 FX: WARA WARA… [plop plop…]

13.1 FX: GARA GARA [klak klak]
13.4 FX: PAN PAN PAN [fwap fwap fwap]
FX: TA TA TA… [tmp tmp tmp…]

14.1 FX: DOSA [whump]
14.4-5 FX: ZABAA [swissh]
14.6 FX: SHA [fwoosh]
14.7 FX: SHA SHA [fwoosh fwoosh]

63.1 FX: KOTSU [tok...]
63.2 FX: SU [fsh]
63.5 FX: KUUU... [zzzz...]
63.7 FX: SU... [fsh...]
63.8 FX: KOTSU KOTSU KOTSU...
[tok tok tok...]

64.2 FX: DOOH [fsssh]
64.3 FX: DOOOH [fssssh]
64.4 FX: DOOOOOOH [fsssssssh...]
64.5 FX: GABA [fwoosh]
64.5-7 FX: DOOOOOH [fsssssssh...]

65.3 FX: GOTO... [tunk...]
65.4.1 FX: ZAAA... [fssssh...]
65.4.2 FX: ZAA— [fsssh—]

66.2 FX: BATAN [thud]

68.4 FX: CHARI [plink]

69.3.1 FX: TA [tmp]
69.3.2 FX: DA [tmp]
69.5.1 FX: TA TA TA... [tmp tmp tmp...]
69.5.2 FX: TA TA... [tmp tmp...]
69.7.1 FX: DA [tmp]
69.7.2 FX: TA TA... [tmp tmp...]

70.1 FX: KAANKAN KAANKAN KAANKAN
[klaang klaang klaang]
70.2.1 FX: PIII PIII [tweeet tweeet]
70.2.2 FX: UU UU— [ooo— ooo—]
70.2.3 FX: ZA ZA ZA... [fsssss...]

71.1 FX: DO DO DO DO...
[glug glug glug glug...]
71.2.1 FX: HISO HISO [mmrr mmrr]
71.2.2 FX: GAYA GAYA [yadda yadda]
71.3 FX: KAANKAN KAANKAN
[klaang klaang]

72.1.1 FX: WAA WAA WAA [ahh ahh ahh]
72.1.2 FX: ZABUN ZABUN...
[plish plish...]
72.1.3 FX: KAANKAN KAANKAN
[klaang klaang]
72.5 FX: HA [huh]

73.3 FX: NUU [foop]
73.4 FX: SA [fwip]

74.4 FX: SORO— [hmmm—]

75.2 FX: HYURURURURURU...
[tweeeee...]
75.3 FX: HYURURURURU... [fweee...]
75.4 FX: KA [thwak]
75.5 FX: ZUZUUN [booomsh]

50.3.2 FX: DOHN DOHN DOHN
[booom booom booom]

51.1.1 FX: GOOH [rrrrr...]
51.1.2 FX: GOOH [rrrrr...]
51.2 FX: GOGOGO... [krr krr krr...]
51.3 FX: GOOH [rrrr...]
51.4 FX: GOOH [rrrr...]

52.2 FX: PA [foop]
52.3 FX: BARA BARA BARA...
[fwap fwap fwap ...]

53.1.1 FX: GYAA [aieeeee]
53.1.2 FX: BASA BASA BASA
[fwip fwip fwip]
53.2-4 FX: BYUUUUU [whooooo]

54.1.1 FX: BYU [fwoosh]
54.1.2 FX: GYAA GYAA [aiee aiee]
54.2 FX: DOKA [thunk]
54.3 FX: ZA [fwish]
54.4 FX: BA [fwoosh]
54.5 FX: BYUU [whoo]
54.6 FX: GYAA GYAA [aiee aiee]
54.7 FX: GYAA GYAA GYAA
[aiee aiee aiee]

55.2 FX: BYUU... [whoo...]
55.4 FX: BASA BASA [fwap fwap]
55.5 FX: GYAA GYAA [aiee aiee]
55.6.1 FX: GYAA GYAA [aiee aiee]
55.6.2 FX: FU [fsh]
55.7 FX: GYAA GYAA [aiee aiee]
55.8 FX: BASA BASA BASA
[fwap fwap fwap]

56.1 FX: KOKEKOKKOH—
[cockle-doodle-doo—]
56.4.1 FX: KURI [krik]
56.4.2 FX: GACHA... [chak...]
56.5.1 FX: BATAN [thud]
56.5.2 FX: KOTSU... [tok...]

57.1 FX: KOTSU KOTSU [tok tok]
57.2 FX: YURA [fwom]
57.4 FX: DOSA [whump]
57.6 FX: DOKA [thunk]
57.7 FX: FUUU— [ooph—]

58.2 FX: HAA HAA [huff huff]
58.3 FX: BIKUN [zing]
58.4-6 FX: ZUZUZUZUZU... [krrrrrr...]

59.5 FX: FUUU... [hnnn...]

60.5 FX: GOTON [thunk]

62.2 FX: SU [fsh]
62.4 FX: KOTSU KOTSU [tok tok]

35.1-2 FX: BYUUU... [whooo......]
35.3 FX: TA [dash]

37.1 FX: GATA [klak]
37.2 FX: GATA GATA [klak klak]
37.3 FX: GATA GATA [klak klak]
37.8 FX: GUGU [tugg tugg]

38.1 FX: ZURU [shloop]
38.2 FX: ZURU... [shloop...]
38.3 FX: SUPO [ploop]
38.4-5 FX: BUUN [twipp]
38.6 FX: BUWA [fwoosh]

39.2 FX: TON [tmp]
39.3.1 FX: KURU KURU [fwip fwip]
39.3.2 FX: TON TON [tmp tmp]

40.4 FX: GIKU [huh?]

41.1 FX: GUSHU GUSHU [pwoosh pwoosh]
41.2 FX: GUSHU [pwoosh]
41.3.1 FX: PIII— [tweeet—]
41.3.2 FX: SHUU— [fsssh—]
41.4.1 FX: GASHA GOSHA [klang klang]
41.4.2 FX: GIII— [whirr—]
41.4.3 FX: GUHE [burrp]
41.4.4 FX: ZUZU... [rrr rrr...]
41.5 FX: SHIIN [silence]

42.2 FX: PYON [bwing]
42.4 FX: PYON [bwing]
42.5 FX: PYON PYON [bwing bwing]
42.6 FX: TON TON [tmp tmp]
42.7 FX: TON TON TON [tmp tmp tmp]
42.8 FX: GU [tugg]
42.9 FX: BUN [fwip]
42.10 FX: PAN [wapp]

44.2 FX: TON TON TON [tmp tmp tmp]

46.2.1 FX: PATA PATA [fwip fwip]
46.2.2 FX: HYUUU... [whooo...]
46.3 FX: ZAZAZA... [zoosh...]

48.4 FX: BYUUU... [whooo...]

49.1 FX: GOHHH... [rrrrr...]
49.2.1 FX: BAKI [krakk]
49.2.2 FX: GARA GARA [klakk klakk]
49.4 FX: KI [hmph]
49.5 FX: DODOHN DODOHN [boosh boosh]
FX: DOHN [booom]

50.1.1 FX: HYURURURU [fweeee]
50.1.2 FX: HYURURURU... [fweeee...]
50.1.3 FX: VOOOHN [vwooom]
50.2 FX: GOOH [rrrr...]
50.3.1 FX: DODOHN [boosh]

103.2	FX: KACHA [chak]	
103.8	FX: KOTO... [tok...]	
104.1.1	FX: HIII... [fwoo...]	
104.1.2	FX: KATA KATA... [klak klak...]	
105.6	FX: HUUU [hmmm]	
107.4	FX: GEH... [urk...]	
107.6	FX: HAAA— [huff—]	
108.4	FX: GABA [fwash]	
110.2	FX: GUGU [zoop]	
112.3	FX: GYU [tugg]	
113.3	FX: KACHIRI [chak]	
113.4-5	FX: FUWAA [swoosh]	
113.7	FX: SU... [fsh...]	
115.1	FX: SA [fsh]	
115.2	FX: GACHA [chak]	
115.3	FX: PATA... [thud...]	
115.6	FX: SU [fsh]	
116.1	FX: GORO GORO GORO... [putt putt putt...]	
116.2	FX: KOTO KOTO KOTO... [tok tok tok...]	
116.3	FX: SHU SHU SHU... [poof poof poof...]	
116.4	FX: BASA [fwap]	
117.2	FX: BASA BASA BASA [fwap fwap fwap]	
117.4.1	FX: SHA SHA SHA [whirr whirr whirr]	
117.4.2	FX: BASA BASA [fwap fwap]	
118.1	FX: SHA SHA SHA [whirr whirr whirr]	
118.2	FX: SHA SHA [whirr whirr]	
118.3	FX: SHA... [whirr...]	
120.2	FX: SUU... [fssh...]	
121.1	FX: TETE... [tup tup...]	
121.3	FX: SUTA SUTA... [tmp tmp...]	
121.8	FX: TETETE... [tup tup tup...]	
121.9	FX: KYORO [hmm]	
121.10	FX: KYORO [hmm]	
122.2	FX: TETETE... [tup tup tup...]	
122.3	FX: HIN! [heen!]	
122.5	FX: SUTA SUTA [tmp tmp]	
122.6	FX: TA [tmp]	
122.7	FX: TA TA TA [tmp tmp tmp]	
123.3	FX: TA TA [tmp tmp]	
123.4	FX: SA... [fsh...]	

88.1-2	FX: OOOOH... [ahhhhh...]	
88.3	FX: GORO GORO GORO GORO... [krrrrrrrr...]	
89.4	FX: NECHA... [gwump...]	
89.5	FX: NECHOH... [gwoop]	
89.6	FX: POTA POTA [plip plip]	
90.2	FX: YORO [fwom]	
91.2	FX: DA DA DA... [tmp tmp tmp...]	
91.3.1	FX: GACHA GACHA [klak klak]	
91.3.2	FX: KIRI KIRI [krr krr]	
91.4	FX: BA [fwoosh]	
91.5	FX: BAN!! [slamm!!]	
92.1.1	FX: ZAAAAAA... [fsssh...]	
92.1.2	FX: TA TA TA... [tmp tmp tmp...]	
92.2-4	FX: ZAAAAAAA... [fsssssh...]	
93.1-3	FX: ZAAAAAAA... [fsssssh...]	
92.4	FX: ZAAAAAA... [fssssh...]	
94.1	FX: ZAAAAAA... [fsssssh...]	
94.2	FX: PYON [bwing]	
94.3	FX: PYON [bwing]	
94.4	FX: PYON [bwing]	
94.5.1	FX: PYON [bwing]	
94.5.2	FX: ZAAAAAA... [fsssssh...]	
95.1	FX: SUTO [tump]	
95.1-2	FX: ZAAAAAA... [fssssh...]	
95.5	FX: TATA [tmp tmp]	
96.1.1	FX: DORO DORO... [glug glug...]	
96.1.2	FX: GII— [kreek—]	
96.1.3	FX: BATAN [thud]	
97.2	FX: GUI [fwish]	
97.5	FX: ZUZUZUZU... [fwoowoosh...]	
98.1	FX: TA TA... [tmp tmp...]	
98.6	FX: HA [huh]	
99.1	FX: ZAA— ZAA— [fssh— fssh—]	
99.2	FX: ZAA... [fsssh...]	
	FX: BATAN [thud]	
100.1.1	FX: PUU PUKUPUPPU [proot proot]	
100.1.2	FX: DON DON [dum dum]	
100.2	FX: PUPPUU— [proot proot—]	
100.3.1	FX: PUPUU— [prooot—]	
100.3.2	FX: DON DON [dum dum]	
101.3	FX: KON KON KON KON [tok tok tok tok]	
101.4	FX: KACHA [chak]	
101.5	FX: GYO [urk]	

76.1.1	FX: ZUUN ZUUN ZUUN [boosh boosh boosh]	
76.1.2	FX: WAAA— [ahhh—]	
76.1.3	FX: KYAHH— [aieee—]	
76.2.1	FX: WAAA— [ahhh—]	
76.2.2	FX: KYAHH— [aieee—]	
77.1	FX: OOHN [womm]	
77.2.1	FX: OOHN OOHN [womm womm]	
77.2.2	FX: BA... [fip]	
77.3	FX: BARA BARA BARA BARA [fwip fwip fwip fwip]	
78.2	FX: WAAA— [ahhh—]	
78.3.1	FX: HAA HAA [huff huff]	
78.3.2	FX: WAAA [ahhh]	
78.4	FX: HAA HAA... [huff huff...]	
79.1	FX: GACHA [chak]	
79.2.1	FX: BATAN [chud]	
79.2.2	FX: ZEHH ZEHH [huff huff]	
79.3	FX: HAA HAA HAA [huf huf huf]	
79.4	FX: HAA HAA [huf huf...]	
79.5	FX: YORO YORO [fwom fwom]	
80.1	FX: TA [tmp]	
80.4.1	FX: GIKU [huh?]	
80.4.2	FX: WAAA [aieeeee]	
80.5.1	FX: DOTAN [whomp]	
80.5.2	FX: BATAN [thudd]	
80.5.3	FX: GASHAN [krrsh]	
81.2.1	FX: YORO [fwom]	
81.2.2	FX: BAN [thudd]	
81.3	FX: YORO YORO [fwom fwom]	
81.5	FX: DA [tmp]	
81.6	FX: DOTA DOTA [tump tump]	
82.1	FX: DOTA DOTA... [tump tump...]	
82.3	FX: DA [tmp]	
82.4-6	FX: DADADADA... [tmp tmp tmp tmp...]	
83.2	FX: GUI [tugg]	
83.3	FX: BA [fsh]	
84.1	FX: DOKI [twump]	
84.4	FX: KUSHA KUSHA [skrrsh skrrsh]	
85.2	FX: YORO [fwom]	
85.3	FX: YORO... [fwom...]	
85.4	FX: GATA... [tunk...]	
86.1	FX: KUSUN KUSUN [sniffl sniffl]	
86.6	FX: KUSUN KUSUN [sniffl sniffl]	
87.3-4	FX: OOH... OOH... [ahhh... ahhh...]	

143.3 FX: HAH HAH [huff huff]
143.4 FX: HAH HAH [huff huff]

144.3.1 FX: SUU— [fwoo—]
144.3.2 FX: PATA [thud...]

145.1 FX: YOTA YOTA YOTA
[fwup fwup fwup]
145.3.1 FX: DO... [shlump...]
145.3.2 FX: GISHI... [kreek...]
145.4 FX: HAAAA [ahhh]

146.1 FX: HAH HAH [huff huff]
146.2 FX: TETETETETETE
[tup tup tup tup tup tup...]
146.5 FX: CHIRA [glance]
146.6 FX: SU [fsh]

147.3 FX: SHU [fsh]

148.1.1 FX: HAH HAH [huff huff]
148.1.2 FX: SURU SURU SURU [vim vim vim]
148.2 FX: HAH... [huff...]
148.3.1 FX: SURU SURU SURU [vim vim vim]
148.3.2 FX: HA [huh]
148.5 FX: SURU SURU SURU...
[vim vim vim...]

149.1 FX: SURU SURU SURU...
[vim vim vim...]
149.2.1 FX: HA [huh]
149.2.2 FX: SURU SURU... [vim vim]
149.4-5 FX: GUASHAAN [krrrsh!!]
149.6 FX: BACHI [zing]

150.1-3 FX: JIIIIN [ziiiiing]
150.4 FX: KA [zapp]
150.5 FX: JIII... [ziing...]
150.6.1 FX: BA [fwoosh]
150.6.2 FX: JIIIN [ziiing...]
150.7 FX: JIIIN [ziiing...]

152.1 FX: KATSU KOTSU [tak tok]

156.4 FX: HIN [heen]

157.5 FX: HAAA— [hufff—]

158.2 FX: KOKUN [nod]

161.2 FX: KARA KARA KARA
[klak klak klak]
161.3 FX: KARA KARA KARA
[klak klak klak]
161.4 FX: KARA KARA [klak klak]

164.4 FX: GATAN [tunk]

165.2 FX: BIKU [urk]

171

134.1 FX: GU... [tugg...]
134.2 FX: YORO [fwom]
134.3 FX: HAH HAH [huff huff]
134.4.1 FX: HA HA [huff huff]
134.4.2 FX: HAH HAH [huff huff]
134.5.1 FX: HA HA [huff huff]
134.5.2 FX: HAH HAH [huff huff]
134.6.1 FX: HA HA [huff huff]
134.6.2 FX: HAH HAH [huff huff]
134.7 FX: HA HA [huff huff]
134.8.1 FX: HAH HAH [huff huff]
134.8.2 FX: HA... [huff...]

135.1 FX: HAH [huff]
135.2 FX: HAH... [huff...]
135.4 FX: HAH HAH [huff huff]
135.5 FX: HAH HAH [huff huff]
135.6 FX: HAH HAH [huff huff]

136.1.1 FX: YORO [fwom]
136.1.2 FX: HAH [huff]
136.2.1 FX: HAH [huff]
136.2.2 FX: YORO [fwom]
136.3 FX: MU [hmph]
136.4 FX: PUI [hah]
136.5 FX: HAH HAH [huff huff]
136.6.1 FX: UN... [ugh...]
136.6.2 FX: HAH [huff]
136.7 FX: HAH HAH [huff huff]

137.1 FX: HA HA HA [huff huff huff]
137.2 FX: HAH [huff]
137.3 FX: HAH HAH [huff huff]
137.4.1 FX: HAH HAH [huff huff]
137.4.2 FX: HAH HAH HAH [huff huff huff]
137.6 FX: HAH HAH [huff huff]

138.1 FX: ZEH ZEH [ooph ooph]
138.2 FX: ZEH ZEH [ooph ooph]
138.3 FX: HAH HAH [huff huff]

139.3 FX: HAH HAH [huff huff]
139.4 FX: HAH HAH [huff huff]

140.1 FX: HAH HAH [huff huff]
140.2 FX: HAH... [huff...]
140.3 FX: SUTO [fup]
140.4 FX: HAH HAH [huff huff]
140.6 FX: HAH HAH HAH [huff huff huff]

141.1 FX: SUSU [tup tup]
141.6 FX: SUU [ooph]

142.2 FX: HAH HAH [huff huff]
142.3 FX: HAH HAH [huff huff]
142.4 FX: HAH... [huff...]
142.5 FX: HAH HAH [huff huff]
FX: ZEH ZEH [ooph ooph]

143.2 FX: HAH HAH HAH [huff huff huff]

124.1 FX: TETETE... [tup tup tup...]
124.3 FX: TA TA [tmp tmp]
124.4 FX: TA TA [tmp tmp]
124.5 FX: TA TA [tmp tmp]

125.1.1 FX: TA TA [tmp tmp]
125.1.2 FX: SUTA SUTA [tmp tmp]
125.2.1 FX: TA TA [tmp tmp]
125.2.2 FX: SUTA SUTA [tmp tmp]

126.3 FX: SHA... [fssh...]
126.4 FX: TA TA TA [tmp tmp tmp]

127.1 FX: TA TA [tmp tmp]
127.2 FX: TA TA [tmp tmp]
127.3 FX: SUTA SUTA... [tmp tmp...]

128.1 FX: TA TA TA... [tmp tmp tmp...]
128.2 FX: TA TA [tmp tmp]
128.3 FX: TA TA [tmp tmp]
128.4.1 FX: TA [tmp]
128.4.2 FX: JI... [fich...]
128.6.1 FX: TA [tmp]
128.6.2 FX: POWAAN [fwuzzz]
128.7 FX: JI [fich]
128.9 FX: POWAAN [fwuzzz]

129.1 FX: TA [tmp]
129.2.1 FX: TA... [tmp...]
129.2.2 FX: YORO [fwom]
129.3 FX: NECHO [gwoosh]
129.4.1 FX: GOTSUN [tunk]
129.4.2 FX: NECHO... [gwoosh...]
129.5 FX: DON [whudd]
129.6 FX: SHA [fssh]
129.8 FX: SHUU SHUU... [foosh foosh...]

130.3 FX: MU [hmph]
130.5 FX: SUPON [pluk]
130.6 FX: SUUU [snifff]

131.1 FX: HEKKSHON [ah-choo]
131.2 FX: BA [fsh]
131.4 FX: BATAN [thud]
131.7 FX: TETETE... [tup tup tup...]

132.1 FX: SUTA SUTA [tmp tmp]
132.3 FX: DOTE [thup]
132.4 FX: GURU GURU [fwip fwip]
132.6.2 FX: BAFU [woof]
132.6.2 FX: HIN! [heen!]
132.7 FX: HIN! [heen!]
132.9 FX: HA [huh]

133.1 FX: CHIRA [glance]
133.2 FX: TA TA [tmp tmp]
133.3 FX: TA TA TA... [tmp tmp tmp...]
133.6 FX: GUI [tugg]
133.7 FX: YORO [fwom]
FX: TA [tmp...]

This book should be read in its original Japanese right-to-left format.
Please turn it around to begin!

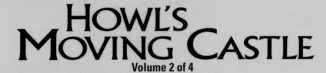

HOWL'S MOVING CASTLE

Volume 2 of 4

From the novel by Diana Wynne Jones
Screenplay written and directed by Hayao Miyazaki

Unedited English-Language Adaptation/Cindy Davis Hewitt & Donald H. Hewitt
Original Japanese Script Translation/Jim Hubbert
Film Comic Adaptation/Yuji Oniki
Lettering/John Clark
Design/Hidemi Sahara
Editor/Pancha Diaz

Howl's Moving Castle (Howl no Ugoku Shiro)
© 2004 Nibariki - GNDDDT
All rights reserved.
First published by Tokuma Shoten Co., Ltd. in Japan.
Howl's Moving Castle title logo © Buena Vista Pictures Distribution.

Printed in Malaysia

Published by VIZ Media, LLC
P.O. Box 77010
San Francisco, CA 94107

First printing, August 2005
Third printing, April 2014

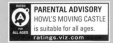

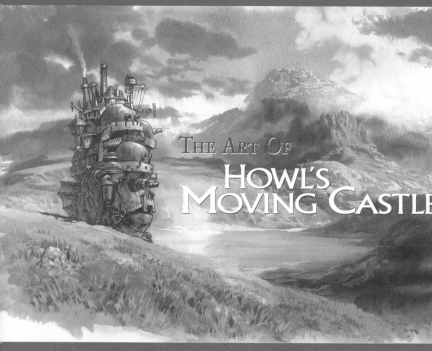

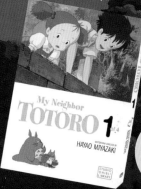